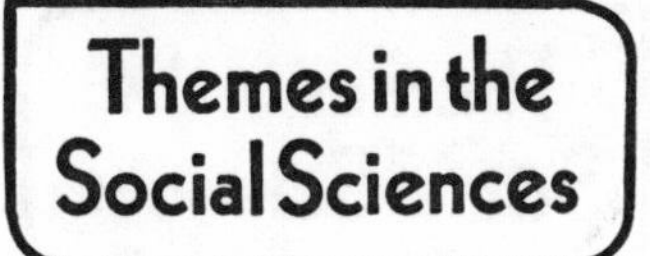

Rational choice and social exchange

Themes in the Social Sciences

Editors: Jack Goody and Geoffrey Hawthorn

The aim of this series is to publish books which will focus on topics of general and interdisciplinary interest in the social sciences. They will be concerned with non-European cultures and with developing countries, as well as with industrial societies. The emphasis will be on comparative sociology and, initially, on sociological, anthropological and demographic topics. These books are intended for undergraduate teaching, but not as basic introductions to the subjects they cover. Authors have been asked to write on central aspects of current interest which have a wide appeal to teachers and research students, as well as to undergraduates.

First books in the series

Edmund Leach *Culture and communication: the logic by which symbols are connected. An introduction to the use of structuralist analysis in social anthropology*

Anthony Heath *Rational choice and social exchange: a critique of exchange theory*

Rational choice & social exchange

A critique of exchange theory

by Anthony Heath

Jesus College, Oxford

Cambridge University Press

Cambridge
London New York Melbourne

Published by the Syndics of the Cambridge University Press
The Pitt Building, Trumpington Street, Cambridge CB2 1RP
Bentley House, 200 Euston Road, London NW1 2DB
32 East 57th Street, New York, NY 10022, USA
296 Beaconsfield Parade, Middle Park, Melbourne 3206, Australia

First published 1976

Typeset by Fuller Organization, Philadelphia, Pennsylvania
Printed in the United States of America by R. R. Donnelley
& Sons Company, Crawfordsville, Indiana

Library of Congress Cataloging in Publication Data
Heath, Anthony, 1942–
Rational choice and social exchange.
(Themes in the social sciences)
Bibliography: p.
Includes index.
1. Sociology. 2. Social exchange. I. Title. II. Series.
HM24.H447 301.1 75-39391
ISBN 0 521 21132 8
ISBN 0 521 29053 8 pbk.

Contents

Preface

I first met exchange theory at one of John Goldthorpe's graduate seminars at Cambridge in 1967. Peter Blau was the Pitt Professor at the time and Goldthorpe had invited him to talk about his recently published book *Exchange and Power in Social Life* (1964). Skimming hastily through the book beforehand, my attention was drawn by the diagrams in chapter 7 in which Blau attempted to apply the economist's indifference curves to the study of sociological problems. He had made some trivial mistakes in this treatment of indifference curves and, for want of anything more important to say, I raised them in the seminar. Blau conceded the point readily enough and asked me to write him a note detailing the errors and any others which I could find. This forced me to re-read chapter 7 with a great deal more attention, and I became rather suspicious of his whole attempt to apply economic theory to sociology. I discussed the problems with a number of economists, most notably David Newbery and Partha Dasgupta, and they confirmed and sharpened my suspicions. As a result my note for Blau developed into a short article and John Goldthorpe encouraged me to develop it into a Ph.D. on exchange theory.

My approach to exchange theory at this time was, then, fairly sceptical, and I must confess that I spent a great deal of my time discovering tautologies, *non sequiturs,* and the like in the works of Homans and Blau. This has always been a favourite sport of critics of exchange theory (see, for example, Boulding and Davis, 1962; Deutsch, 1964; Razak, 1966; Abrahamson, 1970; Mulkay, 1971; Ekeh, 1974), and it is certainly true that the exchange theorists provide plenty of scope for this sport. In my view, Blau's book gives the impression of having been written rather too quickly.

Homans, on the other hand, can never be accused of hasty drafting, but his book *Social Behavior: Its Elementary Forms* (1961) seems to me to have a somewhat perverse quality about it. Perhaps out of a spirit of bravado Homans often seems to choose to fight his battles on rather unpromising territory and to deign the safer ground that lies at hand. I have never understood why he did not abandon his value proposition as a tautology and embrace the economist's much safer notion of revealed preference. I am confident that he could have preserved the essentials of his position in this way, as of course the economists have preserved the essentials of theirs, and he would have denied his critics their favourite target. But a full discussion of this must wait until chapter 8.

Despite the discovery of more and more errors of logic and errors of judgement, however, my attitude towards exchange theory gradually changed from the sceptical to the tolerant and thence almost to the enthusiastic. From the start John Goldthorpe insisted on the distinction between those errors which were ones of faulty workmanship and those which were fundamental to the theory itself. No workman is perfect, and indeed it would not surprise me if subsequent critics discover as many examples of faulty workmanship in the present book as I have, or think I have, discovered in my predecessors'. But I would be very surprised if these errors vitiate what I have called the rational choice approach itself (a rather better expression, as I hope the reader will come to be persuaded, than 'exchange theory'). It really does seem to me that an excellent way in which to begin any explanation of human action is to suppose that the actor is a rational agent with intelligible goals, an agent who chooses rationally between potential courses of action in the light of those goals. (This is not of course a view unique to the exchange theorists, nor is it one discovered for the first time by them. Weber certainly held this view, and so I suspect did Marx). If our rational choice evplanation fails or is unilluminating, then we shall assuredly have to turn to other explanations in terms of unconscious drives, habitual action or other forms of non-rational action. But I think we do well, until firm evidence to the contrary is available, to assume that our fellow men are as rational and intelligent agents as we usually suppose ourselves to be.

What I have tried to do in this book, therefore, is to get away from the logical dissection of Homans and Blau which characterized my Ph.D. thesis and instead to present a more systematic account and evaluation of the fundamentals of exchange theory. This has of course required me to make some judgements about what the fundamentals are, and while I do not think that these judgements have been wildly biased, there is bound to be room for disagreement. There are certainly many interesting developments of exchange theory (such as Anderson, 1971; Coleman, 1966, 1973; Hirschman, 1970; Kapferer, 1972) which I have regretfully had to omit. This concentration on fundamentals, or what I take to be the fundamentals, has also made the book much more 'topic-oriented' than 'author-oriented'. I do not apologize for this. There is, it seems to me, a very strong scholastic tendency in much modern writing on sociological theory. We often seem to place exegesis of the classics above the explanation of behaviour, and an 'author-orientation' is likely to reinforce this, in my view, deplorable tendency. This book was not, therefore, intended to be an exposition of what Homans and Blau really said but rather an attempt to evaluate how far the approach which they began to develop can succeed in explaining social behaviour. Unlike many contemporaries I accept Whitehead's dictum that a science which hesitates to forget its founders is lost. I suspect that I have not followed this dictum closely enough, but I have tried to make a start.

It is customary to conclude a preface with a list of acknowledgements, and I would certainly like to acknowledge the interest and stimulation provided by John Goldthorpe and Brian Barry. But neither (given the exigencies of publishers' deadlines and my own delays) has had a chance to read the book in anything like its present form, and I cannot therefore credit them with removing some errors or exonerate them from missing others. Parts of the book, however, have been read at various seminars, and I have encountered many provocative comments at them. I must confess that I have not always been persuaded by these comments, but they have certainly shaped the present book by raising objections which I felt had to be tackled. Whether their proponents are to be thanked or blamed, perhaps I can leave the reader to decide. Finally, there is no doubt that my thanks are due to Gillian Speirs, who put up with my erratic delivery of manuscript for typing, and the staff of the Cambridge Press, who tolerated my unerring ability to miss deadlines.

Anthony Heath

October 1975

Introduction

Exchange is by no means the prerogative of the economist and of the economic market. Outside the market we find that 'neighbors exchange favors; children, toys; colleagues, assistance; acquaintances, courtesies; politicians, concessions; discussants, ideas; housewives, recipes' (Blau, 1964, p. 88). Nor are these social exchanges minor curiosities of little significance in social life. Rather, the exchanges of gifts and favours between friends, neighbours and kin are strong and enduring threads in the social fabric. It has been estimated that in Britain the cards exchanged at Christmas alone were worth £40 million in 1964 (and no doubt a great deal more now) while over 4 per cent of consumer expenditure – an enormous £1,400.8 million in 1968 and about a third of what we spend on housing – was spent on gifts (Davis, 1972). There are no estimates of the money value of the services exchanged by kin and neighbours in time of need or emergency but there can be little doubt of their importance, or that the welfare services of our society would be overwhelmed if they were to stop.

Many of these social exchanges are readily recognized and described as such by the participants concerned themselves. The language of exchange is commonly used in everyday speech. We say that we are 'indebted' to someone on account of the help he has given us; we say that we 'owe' someone a letter or an invitation to dinner.
commonly recognized as such. Simmel went so far as to suggest that
a great deal more social interaction takes form of exchange than is commonly recognized as such. Simmel went so far as to suggest that 'all contacts among men rest on the schema of giving and returning the equivalence' (Simmel, 1908, p. 387), while in another early work Malinowski (1926) demonstrated that 'give and take' pervades the social life of primitive societies. More recently Homans (1961) has suggested that most (if not all) social behaviour can be viewed as 'an exchange of activity, tangible or intangible, and more or less rewarding or costly, between at least two persons' (p. 13), while Blau has added that 'social exchange can be observed everywhere once we are sensitized by this conception to it, not only in market relations but also in friendship and even in love' (Blau, 1964, p. 88). This broader

conception essentially includes within the category of social exchange all 'actions that are contingent on rewarding reactions from others and that cease when these expected reactions are not forthcoming' (Blau, 1964, p. 6). In other words, any behaviour that is motivated by an expected return or response from another falls under the heading of exchange. Thus if a man conforms with the norms of his group in order to win the praise of his peers (and if he ceases when that praise is not forthcoming), then we can talk of an exchange of conformity for approval; if a supervisor turns a blind eye to certain infringements of the rules in order to secure greater cooperation from his workers in other matters (but tightens up on the rules when the cooperation is not forthcoming), then we can again talk of an exchange.

Excluded from this conception of exchange is behaviour which is not motivated by the return but by a sense of duty or by some other internalized value. The actions of the man who believes in the rightness of his cause and is not affected by the praise or blame of others cannot be included in the category of exchange. Nor can behaviour which is actually lacking in motive. The man who is really 'drunk and incapable' and the housewife who has a neurotic compulsion to go shoplifting cannot sensibly be said to be engaging in social exchange, whatever the views of the police or magistrate may be. *Social exchange may be pervasive but on this definition it is not all-inclusive*

The view which I have described here is essentially that of the sociologist Peter Blau, whose book *Exchange and Power in Social Life* (1964) is one of the most notable recent attempts to develop a theory of social exchange. Blau was heavily influenced by two slightly earlier works, namely Thibaut and Kelley's *The Social Psychology of Groups* (1959) and George Homans' *Social Behaviour: Its Elementary Forms* (1961). These three works are the ones to which the term 'exchange theory' is most commonly applied and they are the ones which will be the primary focus in this monograph. There are also a considerable number of other, essentially similar treatments of social exchange in psychology, sociology, anthropology and political science which could equally well be termed examples of exchange theory. Most notable here perhaps are the 'transactional theory' of Fredrik Barth (which he presents in his *Models of Social Organization,* 1966) and the 'economic theories' of Anthony Downs and Mancur Olson (presented in *An Economic Theory of Democracy* (1957) and *The Logic of Collective Action* (1965), respectively).

While there are numerous differences of detail between these works, they share a common concern with the 'exchange of activity . . . more or less rewarding or costly, between at least two persons'. They also share the economist's 'rational choice' approach to theory construction.

Thus Downs and Olson are in fact themselves economists who are setting out to colonize the virgin territory of political science. Homans and Blau are sociologists who explicitly attempt to learn and borrow some of the rational choice theories of economics and apply them to social exchange generally. Barth, an anthropologist, is overtly influenced by the very similar rational choice approach of game theory. And the social psychologists Thibaut and Kelley, although they seem to have little formal knowledge of economics or game theory, nevertheless come up with theories that are in structure very similar. If a broad conception of social exchange is the first hall-mark of exchange theory, then, the use of a rational choice approach is a second, equally important one.

Broadly speaking the rational choice approach as used in exchange theory, game theory and in economics begins with the assumption that men have given wants, goals, values or 'utility functions'. (The terminology often differs but the meaning is essentially the same.) It then assumes that these goals cannot all be equally realized. Men live in a world of scarcity and therefore must select between alternative courses of action. They will, it is assumed, do so rationally, selecting the course of action which is the most effective means to their goal (if, for example, they have a single goal) or selecting the course which leads to their most preferred goal (if they have many, equally attainable goals). In Robbins' often-quoted words economics is a 'science which studies human behaviour as a relationship between ends and scarce means which have alternative uses' (Robbins, 1932, p. 15). It is this aspect of economics which the exchange theorists try to plagiarize.

On the face of it the more widespread use of this approach in sociology and anthropology seems long overdue. Social life no less than economic life is characterized by scarcity. We may be faced by a scarcity of time rather than of money, but it is true nonetheless that we cannot have all we want. Accordingly men must choose and make decisions. It has been suggested that 'economics is all about how people make choices. Sociology is all about why they don't have any choices to make' (Duesenberry, 1960, p. 233), but, if this is so, it is time that sociology changed. Men are not mere automata programmed by their culture to behave in certain ways. There may be norms and roles which prescribe how people should behave in certain situations, but one of the important results of modern research on roles is that they leave a great deal more latitude for individual decision-making than had previously been supposed (Gross et al., 1958).

A further advantage of the rational choice approach is that the sociologist does not have to think up theories for himself from scratch. Economics and game theory between them have a large stock of intellectually sophisticated and highly prestigious theories for the sociologist to plunder. They can provide a short-cut to scientific success. This is not quite such a flippant point as it might seem. In the natural sciences there is a long history of colonization, reputable and well-attested theories being exported from their original field and set to work in other less-developed areas of enquiry. This has led to some spectacular successes, although doubtless there have also been some spectacular, but less well-publicized failures. Whether this can be repeated in the social sciences, and whether economics in particular can be a successful colonizer, is still a matter for debate. (Among anthropologists, for example, there has been a bitter debate about the applicability of conventional economic theory to the economics of so-called primitive societies. See LeClair and Schneider, 1968; Firth, 1967.) This, then, is an issue to which we must devote considerable attention in this book.

If our exchange theorists simply borrowed existing theories from economics and game theory and applied them more or less as they stood to the exchange of conformity for approval or of advice for status, the task of exposition and evaluation would be relatively simple. Sometimes rightly and sometimes wrongly, however, the sociologists have not been content to leave well alone. They modify the assumptions, add new propositions and, much less excusably, devise new terminologies of their own. Homans is the prime culprit here. While he sets out, reasonably enough, to borrow propositions from other disciplines rather than to invent his own, he decides to borrow both from economics *and* from Skinner's behavioural psychology. This too might have been useful enough but Homans then decides to amalgamate the two sets of propositions in a hybrid terminology that grates on the ear of economist, psychologist and sociologist alike. Homans' world is populated by a 'Person' and 'Other' who 'emit' activities, exchange 'rewards', and pursue 'psychic profits'. I apologize in advance for the results.

Thibaut and Kelley also work within a psychological tradition and, as well as using an idiosyncratic language to describe their theory, draw on the results of experimental social psychology to produce a substantially modified economic theory. Some of these modifications are in fact extremely sound and could usefully be lent to economists in return. (With one or two notable exceptions, however, economists have proved rather arrogant colonizers making little attempt to integrate with the indigenous peoples, and there is no sign as yet that they propose to learn from the other social sciences.)

Of all the exchange theorists (and perhaps of all social scientists), however, Blau is by far the most eclectic. He owes considerable debts to Simmel, to Goffman and the symbolic interactionists, to Parsons and to the anthropologist Marcel Mauss as well as to the economists. The various borrowings are piled together to produce, in Alasdair MacIntyre's words, a vast quarry. (In one's more exasperated moments, however, one is tempted to use a different metaphor and call the result an impenetrable quagmire.)

Of Blau's debts one of the most interesting and important is to Mauss. Some of Mauss's main concerns had been to show that exchange in primitive and archaic societies took the form of reciprocal gifts rather than of economic transactions, that these gifts were governed by a quite different morality from that of the economic market, and that they therefore had a meaning which, in Lévi-Strauss's words, was 'social and religious, magic and economic, utilitarian and sentimental, jural and moral' (Lévi-Strauss, 1949, p. 52). If it is true that the morality of social exchange, not only in primitive societies but also (as Blau supposes) in our own, is quite different from that of the economic exchange, then the applicability of economic theory outside its normal sphere becomes a much more contentious matter. Indeed, it is one of the paradoxes of exchange theory that Blau, having posed the contrast between economic and social exchange, makes virtually no attempt to modify his economic theories accordingly. It must therefore be another one of our tasks to see if this modification can satisfactorily be carried out.

The aim of this book, therefore, is to give an exposition and evaluation of some of the principal features of exchange theory. I shall be asking how far a rational choice approach can be used successfully outside economics. What are the main obstacles to its application? Does it need to be modified to make it applicable not only to 'primitive' economics but also to the exchange of advice for status, of conformity for approval? Can it be integrated with the traditional sociology of exchange or must there be two 'exchange theories', one deriving from economics and another from psychology and anthropology?

In accordance with these aims I shall begin, in part I, with an exposition of the different elements of exchange theory. First will come an outline of the 'pure theory of rational choice', and this will be followed by a description of the main uses to which Homans, Blau and company put it. Next I shall turn to what might be called the 'psychology and sociology of exchange', that is to the principal additions to the pure theory that our various exchange theorists have proposed.

In part II, I shall then be concerned with the task of evaluation. It was Homans himself who said that 'much modern sociological theory seems to me to possess every virtue except that of explaining anything' (1961, p. 10) and who promised that his own book would be a 'book of explanation'. Equally it seems to me that much modern discussion of sociological theory possesses every virtue except that of telling us whether the theory succeeds in explaining anything. The reason for this latter failure is, however, fairly obvious. It is often very difficult to test sociological theories and, even when it can be done, the tests have not always actually been carried out. I do not therefore promise any definitive 'book of evaluation' but I shall at the least try to provide the beginnings of some answers.

PART I

2. *The pure theory of rational choice*

It is one of the paradoxes of exchange theory that we start not with a theory of exchange but with a theory of choice that can be applied much more widely and to many phenomena that do not properly come within our definition of exchange. Thus even altruists whose actions are not 'contingent on rewarding reactions from others' still have to choose between alternative potential beneficiaries, and the theory of choice is in principle as easily applicable to them as it is to the more hard-nosed individuals who engage in social exchange. Altruists, like everybody else, are faced with the problem of 'scarce means which have alternative uses'. They are not exempted from the dilemmas of choice.

The strict economic theory of choice deals separately with situations of *certainty* and situations involving *risk*, while game theory deals with a special class of situations involving *uncertainty*. Situations of certainty are of course ones where each course of action open to the individual has a single, known outcome or consequence, whereas in the case of risk or uncertainty a number of possible outcomes may follow from any given course of action. *In the case of risk a numerical probability can be assigned to the likelihoods of each of the outcomes occurring whereas in the case of uncertainty no such probability can be assigned.* Tossing coins therefore involves risk; guessing whether Germany would invade Poland involved uncertainty.

This set of distinctions is unfortunately one which most exchange theorists ignore. They all start with the theory of choice under certainty (more commonly called the theory of riskless choice) and most rest content there, apparently oblivious of the fact that in real life certainty is a rare and privileged state of existence to be in. A few pay lip-service to game theory and to uncertainty, although fewer still explicitly use the theory of choice under uncertainty. And only Homans of the non-economists really uses the theory of risky choice. The distinctions are, however, useful and important ones and I shall therefore go through each in turn.

The theory of riskless choice

The central elements of this theory are extraordinarily simple, so simple indeed that the theory is frequently claimed to be tautological. It merely assumes that the individual can rank all the alternatives open to him in order of preference and will then select the one that comes at the top of the list. This is sometimes called the principle of 'utility maximization'. To choose the most preferred alternative is to choose the one which yields most utility and to maximize utility is therefore to select the alternative you like best.

While this may seem absurdly simple, there cannot be much doubt that it is a theory of *rational* choice. There could hardly be any other principle that a rational man would follow in situations of certainty. If it is a simple principle it is, I suggest, because situations of certainty are such straightforward ones.

To give the theory rather more bite, however, the economist usually makes a number of additional assumptions, nowadays employing the apparatus of indifference curves. These are not nearly so simple and they have caused a number of people (Blau among them as we shall see) considerable trouble. Briefly, they are geometrical devices used by economists to present information about an individual's preferences for differing combinations of two commodities. Figure 1 gives a typical example of an indifference map (that is of a set of indifference curves). Quantities of the two commodities are measured along the two axes, in this case (borrowed from Baumol, 1961) the number of cummerbunds being measured along the vertical axis and helpings of zabaglione along the horizontal axis. Any point to the 'north-east' of these two axes thus represents a particular *combination* of cummerbunds and zabaglione.

A set of indifference curves is then drawn in this area to the north-east of the axes, each indifference curve being 'the locus of points each

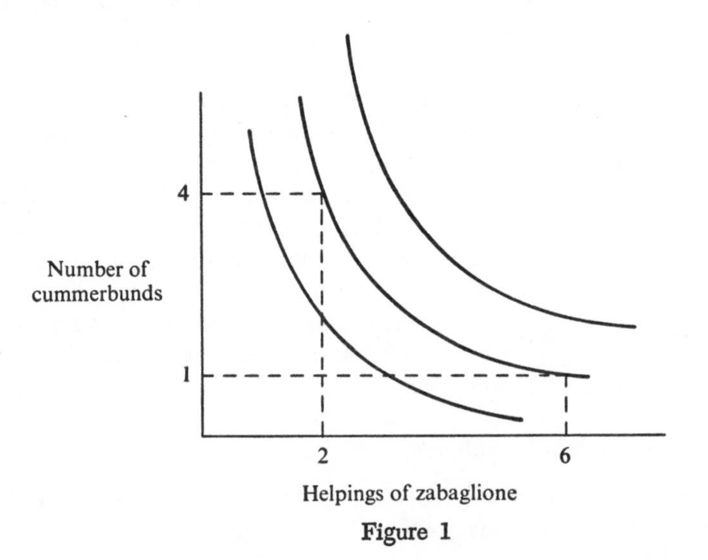

Figure 1

of which represents a collection of commodities such that the consumer is indifferent among any of these combinations' (Baumol, 1961, p. 183). For example, we could confront the consumer with a large number of combinations of commodities and ask him to rank them according to how desirable he found them. Presumably he would like some combinations more than others, but there would also be some 'ties'. He might be just as happy with, say, four cummerbunds and two helpings of zabaglione as he is with one cummerbund and six helpings of zabaglione. We could then draw a line joining these two 'tied' combinations and this would constitute an indifference curve. The indifference curve simply shows a set of combinations which the consumer ranks equally highly in his scale of preferences.

In drawing these indifference curves the economist also commonly makes three assumptions. They are:

1 *Nonsatiety*: the consumer is not oversupplied with either commodity.

2 *Transitivity*: if P, Q and R are any three combinations of commodities, and if the consumer prefers P to Q and Q to R, then he will also prefer P to R.

3 *Diminishing marginal rate of substitution*: the more the consumer has of one commodity, the more he is prepared to give up of that commodity in exchange for a given amount of the other.

Broadly speaking these assumptions mean that, first, the consumer would prefer to have more cummerbunds and more helpings of zabaglione, other things being equal, if he had the chance. He must therefore not be on a diet in this particular case. (For the indifference curves which resulted when subjects actually were on a diet see MacCrimmon and Toda, 1969.) It follows that the further to the north-east a point lies the more the consumer will prefer it. Accordingly any indifference curve lying above and to the right of another will represent preferred combinations of commodities.

Secondly, transitivity means that the consumer must have consistent preferences. (And to have intransitive preferences would be accounted irrational.) It follows from this assumption that indifference curves will not intersect.

Thirdly, the 'diminishing marginal rate of substitution' is a modern version of the old-fashioned notion of diminishing marginal utility: the more we have of one thing the less valuable any further unit becomes. From it follows the conclusion that indifference curves will be convex to the origin and will have a downwards (or negative) slope.

Finally, the economist introduces scarcity in the form of the budget constraint line. The consumer is (reasonably enough) assumed to have a limited amount of money which he can either spend on cummerbunds, on zabaglione, or on some combination of the two. The precise amounts that he can obtain will of course depend on the prices of the two commodities as well as on the actual amount of money available. The first budget constraint line in figure 2 shows that, at the reigning prices, he could get three cummerbunds if he spent all his money on them, six helpings of zabaglione if instead he spent it all on them, or any of the combinations of the two given by the constraint line.

The economist is now at last in a position to give us some predictions. First of all he can predict that the consumer will in fact choose the combination of commodities given by the point of tangency between the budget constraint line and the indifference curve JJ′. This is the point which yields the most preferred combination of cummerbunds and zabaglione available (all other combinations which are actually open to him being on lower indifference curves) and, if he follows the theory of riskless choice and maximizes utility, this is the point which he must choose.

The economist can also predict the consumer's behaviour if his income rises or falls, or if the relative prices of the two commodities change. If his income rises, the constraint line will move to the right and the consumer can move to a higher indifference curve. This is straightforward enough. When relative prices change, however, the results are rather more interesting. Suppose, for example, there is a slump in the cummerbund market and the price falls to half its original level. Even though the consumer's money income has not changed, he is now faced by a new budget constraint line: he can now obtain six cummerbunds instead of the previous three if he spends all his money on them and he can also buy any of the new combinations

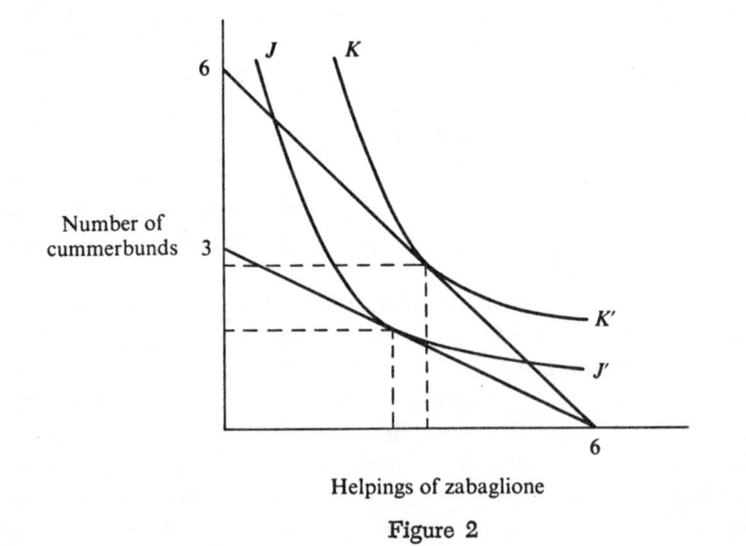

Figure 2

given by the new constraint line. The indifference curve JJ′ is nowhere tangential to this new constraint line and the consumer will be able to move to a higher indifference curve than the old one, going in this case to the point of tangency between the curve KK′ and the constraint line. As might have been expected, at this new point the consumer is buying more cummerbunds (since they are now more attractively priced than they were before). But there is also the much less expected result that *the fall in the price of cummerbunds has led to an increase in the purchase of zabaglione.* This is a much more striking result and, as we shall see in a later chapter, one with some important applications in sociology and anthropology. It occurs because the fall in the price of cummerbunds has enabled the consumer to buy the same quantity of goods as before but at a reduced outlay, thus making some money available for *extra* expenditure on cummerbunds and/or on zabaglione. Given the indifference map shown in figure 2, the consumer will choose to buy rather more of each (although we should note that with a different set of preferences he would have reached a different decision).

Of our various exchange theorists Blau is the one who follows the theory of riskless choice most closely. He puts forward the principle of utility maximization in words almost identical to the economists': 'The only assumption made', Blau writes, 'is that human beings choose between alternative potential associates or courses of action by evaluating the experiences or expected experiences with each in terms of a preference ranking and then selecting the best alternative' (Blau, 1964, p. 18).

Blau next goes on to describe indifference curves (in the course of which he makes some rather horrible elementary mistakes, failing to realize that indifference curves indicate preferences between *combinations* of commodities – see Heath, 1968). He also suggests how they might be used in predicting choices made between, say, giving advice to others on the one hand and relaxing and enjoying oneself on the other. On the vertical axis could be measured units of 'the status enhancement that accrues to [the individual] as a result of using his time for advising others' (p. 172) and on the horizontal axis could be measured time spent on relaxation. (Blau makes some mistakes here too but these are best passed over in silence.) The budget constraint line would now show the opportunities open to the individual given the *time* rather than the money at his disposal and given the 'price' of status (that is, the length of time he has to spend giving advice in order to obtain a given amount of status enhancement). The same kinds of prediction can now be made that the economist had earlier made: the individual will allocate his time in the proportions indicated by the point of tangency between constraint line and indifference curve, and changes in the 'price' of status will lead to consequential changes in the allocation of time.

Blau's example may not be the most compelling one, and his mistakes are rather unfortunate, but it should be clear that it is in principle almost as easy to apply indifference curve analysis to the allocation of time as it is to the allocation of money. If the individual can rank combinations of cummerbunds and zabaglione, there is no reason why he should not rank combinations of work and leisure or of status and relaxation; units of time can be as easily measured as quantities of goods or amounts of money; and even if there is an added difficulty in measuring status enhancement, there are surely other ways of spending one's time that are more easily measurable.

The other exchange theorists (the economists such as Downs and Olson always excluded) do not keep anything like so close to the economists' formulation. Homans gives us a 'value proposition' which one gathers is closely akin to the principle of utility maximization, although it is dressed up in something akin to the language of behavioural psychology. It reads: 'The more valuable to a man a unit of the activity another gives him, the more often he will emit activity rewarded by the activity of the other' (Homans, 1961, p. 55). In rather more prosaic language, 'the more valuable something is to a man, the more likely he is to try and get it'.

Homans makes no use of the apparatus of indifference curves, constraint lines and so forth (and was sharply taken to task by an economist for his omission – see Boulding and Davis, 1962), but he does have a 'deprivation–satiation proposition' which is perhaps a first cousin of the economists' principle of diminishing marginal utility. The proposition reads: 'The more often a man has in the recent past received a rewarding activity from another, the less valuable any further unit of that activity becomes to him' (Homans, 1961, p. 55).

But of all our main writers it is Thibaut and Kelley who have the most unusual terminology. They first introduce the notion of 'comparison level for alternatives' – CL_{alt} for short – by which they seem to mean the level of 'outcomes that the person can achieve in his best available alternative to the present relationship' (Thibaut and Kelley, 1959, p. 100). They then state that 'whether or not an individual attains (or at least expects to attain) reward–cost positions above his CL_{alt} determines whether or not he will remain in a given dyadic relationship' (p. 23). More simply and prosaically, 'a man will only stay in a relationship if it is more rewarding than the alternatives open to him'.

Despite the complicated and sometimes cumbersome language used by the economists and exchange theorists, it is important not to be deterred. The basic idea of the theory of riskless choice is simple enough: in situations of certainty men choose the course of action that yields them the most desirable consequence. And while the apparatus of indifference curves is sometimes found (as indeed it must have been by Blau) to involve an unfamiliar mode of reasoning, it enables us to present, in a convenient form, some general properties of people's preferences.

The theory of risky choices

As I suggested earlier, the principle of utility maximization is not so generally applicable as many have supposed. Take, for example, the man who goes into a betting shop with 50p in his pocket. He can either keep his 50p or he can stake it on a horse. To help him decide what he should do it is of little help to say that he should choose the course of action that has the most desirable consequences. Clearly the most desirable course is for him to stake his money, see his horse win, and get, say, £5 back. But equally the least desirable course is to stake the money, see his horse lose and get nothing back, losing even the 50p. What he wants to know is whether 'the risks are worth it'.

The earliest answer to this problem was that the individual should calculate the *expected value* of the different courses of action: he should weight the possible money gains or losses by the probability of their occurrence. In this case, if the probability of the horse's winning is one in twenty, the expected value of the gamble is 1/20 times £5, that is 25p. Since the expected value of keeping the stake money for oneself is simply 50p (there being no risk involved), it is clear that one should not take the gamble. The risks are not worth it.

The difficulty with this as an explanatory principle, of course, is that most people simply cannot be following it. Insurance companies and bookmakers generally make profits. They must therefore be taking in more in the form of premiums and stakes than they are paying out in winnings and compensation, and the expected value to the individual of his gamble or of his insurance policy must be less than that of keeping his money in his pocket. If it is rational to maximize expected value, the ordinary man in the street (unlike bookmakers and insurance companies) simply is not rational.

However, it can be argued that what is important to the individual is not so much the money that he gets as the utility that he gets from it and that what he therefore should do, and does do, is to act so as to maximize *expected utility*. That is, he should weight the *utility* not the money value of each possible outcome by the probability of its occurrence. This makes it much easier to see why people should insure their property: the large possible loss of all one's property may be exceedingly unpalatable whereas the certain loss of one's premium may have relatively little effect on one's utility. (For a more precise treatment of this see Edwards, 1954.)

The economist, then, assumes that in situations of risk men maximize expected utility and indeed assumes that this is the rational thing to do. This is a much more powerful principle than simple utility maximization (which is indeed merely a special case of expected utility maximization, holding when the probabilties are all unity). And it can be used to give some much more novel and interesting results, as we shall see when we come to Olson's work on the logic of collective action. It is, however, strangely ignored by the exchange theorists, and only Homans really takes it seriously. He first puts forward a 'success proposition' which states: 'The more often within a given period of time a man's activity rewards the activity of another, the more often the other will emit the activity' (Homans, 1961, p. 54). In simpler language, 'the better the chance of getting something, the more likely one is to try and get it'. Homans then, in a later work, correctly suggests that his value and success propositions, taken together, amount to more or less the same thing as the principle of expected utility maximization. He writes: 'The main proposition of the rational theory in one of its forms may be stated as follows: in choosing between alternative courses of action, a person will choose the one for which, as perceived by him, the mathematical value of $p \times v$ is the greater, where p is the probability that the action will be successful in getting a given reward and v is the value to the person of that reward. The effect of value on action in the rational theory is embodied in the value-proposition of behavioral psychology; the effect of the probability of success, in the success-proposition' (Homans, 1967, pp. 38–9). However, while Homans' two psychological propositions may more or less amount to the same thing as the theory of risky choice, they are not actually identical to it. Homans' propositions are based on the common pigeon, and the common pigeon, it seems, learns only from experience of past events; it does not reflect about the future. The rational man of the economists, on the other hand, does hold expectations about the future, and while these may be acquired from his personal experience of similar events in the past, this is not the only possible source of expectations. Thus if an unbiassed coin has come up heads on one trial, Homans' pigeon is apt to believe that it will come up heads on the subsequent trial too. But the rational man who has been told about probability theory does not make this mistake. He knows that there is a fifty–fifty chance of heads on each and every trial. His expectations are thus different from the pigeon's, and so will be his behaviour.

In many cases we will have no objective grounds for assigning numerical probabilities and we will therefore be faced with what were earlier defined as situations of uncertainty, not of risk. Here a different decision rule is called for, and the appropriate one is often supposed to be the *minimax* rule of game theory. Game theory made a spectacular appearance in the intellectual firmament with the publication of Von Neumann and Morgenstern's *Theory of Games and Economic Behavior* (1944). Since then its brightness has become dimmed. There have been no major advances in the theory itself and, while many have advocated its application in almost every branch of social science, few have been bold enough to put it into practice. It may, like many other brilliant theories, eventually turn out to be an intellectual curiosity of passing interest to the historian of ideas alone. Whatever the long-run significance of game theory proves to be, however, its manner of conceptualizing problems, if not its actual results, has influenced a number of exchange theorists (particularly Thibaut and Kelley and Barth), and this is perhaps an additional reason for looking at it.

The most famous part of game theory, and the part from which the minimax rule derives, is the theory of two-person zero–sum games. The game is zero–sum in the sense that the interests of the two participants are directly opposed: one person's winnings are at the expense of the other participant, and the more one wins the more the other loses. (The most common example would be a card game where each of the two players lays a stake and the winner takes all.) The two players are also assumed to be rational, informed actors. Each actor is therefore trying to get the best result for himself and hence the worst result for his opponent, and, more importantly, *each knows that the other knows that this is the case.* My opponent knows that I am out to do him down and will therefore take steps to prevent me, but I know this too and can therefore work out what he will be trying to do. As in chess, I can try to work out what my opponent's best replies are to my various moves, and I will select mine in the light of this information. It is therefore a game of strategy with each participant assessing what the other will do.

Consider, then, a game such as that described in figure 3. It might be a war game, for example, or indeed an actual war. Let us suppose the two opponents are those countries of Middle Earth, Gondor and Mordor. Both countries' sole aim, we assume, is to conquer territory from their neighbour, and each has three options open to it. Gondor could, as one option (a_1), make a pre-emptive nuclear strike against Mordor's capital and wipe it out. Alternatively, it could prepare a

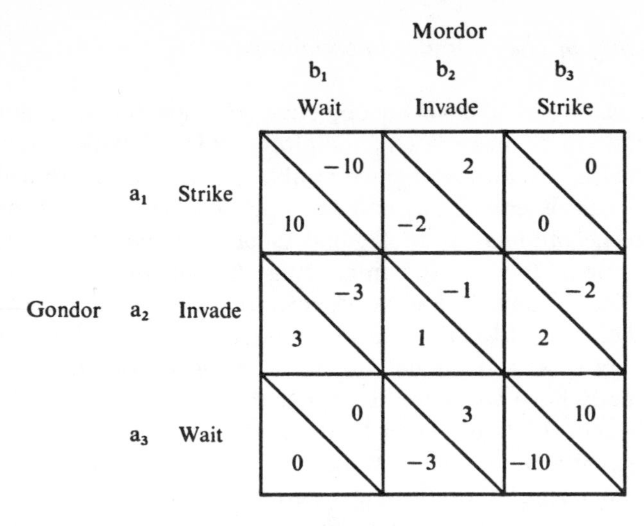

Figure 3

land invasion against Mordor's territory (option a_2), and finally it could simply wait and do nothing for the time being (option a_3).

Mordor equally has the same three options open to it, giving nine possible outcomes in all. The pay-offs associated with each outcome are given in the matrix in figure 3. Thus if Gondor makes a pre-emptive strike while Mordor waits, the result is outright victory for the former, which we will say is worth ten utiles (the unit which game theorists use), to Gondor, and minus ten to Mordor. Alternatively, if Gondor strikes but Mordor invades, the latter's land invasion succeeds in capturing some territory, but it cannot capitalize on its advantage because of the destruction of its capital. This, we shall say, gives Mordor two utiles and Gondor minus two. Similar stories can be told about the remaining cells.

Consider now the likely reasoning of the opponents. Gondor will clearly be tempted to make a pre-emptive strike in the hope of getting the ten-utile pay-off, but he can see that on the same reasoning Mordor will go for b_3. If both choose accordingly, there will be stalemate, neither capturing any territory and both therefore getting a zero pay-off. Gondor, however, can see that he can do better than this by choosing to invade. This guarantees him a gain of one utile and might even get him three utiles. Mordor knows that Gondor knows this, however, and therefore chooses to invade likewise, thus minimizing his loss. The 'solution' of the game is therefore for the two opponents to choose options a_2 and b_2 respectively. Neither has any incentive now to move from this choice. If Gondor switches (Mordor sticking to b_2), he is bound to do worse; and the same applies to Mordor.

Notice that what each player has done is to *select the course of action that minimizes his possible loss.* Mordor has guaranteed himself that he will lose no more than one utile (other courses of action possibly losing him rather more) and Gondor has guaranteed himself a gain of one utile (other courses of action not necessarily doing as well). To follow the minimax rule, therefore, is to compare the worst outcomes that can follow from each course of action and to choose the one which has the least ill effects if the worst outcome should occur. One major achievement of game theory, then, is to show that in a special class of games this is the 'rational' thing to do (rational in the sense that there is no incentive to depart from the minimax solution).

It is, however, a very special class of games that is concerned. First, as we have seen, they are *two-person* games: if we introduce a third person new problems of coalition formation arise. Second, they are *zero-sum* games; if we allow some common as well as some conflicting interests the issues become much more complicated. We have to assume that both are interested only in territory and do not care how many men or material they lose in the process. Third, the players have to be *rational strategists*: suppose for example that Mordor took a flippant view of the game and instead of considering his opponent's possible actions and reactions simply tossed a die to select his own move; in this case b_1, b_2 and b_3 would all be equally likely and Gondor could do best for himself by choosing a pre-emptive strike. He would thus have a one-in-three chance of ten utiles and this (taking into account the one-in-three chance of a small loss) gives greater expected utility than do either of the other options. (The point will perhaps be clearer if we consider a series of plays of the game. If he chooses a_1 every time Gondor gets an average 2⅔ utiles per game. His next best option, a_2, only gives an average of 2 utiles.) This yields the important conclusion *that it is irrational to minimax against an irrational opponent.*

Fourth – and here we come to a new point and to one of the most complicated aspects of game theory – the simple minimax strategy is only appropriate in games that have a *saddle-point.* A saddle-point is an entry in the game matrix which is the highest in its column and the smallest in its row, and it is no coincidence that the cell a_2,b_2 in our matrix happens to be a saddle-point. It was precisely because it was the highest in its column that there was no incentive for Gondor to select a different option, and it was precisely because it was the lowest in its row that Mordor had no incentive to alter his strategy either.

There is, alas, no necessity for every zero-sum game to have a point with such desirable qualities, and this means that there will be many games in which there will be no such unique 'solution' as we found in figure 3. There will be an incentive for one or other player to alter his intended move, leading to the familiar sequence of 'if I do this, he will do that . . . but if he does that, I will try the other . . .', an unending sequence that is so familiar to novice chess players. (In fact, chess does have a saddle-point but fortunately it is not yet known what it is.)

So much for the bad news. Now for the good news. One of the most impressive intellectual achievements of game theory has been to show that in zero–sum games without a saddle-point the rational course of action is not to minimax at all but to follow a 'mixed strategy' in which different moves are played in a specifiable ratio. While the proof of this result is beyond our scope, the actual computations required to work out what the actual ratio is are not all that difficult, and as we shall see later there is one anthropological study in which these computations are made and yield some intriguingly accurate predictions (Davenport, 1960).

It should be clear by now that game theory is not attempting (and could not hope) to provide any general conclusions about how people behave in conditions of uncertainty. Indeed, to be fair to game theory, it does not claim to be about what people actually do under any situations whatever; it merely claims to be a *normative* theory telling people what they *ought* to do in the situations described. Still, we may reasonably hope that some people will prove to be good strategists and to follow the 'right' strategies in two-person zero–sum games, but what people will or ought to do in other situations of uncertainty is a matter to which our theorists have paid remarkably little attention. One possibility (to which I am favourably inclined) is that one should operate on the principle of 'insufficient reason'. That is to say one should, in the absence of information to the contrary, simply assume that each possible outcome is equally probable. Another possibility is that one should take into account only the best and the worst outcomes that could arise from each course (see Arrow and Hurwicz, 1972). But at all events I think it is fair to say that to follow the minimax in *all* situations of uncertainty is an unduly conservative strategy and cannot be accounted rational.

3. *Exchange and power in social life*

We have so far, with the exception of game theory, been concerned only with one side of the exchange. Thus in the theories of riskless and risky choices we simply considered what the rational individual would do when faced with a given range of outcomes with known probabilities of occurrence. We took it for granted, for example, that if a man paid the appropriate price he would get some zabaglione in return, but we did not explicitly consider why anyone else would be prepared to sell him this zabaglione. We simply assumed that it would be forthcoming. We explained Ego's behaviour but not Alter's.

In principle, however, it is easy enough to apply these theories of choice to *both* sides of the exchange, and all our major writers in fact do so. Or rather, they all apply the theory of riskless choice to both sides. They point out (to no one's surprise) that an exchange will take place only if *both* participants believe that the exchange provides them with more utility than does any other option currently open to them. Thus, say Thibaut and Kelley, 'the formation of a relationship depends . . . upon whether or not the *jointly* experienced outcomes are above each member's CL_{alt}' (Thibaut and Kelley, 1959, pp. 22-3). Or suppose, to take Blau's favourite example, that two members of a work group are considering whether to exchange advice for status. The exchange will take place only if (1) the more expert believes that the status gained outweighs the utility he would have obtained from any of the alternative activities open to him (for example, getting on with his own work) and similarly if (2) the less expert believes that the advice he receives outweighs the status lost (status which he could have kept if he had worked out his problem for himself). (More technically, the new combinations of status, work and so on that each participant gets from the exchange must put him on a higher indifference curve than the combinations he would have got from alternative transactions or from no transaction at all.)

The basis for exchange, then, is that each side has something that the other wants. The less expert member of the group wants advice with his work; the more expert wants praise and status. True, the former would like status as well, but at the moment his relative wants are such that he thinks he will be better off giving up some self-respect and getting some help in return than he would be keeping his self-respect and going without the advice. *The exchange, therefore, enables both participants to be better off than they would have been without it.*

Notice, however, that although the two individuals will be better off than they would be if they did not carry out the exchange, *they need not necessarily be better off than they were before.* Indeed, whether or not they are is a good way of defining whether it is a *voluntary* exchange or a *coerced* one. This is a very important distinction and failure to make it can lead to some unfortunate muddles; it can certainly lead us to overlook some of the less palatable aspects of social exchange and to suppose that there is some 'hidden hand' making all for the best in the best of all possible worlds.

Now, the example we have so far used (like most of the exchanges with which economists deal) is presumably a voluntary one. The less expert worker can decide not to ask for advice, in which case he preserves the status quo: he can ensure that he does not end up worse than before. And the more expert worker could perhaps refuse to enter the exchange without incurring any penalty. So he too can preserve the status quo. Suppose, however, that the expert initially refused to give advice and that the other worker then threatened to report his long lunch hours to the supervisor if he continued to be uncooperative. The expert might now change his mind and offer to give the advice, presumably reckoning that he was better off doing so than getting on with his own work and being reported for his infractions of the rules. But he must now be worse off than he was before. If the other worker is serious about his threat, he cannot return to the status quo ante: he has been coerced into the exchange. Admittedly overt threats are probably rather rare in social life, but a norm requiring people to do favours for others when asked would have much the same effect. Failure to comply with the norm may lead to sanctions from onlookers in the group, and may therefore lead the expert to provide the assistance requested even though he would have preferred to be left in peace to get on with his own work.

Puzzlingly, most exchange theorists ignore or omit these coerced exchanges from their theories and concentrate instead on the voluntary exchanges. Thus, for example, Blau writes: 'An individual may give another money because the other stands in front of him with a gun in a holdup. While this could be conceptualized as an exchange of his money for his life, it seems preferable to exclude the result of physical coercion from the range of social conduct encompassed by the term "exchange"' (Blau, 1964, p. 91). It is hard to see why this is preferable. Both voluntary and coerced exchanges are equally amenable to the kind of rational choice explanation which Blau favours, and it seems unfortunate to restrict unnecessarily the scope of a theory. There will be plenty of inevitable restrictions all too soon.

The theory so far, then, simply says that the exchange will take place if both sides find it preferable to the alternatives actually open to them at the moment in question. It says nothing so far of the actual rates of exchange – of the amount of respect and approval which is given in return for the advice in our example. And indeed where we have a single dyadic relationship as in this example, conventional economic analysis has relatively little to offer. We can, however, see that the alternatives open to the two workers will determine the *limits* within which the rate of exchange must fall. Thus if the novice can get the same quality of advice from the supervisor at the cost of a mild rebuke, he is not going to abase himself in front of the expert.

And if the expert has got sycophantic colleagues who will always listen admiringly to his latest exploits, he is not going to tolerate a curt 'thank you' from the novice. Each can do better for himself elsewhere and so the exchange will not take place on these terms.

This can be put into a simple and rather useful diagram if we take a monetary example. Thus figure 4 shows that a gourmet is willing to pay up to £2 for a serving of a rather special kind of zabaglione. Above that price he decides that it is not worth it and that he would prefer to spend his money on the rather larger helpings of inferior zabaglione that he can obtain elsewhere. At anything below £2, however, he thinks it definitely is worth it, and the lower the price the better. Conversely, the restauranteur is not prepared to go below 50p, for he knows that he can always find another customer at that price to buy the zabaglione which he has prepared. Anything above 50p is worth it, and this time, of course, the higher the price the better.

This gives us the limits for the two participants and the two ranges over which each will find the transaction worthwhile. The area of overlap therefore determines the range of prices which are actually feasible. If there had been no overlap, no exchange would have taken place. Since there is an overlap, however, there will presumably be an exchange; the price must fall somewhere within the range of overlap; but where it will fall will depend on a variety of other factors such as the bargaining skill of the two participants.

It is in fact possible to give a slightly more sophisticated analysis of the exchange if we use indifference curves once more, and Blau does in fact attempt to do so. The analysis is a rather complicated one for the reader who is unfamiliar or unhappy with the geometrical de-

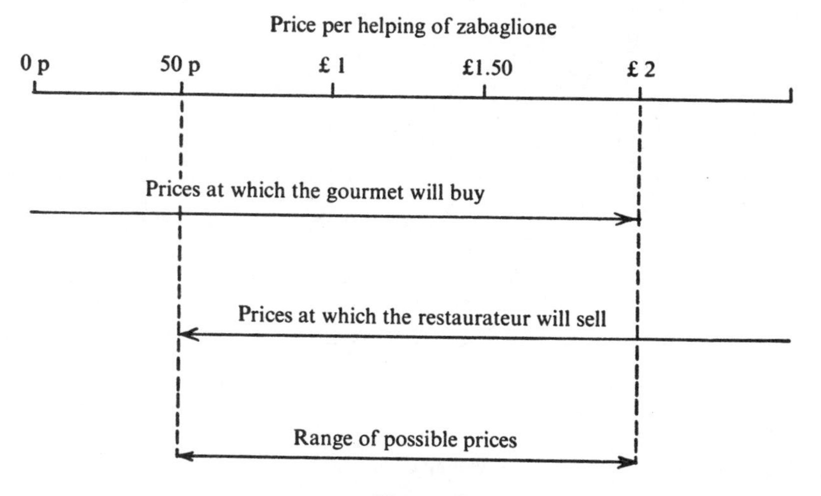

Figure 4

vices beloved of economists and, since it does not really add a great deal, little will be lost by skipping the remainder of this section.

Blau begins with a 'box diagram' as in figure 5. On the vertical axes he measures 'problem-solving ability' and on the horizontal axes 'resources of willing compliance'. To the north-east of the axes O_aY and O_aX he then draws the expert's indifference map and to the south-west of the axes O_bX and O_bY he draws the non-expert's map. By this ingenious device we have the two participants facing each other as if across the bargaining table. The next stage is to assume that each comes to the transaction with an existing stock of resources. The expert, Blau assumes, has O_aK_a problem-solving ability and O_aH_a resources of willing compliance, putting him at the point P_0 and on the indifference curve P_0A_0. Conversely the non-expert has O_bH_b resources of compliance but only O_bK_b worth of problem-solving ability, putting him also on the point P_0 but of course this time on his own indifference curve curve P_0B_0.

This all means that the total resources of compliance available to the pair is the amount O_aX and that the total problem-solving ability is O_aY. It also means that it is possible to redistribute the compliance and problem solving between the two participants so that both end up on higher indifference curves and thus are better off. As can be seen any point within the melon-shaped area $P_0A_0Q_0B_0$ puts both of them on higher curves than they were on originally at point P_0.

This does not yet really add very much to the earlier analysis of exchange. We have simply rediscovered the area of possible transactions. Consider, however, a point such as R_0. Both sides will clearly

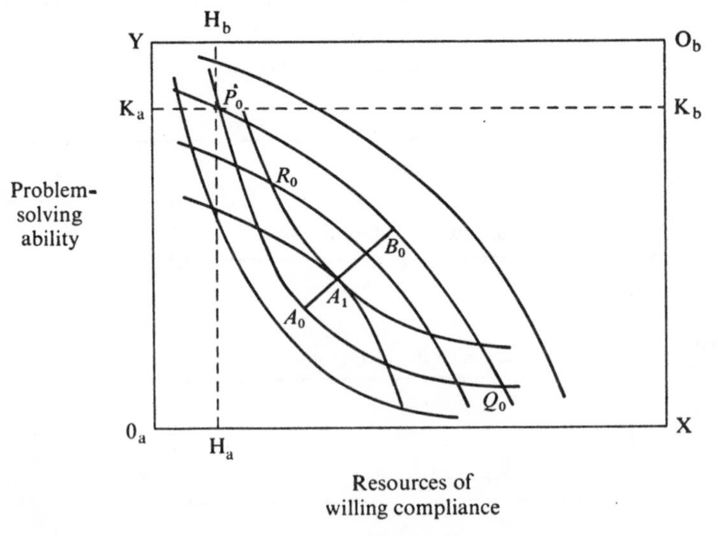

Figure 5

find this preferable to P_0. But it is still possible for one or other side to become better off still without making the other worse off. They could, for example, move along the expert's indifference curve until they reach A_1. Here the expert is by definition just as content with the combination of services that he is getting as he was with the one at R_0. Equally clearly the non-expert is better off, for he has moved to a higher indifference curve.

It can easily be seen that further movements along the expert's indifference curve will now make the non-expert worse off and will do so without bringing any advantage to the expert either. Point A_1 will therefore be a kind of 'sticking point'. It can also be seen that the same kind of argument can be applied to other points within the area of possible transactions. One side will always become better off, and will do so without making the other worse off, if they move along an indifference curve until they reach the line A_0B_0. This line is called the 'contract line'. Once on it, however, it is possible for one participant to improve his position only at the expense of the other and clearly a rational opponent (for such he now becomes) will not stand for this. The theory therefore enables us to infer that the actual exchange will take place somewhere on the contract line, but precisely where on the line it cannot tell us.

Power and dependency

Much simpler, and also much more useful, than the 'box diagram' analysis of exchange is a rational choice theory of power that has long been current among sociologists. The basic idea is a beautifully simple one that follows directly from the elementary analysis of exchange. It is simply the idea that *the less satisfactory are the alternatives to a particular supplier, the more dependent one is on him and the higher the price that he will be able to obtain.* Thus the more that a worker wants advice from a particular expert colleague, or the less expert are other potential advisers, then the higher will be the price that he will tolerate, if he is rational, before deciding not to enter the exchange. Conversely, the less the expert wants status and praise, and the more willing others are to accord him it, the higher will be the price that he will require before entering the exchange.

The same points can easily be made using the diagram (figure 4) that we used for the elementary analysis of exchange. If the zabaglione is already made (or at least the ingredients all prepared) and it is already late at night (so that no further customers can be expected), the restaurateur will have no satisfactory alternatives to our gourmet and almost any price however low will be preferable to throwing the ingredients away. The restaurateur's 'comparison level for alternatives' is thus much reduced and the area of overlap is much increased – to the considerable potential benefit of the gourmet. (One may ask, perhaps, why restaurant prices do not therefore fall drastically in the early hours of the morning. I suppose that one reason might be that real restaurants are more efficient than our hypothetical restaurateur and do not prepare their ingredients beforehand. Another might be that they have to pay their staff overtime after midnight, thus raising the comparison level for alternatives once more.)

Again we have not been able to predict what the price will actually be. This will still be a matter for bargaining. All we have really done is to point out that the *bargaining power* of the participants will vary according to the alternative sources of supply open to them. Men may use their bargaining power more or less adroitly, and it is certainly possible that changes in the available alternatives will not be reflected at all in the price. By and large, however, it seems a reasonable enough inference that the two will be correlated.

Theories of bargaining power on essentially the same lines as the one just outlined appear in many different areas of sociology and in many different guises. Thus Ross (1921) advanced an essentially similar 'law of personal exploitation' which he held applied even (or indeed especially) to intimate social relationships. 'In any sentimental relation', he wrote, 'the one who cares less can exploit the one who cares more' (p. 136). And Waller and Hill (also interested in sentimental relations) put forward a very similar 'principle of least interest'. They write: 'That person is able to dictate the conditions of association whose interest in the continuation of the affair is least' (Waller and Hill, 1951, p. 191). 'A boy and girl are thrown together', they state. 'They are of the same general class standing, but one stands recognizably higher in the scale of dating desirability than the other. The more desirable person has many more opportunities for courtship association than the other, and both recognize that he could, if he wished, "date" someone more desirable. An interaction ensues based upon the fact that the person in the higher position has little motivation to continue the relationship, whereas the other intensely desires its perpetuation. Control of the relationship follows the principle of least interest, and the relationship, if it is continued, comes to give the dominant partner everything that he desires of such a relationship (and what he may desire is by no means limited to sexual demands) while the other partner gains nothing but the continuance of the relationship' (p. 166).

The modern exchange theorists put forward essentially similar theories of power too. Thibaut and Kelley put the point most simply. They argue that the level of a man's CL_{alt} determines his dependence upon a relationship and hence his power within it. They also manage to get us away from 'sentimental relations' and instead illustrate their argument with an example from Wilensky's study of intellectuals in trade unions (Wilensky, 1956). 'The replaceability of the staff expert's skill is an important factor in determining the amount of influence he will have on decision making in the union', they say. 'His power is increased to the degree that his skill and experience are not replaceable' (Thibaut and Kelley, 1959, p. 109).

Blau gives us a rather more complicated (and, I fear, muddled) account. He presents four conditions which, taken together, give men no option but to submit to the power of another and comply with his requests. The conditions are:

1 They have no services to offer which the other would like in return.

2 They cannot obtain the needed service elsewhere.

3 They cannot coerce him to furnish the service.

4 They cannot resign themselves to do without the service.

At first sight this all seems sensible enough, for it is not difficult to show that from these and a few other assumptions (that men are rational and informed, for example) the individuals concerned will have to submit. Where the account is unsatisfactory, however, is that it equates power with the ability to secure submission and compliance (following the Weberian tradition) and thus makes power a product of the *extreme* case where there is a 'unilateral exchange' of services. Now it may be true that individuals with pressing needs, no services to give in return, no satisfactory alternatives, and no means of coercion simply have to submit to another and comply with whatever requests he may care to make. But surely we do not want to restrict the concept of power to such unusual and bizarre situations, which seem virtually to be ones of slavery. Surely we would want to say that power and exploitation are more prevalent in social life than this analysis would allow. Surely, if men have some services to offer in return – but not particularly valued ones; if men have some alternative sources of supply – but not particularly satisfactory ones; if men can have some recourse to coercion – but only at considerable risks to themselves; if men could steel themselves to do without – but only at the cost of some personal suffering – then surely we could expect reciprocal exchange of services, not slavery; but it would be an exchange on very unfavourable terms and we would hardly want to say that the two sides had equal power.

More bluntly, a man's power may be reflected in the *price* that he can secure for his services, and not only in his ability to get others to do whatever he wants. Indeed, this is surely the great advantage of the rational choice theory of power. To use the theory we have to know about the alternatives open to men and their valuation of them, and we can then make predictions about the consequential rate of exchange. *But we do not actually need to measure power itself directly.* Since power seems to be just about the most difficult thing to measure in social science this must be counted a notable success for rational choice theory.

The theory of price

The theory of power has told us that the more dependent one is on a relationship the higher the price that one may have to pay, but it does not tell us what the price actually will be. In the cases we have considered there has always been some bargaining area within which the price would lie, but precisely where, we had no way of knowing. Under some rather special conditions, however, the bargaining area disappears and we are left with a unique, determinate price. The conditions are as follows:

1 *Homogeneous commodities*: in the eyes of the buyers and sellers a unit from one source of supply must be an equally satisfactory alternative to a unit from any other source.

2 *Perfect knowledge*: all buyers and sellers must know the prices at which other transactions are being carried out and at which others are willing to buy and sell.

3 *Large numbers*: there must be many buyers and sellers and none should have such a large market share that he can independently have a significant effect on the volume of transaction.

From the first two conditions it follows that there will be a single price reigning in the market. No buyer (or seller) will be able to discriminate against anyone else and no one will be able to hold out for more favorable terms than others are getting. Thus if one expert worker is willing to provide advice in return merely for a polite 'thank you', it will be no use for another to demand a higher price, for he will simply get no takers. And from the third condition it follows that strategic considerations can be ignored, and that instead the actual price will be determined by the overall demand and supply. A single large buyer might be tempted to try and rig the market whereas a single small buyer would have absolutely no scope for doing so.

The actual price is now given by the intersection of the demand and supply curves (see figure 6). The supply curve indicates the total amounts which all the suppliers in the market, taken together, would be prepared to sell at each price level. It slopes up from left to right indicating the conventional assumption that they will be prepared to supply more the higher the price. Correspondingly the de-

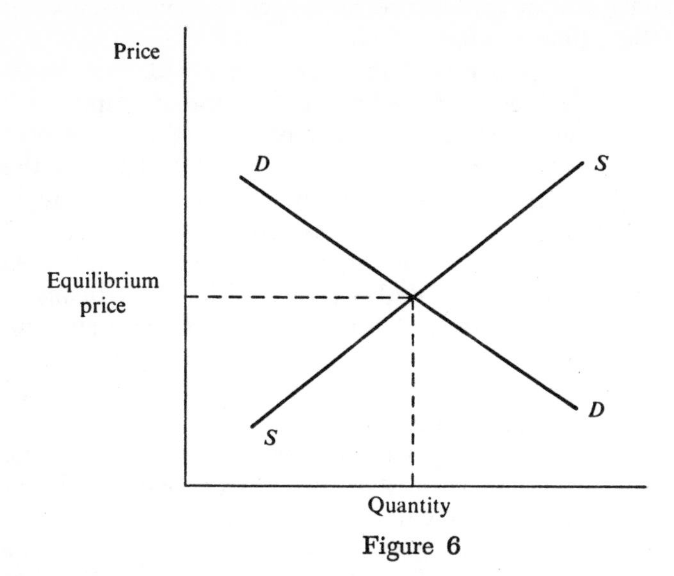

Figure 6

mand curve indicates the total amounts which the buyers would be prepared to purchase at different prices and slopes down from left to right. That the equilibrium price will be given by the intersection of the two curves can easily be seen. If the price were higher, there would be unsatisfied sellers who could find no purchaser, and it would be rational for them to offer a lower price in order to obtain some custom. Conversely, if the price were lower than the equilibrium one, there would be some unsatisfied buyers who could find no one to sell them goods, and it would be rational for them to offer a higher price. Competition would thus force price down and up respectively until supply equalled demand.

Of our main exchange theorists, only Homans and Blau really make any use of the theory of price. They both seem to suppose that there will sometimes be social markets in which services such as advice will be purchased with approval and compliance (the latter being the equivalents of money in social markets). 'The consulting relations in a work group do not exist in isolation from each other . . .', writes Blau, for example. 'The very existence of alternative opportunities invites their exploration, and as some workers explore various exchange opportunities they tempt others who have already become relatively settled in consulting relations with promises of more profitable alternatives. In consequence of this proliferation of exchange, experts must compete for the compliance of colleagues and for superior status in the group, and those in need of advice must compete for the consulting time of experts. In the course of this double competition, an approximate going rate of compliance for advice becomes established in the group' (Blau, 1964, p. 176).

Not only do these competitive processes uniquely determine the price, but we can also see how changes in demand or supply will affect the price. Suppose, for example, some of the established experts are promoted and leave the work group. The amounts of advice that they were willing to supply at each group will clearly have to be subtracted from the aggregate supply curve, and the new curve will now be further over to the left (see figure 7). At each price, then, less advice is now available from the (now reduced) company of experts. The new point of intersection between the demand and supply curves is now further to the left too (indicating a smaller volume of transactions) and of course higher up (indicating a higher price). Increased scarcity has increased the price.

We can also see that the steeper the demand curve (in the economist's language, the more inelastic it is), the bigger will be the increase in price and the smaller will be the reduction in quantity of advice provided. Conversely, the less steep the curve, the smaller the increase in price and the larger the reduction in quantity. This now enables Blau to reach one of those counter-intuitive conclusions beloved of theorists. He writes: 'Changes in the number of experts in a work group will affect the volume of consultation if the task is relatively easy [i.e. if the demand curve is not a steep one] but not, or

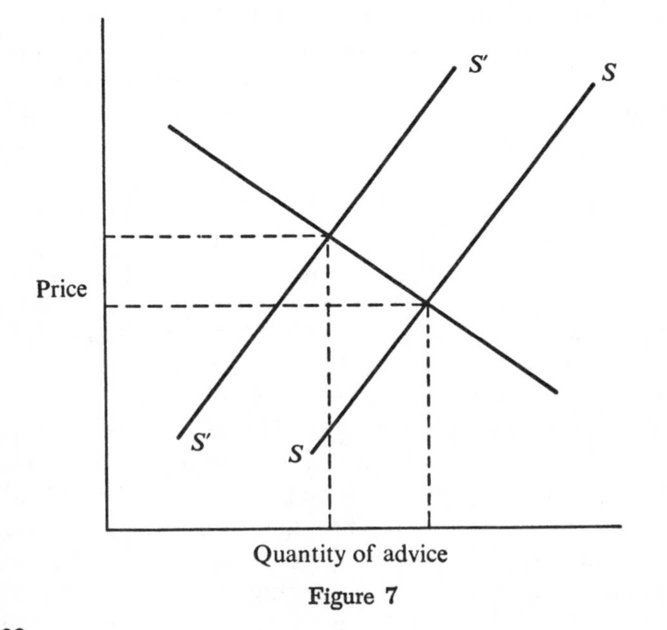

Figure 7

much less, if it is very difficult. Contrary to what common sense would lead one to expect, the supply of advice in a work group will influence the amount of consultation *less* if task performance is of great importance to group members [i.e. if the demand curve is inelastic] than if it is of little importance relative to informal status' (Blau, 1964, p. 169).

Whereas Blau is largely interested in the price changes for a given commodity, Homans is more interested in the relative prices of different commodities. His is the kind of question that used to puzzle the early economists: why is the price of diamonds so much higher than that of water when water is so much more useful and essential than diamonds? The answer of course is that the *supply* of water is much more ample. If there were no more water in the world than there are diamonds, their relative importance for human life would no doubt be reflected in their prices.

Homans does not take such a paradoxical case as diamonds and water but the more mundane one of conformity and expertise. A service such as conformity, he points out, is in ample supply. 'Any old fool, so to speak, can conform' (1961, p. 146). Predictably, however, we find that expert advice with one's work is relatively scarce – the supply curve is further over to the left – and the price will thus be higher. This gives Homans the basis for a theory of social status. He assumes that advice will be paid for in the coin of social approval and that those who supply it to other members of the group will therefore acquire higher social status. 'Whereas a common service like conformity tends to make the members of a group equal in the amount of approval they received from one another, the capacity to supply a rare service gets the men who actually do supply it a larger amount of social approval than the other members of their group get. They are superior to the others and no longer their social equals' (Homans, 1961, p. 148).

4. *The logic of collective action*

Our main writers stop with the theory of price, but there is still a great deal more that can be done with economic theory. We have dealt with 'trade' but we have not yet done anything about 'production'. Fortunately a number of political scientists and economists, such as Downs and Olson, have developed some stimulating and provocative theories that go some way to filling the gap. They are basically theories of *collective action* rather than of exchange pure and simple. They deal with situations where a number of individuals have to get together and organize if a particular benefit is to be obtained; they deal with pressure group activity, with clubs and with coalition formation.

To begin with, an important, indeed fundamental, distinction is necessary between a public good and a private good. *A private good is one whose enjoyment can be restricted to those who have paid for it, whereas a public good is one which, if it is provided at all, must be made available to all potential beneficiaries whether they have contributed or not.* Thus the conventional consumer good is a private good: the shopkeeper can simply refuse to hand it over to anyone who has not paid for it. Equally sports facilities such as swimming baths constitute private goods since those who have not paid their entrance fee can be excluded. Again, the 'spoils of office' in politics constitute private goods since the Prime Minister can exclude his political enemies (even those within his own party) from any share in them. Of course, we may choose to provide these benefits free to all comers, but the important point is that we have the choice whether to or not. We are not bound to provide them to all irrespective of the recipient's contributions.

Quite the reverse is true with public goods. The classic example here is national defence. If national defence is provided in times of war, tax evaders and conscientious objectors get the benefit just as much as those who pay for the defence or who actually do the fighting. Short of rounding up the tax evaders (which might be very difficult) and conscientious objectors (rather easier) and shipping them off to an undefended offshore island, there is no way of excluding them from the benefits of the defence services. Situations of this kind, moreover, are by no means unusual. If a group of activists campaign against, and prevent, a new airport, the local residents who took no part in the campaign get the benefits of the resulting peace and quiet just as much as do the activists. Again, all women, homosexuals or blacks get the benefit of anti-discrimination measures whether or not they have joined Women's Lib, Gay Lib or Black Power.

Whether a particular benefit is a public or a private one is extremely important for the potential beneficiaries, and indeed whether the benefit is actually provided or not may well depend upon it. The major contribution to our understanding of this, and indeed one of the most important contributions to rational choice theory, has been provided by Mancur Olson in his study of public goods, and it is to this that we now turn.

The theory of public goods

Olson's major achievement is to show that public goods may not be provided *even if everyone concerned might actually be better off making the required contributions and receiving the benefits in question.* Suppose, for example, that if the workers in a particular industry organized and formed a trade union they would as a result secure a £1 per week wage increase. Suppose, moreover, that dues of only 10p per week, if paid by all the potential beneficiaries, would be sufficient to finance the organization. All members would thus make a gain of 90p a week. This sounds like a good bargain for the workers, but what Olson is able to show is that, even in this situation, it may be quite rational for no one to contribute and thus for no wage increase to be secured.

The explanation is as follows. In deciding whether or not to join the trade union and make the required contribution to union funds the rational, self-interested individual will consider the expected utility of his contribution and will compare it with the alternative uses to which it might be put. Now the expected utility of the contribution is not the £1 a week wage increase which the worker will obtain, for he gets that increase whether or not he contributes. The question is not simply 'What is the size of the benefit provided by the group?' (as it is in the case of a private good). Rather, it is 'What difference does my contribution make to the group's chance of success?' 'Since I get the benefit whether or not I contribute', the rational worker reasons, 'it is only worth contributing if it makes a significant difference to the chance of success.' More precisely, the rational worker must consider the *difference* which his contribution makes to the likelihood that the benefit will be provided and then multiply this by the utility of the benefit in question. In this case if he thinks that his 10p contribution raises the probability by 0.01 (a rather optimistic estimate, one might imagine), then the expected utility of his contribution is equivalent to $0.01 \times £1$, that is to 1p (assuming that utility is a linear function of money). The individual is therefore clearly better off keeping his 10p dues and spending them on something else. All the other potential contributors will reason likewise; none of them will contribute; no union will form; and no wage increase will be obtained.

Armed with this argument Olson is now able to overthrow the conventional wisdom which asserts that individuals with common interests will join together to further those interests. It will not be enough, says Olson, for the members of the working class to come to an individual appreciation of the fact that it is in their common interest to overthrow capitalism. This will in no way guarantee the occurrence of class action, for each worker will also realize that his own efforts have no noticeable effect on the success of the revolution. Rather, in the absence of special conditions (to which we shall come shortly), *rational, self-interested individuals will not act to achieve their common or group interests* (Olson, 1965, p. 2). Similarly, rational self-interested individuals will not join trade unions or other pressure groups in the absence of special conditions, nor will they vote or pay their taxes.

Since individuals do of course sometimes do these things, Olson concludes that special conditions must be present. The main ones which concern us here are what he calls 'selective incentives'. Essentially these are private goods, additional to the public good in question. 'Only a *separate and "selective" incentive* will stimulate a rational individual in a latent group to act in a group-oriented way', writes Olson. 'In such circumstances group action can be obtained only through an incentive that operates, not indiscriminately, like the collective good, upon the group as a whole, but rather *selectively* towards the individuals in the group. The incentive must be "selective" so that those who do not join the organization working for the group's interest, or in other ways contribute to the attainment of the group's interest, can be treated differently from those who do' (p. 51). Thus the penalties imposed on tax evaders constitute a selective incentive and so do benefits such as protection against unfair dismissal provided by a trade union. Equally, the 'closed shop' rule is a device used by trade unions to make employment in a particular firm a selective incentive. The closed shop, therefore, is not merely a restriction on individual freedom, as many have supposed. It is also a device which makes it rational for working people to join a union and so to further their collective interests. Accordingly it would not come as a surprise to find that the stoutest advocates of individual freedom, and the stoutest opponents of the closed shop, are those members of the bourgeoisie who stand to gain most from a disorganized and ineffective labour movement.

In addition to the presence of selective incentives there is a second, probably less important factor, which may lead to the provision of a public good. This is the presence of some individual or individuals who obtain disproportionately large benefits from the public good. For example, a large landowner may find that the benefits he obtains by mounting a campaign himself against a new motorway are so large that it is in his interest to do so even though it is a public good. Note, however, that it will not be rational for other villagers to join the campaign unless there are selective incentives which the landowner can impose upon them; the earlier argument applies to them just as it did before and they will therefore prefer to be 'free riders'. They will, if they are rational, leave the whole of the burden to be carried by the large landowner thus occasioning a paradoxical exploitation of the great by the small.

A similar situation to this, Olson suggests, is provided by NATO (see Olson and Zeckhauser, 1966). Defence of the west against the supposed communist threat might in some ways be regarded as a public good: if the domino theory is correct effective defence of any one country requires the provision of defence for its neighbours too, and so countries which support no armies or make no provision to NATO would nevertheless be able to shelter under a common nuclear umbrella provided by a neighbour. Now large countries such as the United States presumably get disproportionate benefits from this defence and will accordingly find it in their own interests to provide a certain amount of it from their own resources. But once this amount has been provided, there is no rational reason for smaller countries to make any contribution of their own towards NATO, and indeed it would seem rational for them to remain neutral, as in fact many of them do. True, countries such as these might believe that the communist threat was non-existent, or that American interference in their affairs was an even worse threat, but the important point is that, even if they did value defence against the Soviet Union, it would be rational for them to leave its provision wholly or disproportionately to the United States.

Finally, a public good may be provided if the number needed to provide it is relatively small. In the first place, the difference that one's own contributions make is very much larger (by definition), thus increasing the expected utility of the contributions. And, secondly, when we get a small group there may be scope for strategic bargaining. Neither Britain nor France on her own, for example, might have sufficient resources to provide a truly effective nuclear deterrent, but if they agreed to share the costs it might become feasible. If they got together and made some kind of agreement that could stick, it would therefore be rational for them to go ahead, but they would have to be sure that neither party could renege at a later stage. Organizing this kind of agreement might be rather difficult and costly, of course, and neither party might think it worthwhile to make the effort to do so. Moreover, the larger the group involved, the greater the organization costs will be and the less likely it is that we shall find any one individual prepared to act as organizer. We must reach the conclusion, therefore, that *the larger the number of individuals re-*

quired to participate if a public good is to be provided, the less likely they are to do so.

The theory of private goods

When we turn to groups such as sports clubs or social clubs which provide private goods to their members we find that, other things being equal, they are much more likely to form. In deciding whether to join or not the individual's calculus is in principle the same as before: he has to compare the expected utility of membership with the alternative uses to which he could put the entrance fee. The difference, of course, is that in the case of the private good the individual *must* join if he is to get the benefits. Paying his fee does not merely raise the probability that the club will survive but it also crucially affects the probability that he will share in the benefits. Thus, in the case of an existing sports club which is willing and able to take on new members, paying the fee changes the probability that he will get the benefits from zero to unity, and all he has to do therefore is to compare these benefits with the alternative uses to which he could put the fee. We have no *a priori* way of knowing what the results of this calculus will be, but we can of course say that, other things being equal, he is much more likely to join than he would have been had the good been a collective one.

More interesting questions arise, however, when we consider the actual formation of a club and its willingness to accept new members. It is reasonable to assume that there will be some organization costs (analogous to the production costs faced by a firm), and that these are likely to follow the U-shaped curve traditionally assumed for the business firm (see figure 8). To get a club off the ground may require quite a high initial outlay on premises and so on, making the costs per head rather high, but as the club expands there will then be some economies of scale (the fixed costs being shared among a larger number of people) giving a falling cost curve. Eventually, however, congestion may set in and per capita costs will thus rise again.

To complete the analogy with the business firm we now need to discover the demand for use of the club's facilities. The normal assumption, which seems fair enough here, is that demand will be greater the lower the price charged, and so we can draw the customary downward-sloping curve. We can now also draw the marginal revenue and marginal cost curves, and we can conclude that the club's size, and membership fee, will be given by the intersection of the two curves. At this point marginal cost will equal marginal revenue and the fees brought in by additional members would fail to offset the

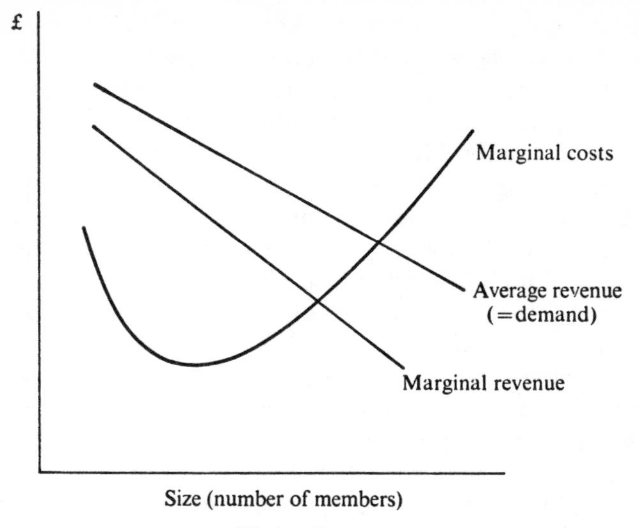

Figure 8

extra costs they would cause. (For a full treatment of the conventional economic analysis see Lipsey, 1975.)

Unfortunately it is not quite this easy with a sports club or social club. Whereas the business firm can realistically be assumed to be maximizing money profit (and so can the commercially run sports club), this would be nonsense in the case of a voluntary association whose 'owners' receive not a share in the money profit but non-monetary enjoyment from the use of the club's facilities. What we have to look at therefore is not the money cost curve of the enterprise as a whole but at the individual utility curves of the different members. These will probably still be U-shaped, but a crucial point will be that different members will find congestion more or less distasteful, some perhaps getting maximum utility when the club has expanded to fifty members and others when it has expanded to two hundred.

Now it would be very convenient if we could add different individuals' utility together in the way that we can add sums of money, and we could then see what size of club would maximize total utility. But of course we cannot do this, or at least economists will not allow us to do so. Inter-personal comparisons of utility cannot be made, they say, and therefore we must face the club with an array of individual 'cost' curves and not a single aggregate one. There will therefore be no unique point at which we can say that the club has reached its optimum size. As we have seen, some members would like to keep it small; others would be happy to expand.

It is of course precisely to deal with cases such as this where there is an array of different individual preferences that decision procedures such as voting are required. And this gives us one useful result: organizations whose members have divergent goals will require different decision-making procedures from those whose members all have identical goals. It may therefore be rational for shareholders, who all presumably prefer higher dividends to lower ones, to delegate all decision-making about the size of the firm, its output, production and so on to one of their number (for his preferences on these matters will be identical to their own), but it will not be so obviously rational for members of a club to allow one of their number to take decisions on their behalf, and if they do one can expect rather more complaints about his behaviour. Thus oligarchy is likely to be more acceptable to shareholders than it will be to the rank and file of political parties, residents' associations or other groups whose members have conflicting as well as common interests.

It might appear that a rational choice theory of clubs and organizations would not be able to make a great deal more progress, for to make further predictions we would need to know what decision-making procedures were in force, who was entitled to participate in them, what their preferences were and so on. With this information we could go on to make specific predictions but it would not appear that any general results would be possible. There do, however, seem to be some cases, notably concerning political parties, where it is perhaps not entirely unreasonable to assume that all participants have, in the relevant respects, identical preferences. Parties and their members, it may be assumed, invariably prefer to be in office rather than out of office, and if they are in office as part of a coalition it may be assumed that they prefer more governmental posts to fewer. On these foundations two important theories have been built. One, with which Anthony Downs's name is usually associated, deals *inter alia* with the strategy that parties will employ in seeking office, and the second, put forward by Riker and others, deals with the coalition-building that may follow an election.

Party competition

Downs's theory is in essence very simple. He borrows a theory developed by the economists Hotelling (1929) and Smithies (1941) to account for the spatial location of shops and uses it to account for the 'ideological' location of political parties. Just as competing shops will place themselves side by side in the centre of the town, so, it is argued, competing political parties will take up positions side by side in the centre of the spectrum of voters. Customers (or voters) will choose the nearest shop (or party), and a shop (or party) which is out on a limb will therefore attract relatively little business and will have to move closer to the centre of things if it is to survive.

More rigorously, Downs begins by assuming that the parties operate within a democratic political system where, *inter alia*, the following conditions hold:

1 A single party (or coalition of parties) is chosen by popular election to run the governing apparatus.

2 Such elections are held at fixed intervals.

3 All adults who are permanent residents of the society are entitled to vote.

4 Each voter may cast one and only one vote in each election.

5 Any party (or coalition) receiving the support of a majority of those voting is entitled to take over the power of government until the next election.

6 There are two or more parties competing for control of the governing apparatus in every election.

Next Downs assumes that political parties are teams of men seeking to control the governing apparatus by gaining office in a duly constituted election. 'By *team*', Downs says, 'we mean a coalition whose members agree on all their goals instead of on just part of them. Thus every member of the team has exactly the same goals as every other. Since we also assume all the members are rational, their goals can be viewed as a single, consistent preference-ordering' (Downs, 1957, p. 25). Specifically, their goals are to maximize votes in any forthcoming election, just as business firms' goals are to maximize profits. (Downs is in fact carried away by his analogy here. He would have gained in logical consistency if he had assumed that parties aim simply to obtain a *majority* of the votes.)

In the case of voters Downs's assumptions (and conclusions) are rather more complicated. Summarizing and simplifying drastically we can say that the voters will cast their votes for the party whose policies they believe will give them most utility if it obtains office. To avoid the public goods problem that we met in the first section of this chapter we must either assume that voting is costless, requiring neither time nor energy, or that some selective incentives are present. As in Australia, for example, it might be the case that every citizen is required by law to vote. Given either of these assumptions, it will be rational for the citizens to cast a vote providing they believe there to be some difference between the parties, although on the former assumption (which is the one Downs initially makes) they will no longer vote when they fail to observe anything between them. But without one of these assumptions it is not at all apparent that rational voters would go to the polls. Since each voter's vote makes an infinitesimal difference to the outcome, almost any costs at all would outweigh the expected utility of voting.

We are not yet through with assumptions, I fear. We now assume that the main sphere for political action, and hence for affecting voters' utility, is government intervention in the market. At one extreme a government could socialize all production and distribution. At the other it could allow an entirely laissez-faire economy. This gives us a one-dimensional left–right continuum, and each party will be located at some point on the continuum. Equally, voters will be located at different points on the continuum, some preferring complete socialism, others a mixed economy, and so on, and each voter will accordingly support the party which comes closest to his own position. (While Downs presents us with this one-dimensional continuum, it is in fact easy enough to apply his theory to a two-dimensional space. See Tullock, 1967.)

The positions which the parties will now take up in their efforts to secure office will, Downs argues, simply depend on the distribution of voters along the continuum. If they are evenly distributed along it, then the parties must if they are rational converge to the centre. This is easily seen from figure 9. If there are two parties, one at a_1 and the other at b_1, all people to the left of a_1 must vote for party A, since it is closer to their preferred positions than party B, and correspondingly all people to the right of b_1 will vote for party B. Even if they are extreme proponents of laissez-faire, it will still be rational for them to vote for B because its policies, unpalatable though they may be, are still preferable to A's. Failure to vote, therefore, could result in the even worse disaster that party A will be returned to power.

Between a_1 and b_1 it can be seen that the voters will divide evenly between the two parties, and party B will therefore win since it is closer to the centre and thus has more people 'outside' it than does party A. Faced with this, party A must change its position if it is to have any hope of winning. Movement to the left will clearly be of little help, but movement to the right might succeed. If the party moves to a_2, it will still get the support of all the voters to its left, since it is still preferable to B, and it will still divide the middle ground evenly But since it is now closer to the centre than B it gets

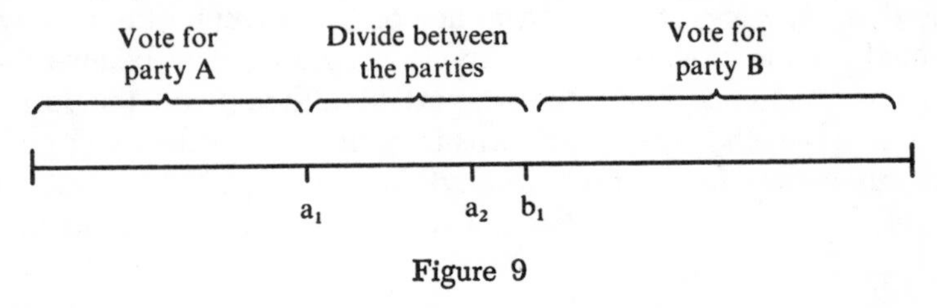

Figure 9

more support in total and must win the election. B also sees this, and equilibrium is reached when both parties are side by side at the centre; only when this point has been reached is there no further incentive for either party to alter its position.

Unfortunately, when both parties have reached this equilibrium position there may be no noticeable difference between them and accordingly no one may bother to go to the polls. Since in real life people *do* go to the polls, Downs goes to some pains to keep the parties apart and thus to give the electorate some reason for turning out. He suggests various mechanisms, the main one being abstention by extremists. As the parties move closer together in the centre, Downs argues, so voters at the two extremes of the continuum will become less inclined to vote, abstaining either because they cannot now perceive any difference between the parties or in an effort to compel their preferred party to move back to a more extreme position. 'Abstention thus becomes a threat to use against the party nearest one's own extreme position so as to keep it away from the center' (Downs, 1957, p. 119).

The efficacy of the threat will be less, Downs asserts, if the voters are concentrated in the centre of the spectrum (as in figure 10) than it will be if they are polarized (as in figure 11). In the former case the possible loss of extremists will not deter the parties from converging since there are so few voters to be lost at the extremes compared with the number to be gained in the middle. In the latter case the reverse is true and so Downs feels able to conclude 'If voters' preferences are distributed so that voters are massed bimodally near the extremes, the parties will remain poles apart in ideology' (p. 118).

Finally, consider a polymodal distribution of voters as in figure 12. Here we might expect a stable multi-party system to develop with a party at each 'mode'. Clearly the centre parties have no incentive to

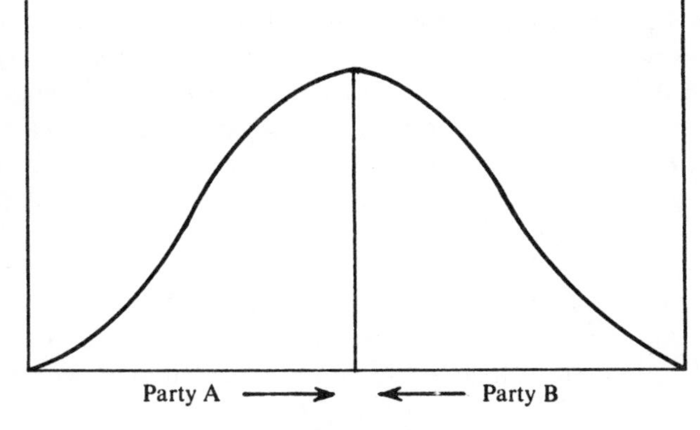

Figure 10

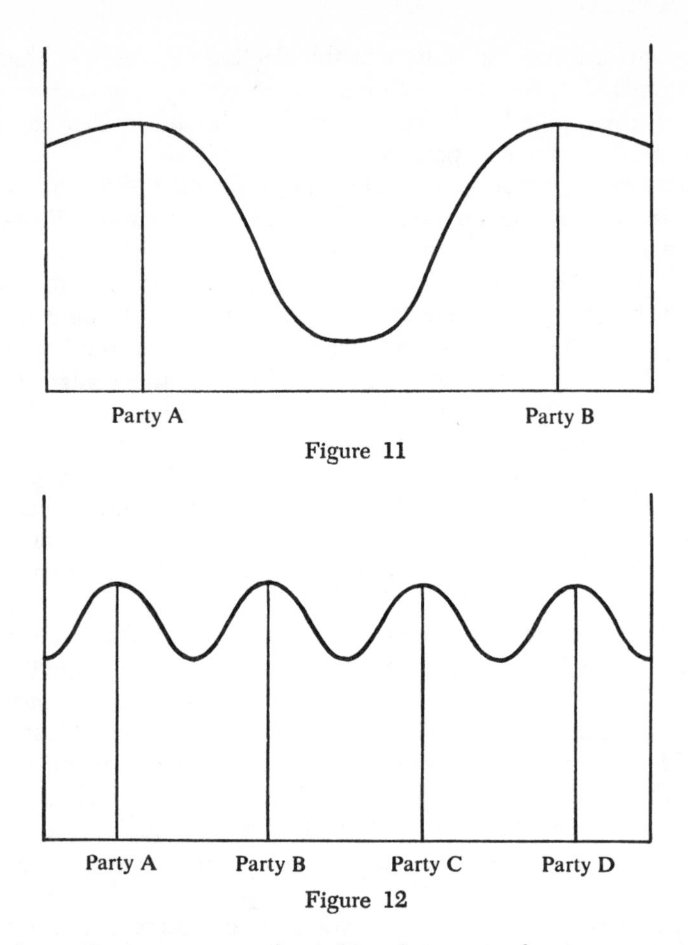

Figure 11

Figure 12

move from their positions, for what they gain from one party they lose to another. The two extreme parties, however, do have an incentive to start moving inwards, setting up a chain reaction, but again abstention by extremists might serve to keep them apart. We thus reach the conclusion that 'in multi-party systems, parties will strive to distinguish themselves ideologically from each other and maintain the purity of their positions; whereas in two-party systems, each party will try to resemble its opponent as closely as possible' (pp. 126–7).

Downs deals with a great deal more than the ideological position of the parties, and his theories are always provocative, if also frequently tendentious. Unfortunately I do not have the space to summarize more of them here, and indeed I fear that I have had to take a number of short-cuts already in presenting the theory of party competition. I propose to conclude this summary of rational choice theory, therefore, with an exposition of the theory of coalition formation instead.

Forming coalitions

As with Downs's theory we begin by assuming the existence of a democratic political system, but this time we are concerned with a multi-party system rather than a two-party one. We assume that the elections have taken place and hence that each party has now a certain number of seats in Parliament. Accordingly a party or coalition must obtain a majority of the seats if it is to take over the government until the next election. As before we assume that the members of a party form a team every member of which has exactly the same goals as every other. Their goals, however, are not merely to obtain office but to maximize their party's share of the spoils of office.

Now there may be several potential coalitions which would have enough seats to obtain a majority and thus win the spoils of office, and the question which has been most commonly tackled is which of these potential coalitions will actually form. Suppose, for example, that there are five parties with seats in Parliament: the Communists with 5, the Socialists with 40, the Liberals with 26, the Conservatives with 25 and the Monarchists with 4. At one extreme all five parties could join together and form a Government of National Unity while at the other a two-party coalition of Socialists and Liberals would still have an overwhelming majority. In between a coalition of the four smaller parties or of the three right-wing ones would also obtain a majority.

The first conclusion reached by the theory is that, of these potential coalitions, only *minimum winning coalitions* are likely to form. That is to say, only coalitions which cannot lose a member party and still retain a majority of the seats will actually form. Thus a coalition of the three right-wing parties is not a minimum winning one since it could exclude the Monarchists and still retain a majority. Even without the Monarchists a Liberal–Conservative coalition still has 51 seats. There are in fact only three possible minimum winning coalitions – a coalition of the Liberals and Socialists, a coalition of the Liberals and Conservatives, and a coalition of the Socialists and Conservatives. According to the theory it will be one of these three that actually forms.

This result, hardly a surprising one, follows from the assumption that the prize (the spoils of office or the seats in the cabinet) is in the language of game theory a *constant sum* payoff. That is, the prize is fixed in size and does not vary with the number of parties in the coalition or the number of seats they possess. The more parties there are in the coalition, therefore, the less there is for each, and if one of the member parties is unnecessary it is clearly rational to get rid of him, leaving a bigger share for each of those that remain. (Riker in fact assumes that the prize is a zero-sum rather than a constant sum payoff, but this is an absurd assumption and one that is quite unnecessary.)

More interesting are the attempts to predict which of the various minimum winning coalitions will form. Will it be the Socialists and Liberals, who control two-thirds of the seats between them, or will it be the Liberals and Conservatives with their bare majority? One answer to this is given by the 'size principle' of Riker (1962), Caplow (1968) and Gamson (1961). They assume that the spoils are distributed according to the 'strength' of each member of the winning coalition, strength in this case being the number of seats that each party holds. If, therefore, the Liberals decide to cast their lot with the Socialists they will get 26/66 of the spoils while the Socialists will get 40/66. If on the other hand they go in with the Conservatives their share will increase to 26/51, which is clearly a much better bargain. Moreover the Conservatives will not be able to do any better than the 25/51 which the Liberals would allow them, and so a Liberal–Conservative Government will form.

Two points are worthy of notice here. First, according to the size principle, *the coalition which forms is the one that has the smallest surplus of seats.* Thus in this case the winning Liberal–Conservative coalition had a bare 51 per cent of the seats – enough and no more than was needed to win – whereas any coalition with the Socialists would have had a very substantial surplus. It is easy to see why this must occur. A party which has x per cent of the seats must obtain its maximum possible share in the cabinet when the other members of the coalition have $51 - x$ per cent of the seats between them.

A second point is that *it may actually be a handicap to be large.* In this particular case, for example, the Socialists, who were after all the largest single party, were actually excluded from the final coalition. True, this was largely a matter of chance. They were unlucky that none of the other four parties had the eleven seats needed to bring about a bare majority. But when we are faced with coalitions within the triad it is no longer merely a matter of chance. On the assumptions of our theory, *within the triad it is inevitably a handicap to be strong.*

This point is most forcefully made by Caplow, who seems willing to apply his theory to any instance of coalition formation within the triad, even those in the family or in Hamlet! His most convincing case, however, concerns three pirates, Ahab, Brutus and Charlie. They are on a lonely island far from civil authority and have the problem of dividing up the loot. Brutus and Charlie are evenly matched, while Ahab is rather more dangerous and could overpower either of the others in a fight on their own (but not the two together). Clearly neither Brutus nor Charlie will want to form a coalition with Ahab and run the risk of being overpowered. They will therefore join together, defeat Ahab, and share the loot equitably between themselves (being of equal strength). In this way then the triad has transformed 'strength into weakness and weakness into strength'. As Caplow puts it: 'The margin of superiority Ahab enjoys as he lands on the island insures his defeat. If he could divest himself of this superiority, becoming equal to Brutus and Charlie, his chances of joining a winning coalition would then be 2 to 1, since all coalitions are equally likely in egalitarian triads. More surprising still, if Ahab's loss of strength were to continue until he became much weaker than Brutus or Charlie, he might be certain of a good share of the spoils . . . both Brutus and Charlie, now giants to his pygmy eyes, are enthusiastic about a coalition partner whom they can readily dominate and with whose help they can subdue an otherwise equal adversary' (Caplow, 1968, p. 3). Unfortunately Caplow seems to ignore the point that a pygmy Ahab can now be easily subdued by his giant partner. It may be a handicap to be strong, but in this case it is no advantage to be weak either.

5. *The social psychology of exchange*

The rational choice theories that we have looked at in the preceding chapters all derive in an almost pure line of descent from economic forebears. A little intermarriage has been inevitable, but otherwise they are hardly tainted with sociology, psychology or anthropology. In Homans' words we have merely had to extrapolate from 'apples and dollars, physical goods and money . . . to the exchange of intangible services for social esteem' (1961, p. 12). Thus, rather than firms that pursue profit we have had political parties that pursue office; rather than financial constraints we have had temporal constraints. But aside from these the changes have been minimal. Like the economist we have assumed that men have stable tastes and preferences, preferring more to less of the 'good' in question (be it social approval or the spoils of office). Like the economist we have made simplified assumptions about the social environment in which men find themselves (be it a market in which many buyers compete for homogeneous services or a democratic political system in which parties must compete for votes). And finally, and this is the whole point of the exercise, we have been able to make more or less rigorous deductions about the behaviour that rational men will adopt given the assumed preferences and environment. How successful this all is we shall consider later, but for the moment there can be no doubt that it yields us one of the very few systematic and integrated bodies of theory in sociology.

While the economists such as Downs and Olson have been content to rest their colonizing activities here, native exchange theorists such as Blau, Homans and Thibaut and Kelley have attempted to supplement and modify the rational choice theories with various additions from the sociological tradition. As I mentioned in the introduction, these additions have not always been very well integrated with the rational choice theories, and in Blau's work in particular we seem to find the two traditions side by side more in a state of cold war than peaceful coexistence. But whether or not they are reconcilable with each other, both are clearly major components of exchange theory as it is now understood and neither can be ignored.

The sociological tradition unfortunately does not have the same rigour and coherence as the economic, and it is by no means so clear which parts of it to include or exclude. In this chapter, however, I have decided to look at the discussions of *comparison processes* which are contained in all three of the main contributions to exchange theory. In the following chapter I shall look at the work of Blau and the anthropologists on the morality of social exchange, and I shall conclude with a discussion of what Blau calls 'emergent processes'.

Comparison processes and comparison levels

'Economic man' is often misunderstood and wrongly vilified, and no doubt the 'rational man' who has walked the previous pages will suffer likewise. True, he cannot be accused (as Homans accused economic man) of being 'anti-social and materialistic, interested only in money and material goods and ready to sacrifice even his old mother to get them' (Homans, 1961, p. 79) but perhaps he will be accused instead of being interested only in status and power and willing to sacrifice his principles to get them. Neither accusation would in fact, be fair, but another, rather more powerful one might be that he is some kind of social innocent, totally oblivious of the successes and failures around him and totally absorbed in his own happiness and disappointment. He is a man quite untouched by envy or jealousy.

Like economic man, the rational man with whom we have dealt so far has fixed, unchanging tastes. His happiness (or, more strictly, his utility) depends solely on the actual combination of goods and services that he himself possesses. How he performs relative to others or relative to his past is of no consequence. Nor surprisingly, however, a great deal of sociological and psychological research (not to speak of everyday experience) has shown this to be a naive and unrealistic picture of man. Thus it is a commonplace that men's expectations reflect their past experiences. That men have rising expectations is a commonplace of sociology. Once a man has achieved some target on a task he will raise his aspiration level and thus no longer obtain as much satisfaction or utility from his original performance as he did before. (The classic investigation here is Lewin et al., 1944). Again, his satisfaction or utility will not depend simply on the absolute quantity of goods and services that he possesses but on the amount he has relative to that possessed by his 'significant others' or 'comparative reference group'. Indeed, it is one of the central tenets of sociology, and one of the principal features that distinguish it from economics, that men compare themselves with others (the classic statements here being Stouffer et al., 1949, and Merton, 1957).

Of the exchange theorists Thibaut and Kelley present perhaps the most cogent account of these comparison processes (although Blau deals with them too). They begin by introducing the notion of *comparison level* (CL). This is quite different from the *comparison level for alternatives* (CL_{alt}) which we met earlier. The CL_{alt} was the level of outcomes which a man could get in his best alternative relationship. It was a measure of the alternative opportunities open to an individual. The CL on the other hand is 'a psychologically meaningful mid-point for the scale of outcomes – a neutral point on a scale of satisfaction–dissatisfaction' (Thibaut and Kelley, 1959, p. 81). In the language of economics we could say that the CL is a zero-point on the utility scale. Points above it represent positive utility, points below represent negative utility (or disutility).

Next Thibaut and Kelley argue that the actual level of outcomes (that is, of goods and services) which yields this midpoint on the satisfaction–dissatisfaction scale will depend on the level of recently experienced outcomes, on those outcomes for which the individual himself had major causal responsibility, and on those outcomes achieved by people similar to himself. It further follows that a man may be dissatisfied with a relationship (since his outcomes fall *below* his CL) but yet forced to remain in it (since the outcomes are *above* his CL_{alt}). Not only are the CL and the CL_{alt} different things, then, but their determinants are different too. The position of the former may be determined by the level of success achieved by a man's peers; the position of the latter by the alternatives currently available not to his peers but to himself.

This distinction between CL and CL_{alt} is itself an extremely useful one, and it exposes a lot of muddles in ordinary thinking. Thus it is sometimes said that a battered wife 'must like it really because otherwise she would have left him long ago'. Students who complain about their courses are told that they should 'put up with it or go'. And we are told not to worry about the poor because 'if they were really dissatisfied they would do something about it for themselves'. All these assertions are based on a failure to see the difference between CL and CL_{alt}. The decision whether or not to stay with one's husband, one's university or one's job depends on one's CL_{alt} – the alternative opportunities open to one – as well as on the level of rewards provided by husband, tutor or employer. If, for example, great stigma attaches to the divorced woman (once true), to the failed student (still true) or to the 'feckless' job changer (also true), the alternatives open to them may indeed be very poor and they may reasonably enough decide, *faute de mieux,* to stay where they are. But one's CL is not determined by the alternatives now open but by one's past experiences or by one's contemporaries' present successes. The wife who has lost her freedom, the student who is made to pursue a pedestrian course when the syllabus had promised intellectual excitement, the employee passed over for promotion may all have quite genuine (and I may add justified) feelings of grievance. It is quite illegitimate to suppose that these feelings are not 'real' ones merely because they are not so great as to outweigh the hardships of leaving.

While the introduction of the CL represents a considerable advance on the economists' model of man, it is not one that is in principle inconsistent with a rational choice approach. The notion that one's utility or satisfaction depend on, say, one's income relative to others' and not simply on one's absolute income can be put into effect easily enough by re-labelling the axes of our indifference map. It may also improve the force of our arguments. Consider, for example, the decision to allocate one's time between work and leisure. If we draw the conventional diagram with the income derived from work on the vertical axis and leisure on the horizontal axis, we are inclined to the conclusion that an increase in the wage-rate will increase the amount of time devoted to leisure. (The situation is analogous to the one in which a fall in the price of cummerbunds increases the consumption of zabaglione.) The individual does not have to spend as much of his time as before to get the same amount of income and leisure. He has now got some 'spare' time which he can reallocate as he pleases on work or leisure. Presumably some of it will go on leisure.

In practice of course, increased wages have not usually led to any increase in leisure. As a result, the economist is forced to the rather desperate, *post hoc,* expedient of redrawing the indifference map. He has to assume that the individual's preferences are such that he will allocate the *whole* of his 'spare' time to work, and he has to redraw the indifference map accordingly. *Post-hoc* expedients are not in themselves improper, but it would be comforting if the economist could give us some reasons (or better still, some independent evidence) for accepting the redrawn map. Why, in this particular case, should the 'substitution' effect outweigh the 'income' effect (as the economists' jargon has it)?

If, however, we adopt a sociologically more informed view, the situation becomes much simpler. On this view an increase in wages, *shared by all workers,* in no way alters the allocation of time between work and leisure. If the worker's utility depends on his *relative* income, not his *absolute* income, a general increase in wage rate leaves him exactly where he was before and the failure of increased wages to reduce hours of work causes us no problem. In this way a rational choice approach can cope perfectly happily with comparison processes. They make life easier for the theorist, not more difficult.

Equally, the notion that one's past record of success or failure affects one's CL can easily be incorporated into a rational choice model. It is best represented by a shift in the location of the indifference map or utility curve rather than by any re-labelling of the axes. The point can be made most easily if we look at an old-fashioned utility curve such as that in figure 13 rather than at a modern indifference map. Here the curve simply shows the utility an individual gets from differing amounts of a *single* commodity (and has nothing to do with the *combinations* of commodities of the indifference map). In this particular case the 'commodity' in question is success in the 'A' level examinations. The curve U_1 shows that, in his first shot at the exams, the candidate would feel more or less neutral about a D grade (which would, in Thibaut and Kelley's terms, be his comparison level), very pleased with a B grade, and only slightly more pleased than this with an A (since we are making the conventional assumption of diminishing marginal utility). If he in fact only manages to obtain an E, we should expect him to be initially very disappointed but subsequently to lower his expectation so that by the time he took the exams the second time round, his curve would have shifted bodily to the left, now giving curve U_2.

It is this bodily shift of the curve which distinguishes our sociological approach from that of the economists. The economist simply assumes that people have a consistent, unchanging utility curve and that as they get richer or poorer, or more or less successful, they simply move *along* the curve getting the same utility from a real income of £2,000 or from a C grade at 'A' level that they would have got last year or will get in ten years' time. Now this may have been a reasonable enough assumption for the economist to make, given the particular phenomena which he wishes to explain. But it is not one that will do for the sociologist. Changing aspirations are one of the

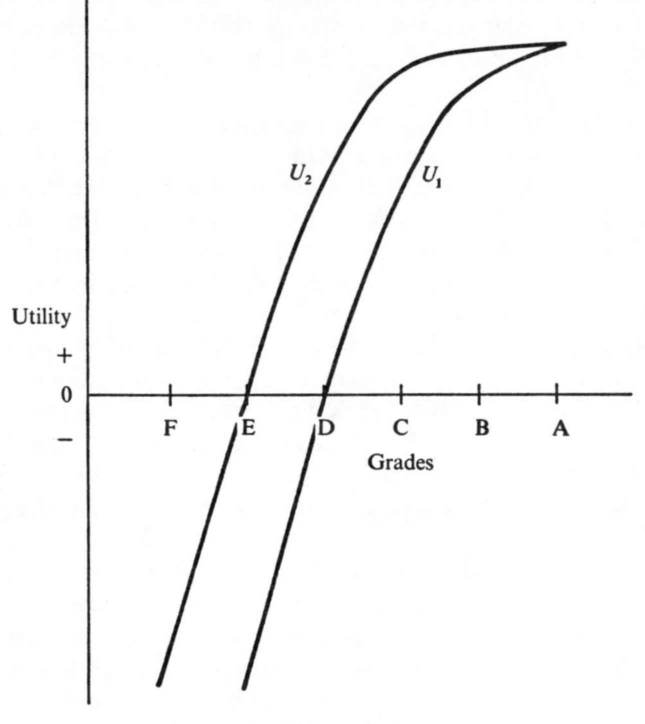

Figure 13

sociologist's main explanatory tools and, luckily, the exchange theorist need not be deprived of them.

Comparison processes and distributive justice

Closely related to Thibaut and Kelley's notion of comparison level, although independently invented, is Homans' concept of distributive justice. Like Thibaut and Kelley, Homans argues that men are influenced by the outcomes they have obtained in the past and by the outcomes that others like them have obtained. (Whatever else can be said about him, Homans' man is no social innocent.) And, also like Thibaut and Kelley, Homans suggests that men will tend to be satisfied if they get more than they expect on these counts and dissatisfied if they get less.

Homans' main concern, however, is not with satisfaction but with 'the emotional behavior we call anger', and this I take to be something different from, or at least additional to, satisfaction. It is also something quite different from any of the phenomena that the economist tries to explain. True the economist is concerned with behaviour, but the behaviour that interests him is the allocation and expenditure of money – never the expression of emotion. Economic man is not only an innocent but a rather repressed one as well.

Homans' man, at any rate, is no innocent and he expresses anger when he does not get as much by way of reward as his past history has taught him to expect, as others like him have received, or as his partner in the exchange should have given him. More specifically Homans formulates a rule of distributive justice (which seems to be a rule that men will have learned from their past history). It states: 'A man in an exchange relation with another will expect that the rewards of each man be proportional to his costs – the greater the rewards, the greater the costs – and that the net rewards, or profits, of each man be proportional to his investments – the greater the investments, the greater the profit' (Homans, 1961, p. 75). And finally Homans presents a justice proposition which states: 'The more to a man's disadvantage the rule of distributive justice fails of realization the more likely he is to display the emotional behavior we call anger' (p. 75).

One of Homans' examples may make this clearer. He takes the case of the 'ledger clerks' and the 'cash posters' employed in the Customers Accounting Division of the Eastern Utilities Co. The ledger clerks were regarded as senior to the cash posters. They had put in a longer time in the company and did more responsible (although more interesting) work than the cash posters. Accordingly, says Homans, their investments (of time put in with the company) and their costs (the responsibility of their jobs) were higher and they would therefore expect to get higher rewards, and hence profits, as well. This is what the rule of distributive justice would require. However, while their jobs were more interesting, they got exactly the same amount of pay as the cash posters and, to add insult to injury, were sometimes taken off their 'own' jobs and put 'down' on posting. Distributive justice failed of realization, and the girls complained bitterly as a result.

Before we leave it, a number of observations need to be made about Homans' theory. First of all, although it is couched in the language of economics with talk of profits, costs and investments, it really has nothing to do with economics at all. Profit does not of course refer to *money* profit but to a man's net gain from the exchange (although whether gain is to be measured in terms of *utility* or in terms of goods and services is somewhat obscure). And investments are not outlays incurred in order to manufacture a product or even to acquire a skill but seem to be any background characteristic whatsoever that a man may deem relevant. Investments therefore may include not only educational qualifications but also age, seniority, even the number of children that one has, and possibly ascribed characteristics like sex and race as well. Of course, the fact that it has nothing to do with economics does not make it a bad theory. It is just a different kind of theory from any that appear in economics.

Secondly, we should note one respect in which Homans' theory differs radically not from economics but from Thibaut and Kelley's theory of comparison levels. Whereas Thibaut and Kelley argued that a man would obtain positive satisfaction if he exceeded his comparison level (indeed this is part of the definition of comparison level), Homans does not claim that men will display the emotional behaviour we call delight if they do better than the rule of distributive justice warranted. Not at all. Instead he claims that they will feel guilt. True a man 'is less apt to make a prominent display of his guilt than of his anger. Indeed a man in this happy situation is apt to find arguments convincing to himself that the exchange is not really to his advantage after all' (p. 76). But in principle at any rate the pleasure from doing well is tempered with guilt. Thus whereas in Thibaut and Kelley's theory the obverse of dissatisfaction is satisfaction, in Homans' the obverse of anger is guilt.

This need not necessarily mean that the two theories are actually in conflict. Broadly speaking, to exceed one's CL is to do better than one *expected* whereas to do better than the rule of distributive justice requires is to do better than one *ought*. The former is thus a theory of expectations, the latter a theory of internalized norms (although Homans never actually calls it as much). And while we often expect to get what we ought, and sometimes we ought to get what we expect, the two need not always go together. Unfortunately, neither Homans nor Thibaut and Kelley tell us precisely when either of their theories can be expected to apply, but it is not hard to imagine some of the factors that might be involved. Thus, if we do better than expected in our 'A' levels, our achievement has been at nobody else's expense and we may justifiably feel satisfied not guilty at our success. But if we get a bigger present from a friend at Christmas than we gave him, our gain has been at his expense, and the rule of distributive justice may thus come into force.

6. *The morality of social exchange*

With distributive justice, morality at last entered our discussion of exchange theory, and it now takes the limelight for itself. Many writers, particularly anthropologists, have pointed out that the morality of social exchange is in many respects quite unlike that of the economic market. Since one might expect the existence of this distinct morality to be a major obstacle to the application of 'economic' theories to social exchange, we thus come to a crucial aspect of exchange theory. The classic contribution here is Marcel Mauss's *Essai sur le don* (1925) in which he deals primarily with what might be called institutionalized or ceremonial exchanges of primitive or archaic peoples. Both he and later sociologists have dealt with the gift exchanges of our own society too, but it is with the former category that we need to start.

Ceremonial exchange

Mauss's attention had been drawn to two notable examples of ceremonial exchange, the Kula and the potlatch, and it may be useful to give some account of these first. The Kula is a form of exchange practised by, among others, the Trobriand Islanders of the Western Pacific (see Malinowski 1920, 1922). The communities concerned formed a wide ring of islands and the objects exchanged – long necklaces of red shell called 'soulava' and bracelets of white shell called 'mwali' – moved around this ring. Essentially what seemed to happen was that an expedition would set off from one island, after the appropriate rituals and magic, and sail to some other more or less distant island, the journey perhaps taking several days. On arrival the visitors would be welcomed by their hosts and would be given gifts either of mwali (if they had travelled in a clockwise direction) or of soulava (if they had travelled anticlockwise). These shells were much prized (although of no intrinsic usefulness), some of them having long and well-known individual histories. To obtain as a present a particularly famous one was a matter of great pleasure and honour to the recipient and would be the central aim of the expedition and indeed of Trobriand life.

In the Kula, however, there could be no haggling or bargaining about the gift. While the host was obliged to make a gift, and the guest to receive it, precisely what was given was left to the discretion of the donor. Moreover the transfer itself would be carried out with great solemnity. The donor would affect an exaggerated modesty, apologize for bringing only his leavings, and throw the shell at his partner's feet.

In due course, perhaps as much as a year later, the erstwhile hosts would make a return expedition to their partners and receive appropriate gifts in return. If they had given soulava, they would now receive mwali; if mwali, then now soulava. As before the equivalence of the return gift would be left to the host. The partner who had already received a Kula gift would be expected to give back a fair return, but the equivalence between the two objects could not be openly discussed, bargained about or computed by the two partners. The decorum of the Kula transaction has to be strictly maintained and there could be no question of it changing into barter (for which there was a separate term, 'gimwali'). Indeed, when criticizing an incorrect, too hasty or indecorous procedure of Kula the islanders would apparently say: 'He conducts his Kula as if it were gimwali.' The morality of the ceremonial Kula transaction was thus quite different from that of the economic gimwali.

One of the more remarkable features of the Kula was that the shells exchanged, although highly prized, were not retained for long. They had to be given away in turn to other Kula partners when they came as guests, and they thus moved in great circles around the ring of islands. Any given mwali or soulava was thus always to be found travelling and changing hands, never settling down. However, while the shells moved on, they nonetheless left behind a permanent and lifelong relationship between the partners concerned. As Malinowski reported, 'The Kula partnership provides every man within its ring with a few friends near at hand, and with some friendly allies in the far-away, dangerous, foreign districts' (Malinowski, 1922, p. 22).

While the ceremonial exchange of shells was the fundamental aspect of the Kula, there were associated with it, and carried out under its cover, a great number of secondary activities and features. Side by side with the ritual exchange of armshells and necklaces, the islanders carried on ordinary gimwali, bartering various 'utilities' as Malinowski called them. In this way the Kula, Malinowski concludes, 'is an extremely big and complex institution, both in its geographical extent and the manifoldness of its component pursuits. It welds together a considerable number of tribes, and it embraces a vast complex of activities, inter-connected, and playing into one another, so as to form one organic whole' (p. 83).

The potlatch, an institution found at the opposite side of the Pacific among the North-West American Indians, seems to have been very similar to the Kula, although it is not so well understood (see Boas, 1897; Curtis, 1915; Codere, 1950; Piddocke, 1965). It seems likely that the potlatch involved a ceremonial feast, given by a chief and his group as hosts to guests composed of another chief or chiefs with their respective groups. As with the Kula, then, the guest–host relation was crucial. The overt purpose of the potlatch, however, was the announcement of some event of social significance. It might be the marriage of an important person, the birth of a potential heir to one of the group's 'titles', or the formal assumption of one of these titles by the heir. The guests and the other spectators would act as witnesses to the announcement and would thus in essence validate it. Thus a person might be recognized as the only proper heir to the highest-ranking title, but until a potlatch had been given at which he formally claimed the position and its privileges, he had no right to use them.

As with the Kula the actual procedure of the potlatch was complex and highly formal. First an invitation party would be sent to the guests' village. They would be feasted and would then deliver the invitation orally to the assembled group, setting the date on which the guests would be expected. At the actual potlatch itself there would be speeches of welcome and then the formal announcement itself – in the case of a title including an account of its origin, how it had been acquired by an ancestor, how it had been transmitted down the family line and so on. Gifts (for example, of blankets) would be distributed to the guests in order of precedence and there would be lavish feasting, the guests taking home with them the food that they could not eat at the feast.

In due course the hosts would expect to be guests in their turn, and again would expect to be lavishly feasted and to receive generous gifts. But it is here that the character of the potlatch becomes disputed. It has frequently been assumed that competitive or 'agonistic' gift-giving would occur, each host in his turn trying to outdo his partner in the size and magnificence of what he gave away. Indeed, it has been suggested that the return gift would have to be *double* the original. Thus Codere in one of the standard accounts wrote: 'The property received by a man in a potlatch was no free and wanton gift. He was not at liberty to refuse it, even though accepting it obligated him to make a return at another potlatch not only of the original amount but of twice as much, if this return was made, as was usual, in a period of about a year. This gave potlatching its forced loan and investment aspects, since a man was alternatively debtor and creditor for amounts that were increasing at a geometric rate' (Codere, 1950, p. 68). Furthermore, the failure in this competition was supposed to entail loss of social rank and status for the chief and his group. 'The rich man who shows his wealth by spending recklessly is the man who wins prestige. The principles of rivalry and antagonism are basic. Political and individual status in associations and clans, and rank of every kind, are determined by the war of property' (Mauss, 1925, p. 35).

Whether this was ever generally true of the potlatch is rather doubtful. Certainly the account of one early ethnographer, Curtis, suggests that there could hardly have been a 'geometric rate' of expansion and that balanced exchange was more appropriate. 'It has been said of the potlatch', Curtis wrote, 'that "the underlying principle is that of the interest-bearing investment of property". This is impossible. A Kwakiutl would subject himself to ridicule by demanding interest when he received a gift in requital of one *of like amount* made by him' (my emphasis). True, a guest might call 'attention to the fact that he is not receiving as much as he in his last potlatch gave to the present host' and he might 'refuse to accept anything less than the proper amount'. But, again as with the Kula, such haggling brought one into disrespect. 'Even this action is likened to "cutting off one's own head", and results in loss of prestige; for the exhibition of greed for property is not the part of a chief; on the contrary he must show his utter disregard for it' (Curtis, 1915, pp. 143-4; quoted in Piddocke, 1965).

Whatever the precise details of the potlatch, it is clear that it shares many characteristics with the Kula. Moreover, Mauss found many other examples of broadly similar institutions throughout the world, and it became apparent from his work that they are by no means rare and exotic 'sports' but widespread institutions which exemplify some of the fundamental characteristics of social exchange. Mauss called them 'total prestations' since they constituted 'un fait social total', having a meaning that was social, religious, magical, emotional, legal and moral, as well as economic and utilitarian. Their main characteristics, he suggests, were as follows:

1 The exchanges were carried out by groups, not individuals. 'The persons represented in the contracts are moral persons – clans, tribes, and families; the groups, or the chiefs as intermediaries for the groups, confront and oppose each other' (1925, p. 3).

2 It was not exclusively 'goods and wealth, real and personal property, and things of economic value' which were exchanged, but rather 'courtesies, entertainments, ritual, military assistance, women, children, dances and feasts' (p. 3).

3 Whereas with the economic transaction there is overt self-interest, with these ceremonial exchanges there is a pretence of disinterested generosity. 'The form usually taken is that of the gift generously offered; but the accompanying behaviour is formal pretence and social deception, while the transaction itself is based on obligation and economic (or political) self-interest' (p. 1).

4 The central obligation involved is that of making a return for the gift received (the obligation that is now known as the norm of reciprocity – see Gouldner, 1960). 'Many ideas and principles are to be noted in systems of this type. The most important of these spiritual mechanisms is clearly the one which obliges us to make a return gift for a gift received' (p. 5). Almost equally important, however, are two others: 'the obligation to give presents and the obligation to receive them' (pp. 10-11).

5 Unlike the economic transaction, gift exchange has many more consequences than the mere transfer of property. It transforms the relationship between the partners and establishes a bond between donor and recipient. 'The objects are never completely separated from the men who exchange them; the communion and alliance they establish are well-nigh indissoluble' (p. 31).

6 The gift received puts the recipient in debt to the donor, and failure to make an equivalent return lowers his reputation and status. 'The obligation of worthy return is imperative. Face is lost for ever if it is not made' (p. 41).

Gift exchange

Mauss sees the ceremonial exchange or total prestation as the form of exchange most remote in character from that of the modern economic transaction. In addition, however, he recognizes a simpler form of exchange which is intermediate between the total prestation and the economic transaction. This intermediate form he terms 'gift exchange' *tout court.* He sees it as 'characteristic of societies which have passed the phase of "total prestation" (between clan and clan, family and family) but have not yet reached the stage of pure individual contract, the money market, sale proper, fixed price, and weighed and coined money' (p. 45). Even in our own society, however, which is dominated by the market, 'it is our good fortune that all is not yet couched in terms of purchase and sale' (p. 63). Even today, says Mauss, the morality of gift exchange is still widespread.

It is not entirely clear how Mauss distinguishes gift exchange from the total prestation, but there seem to be two main features where it varies from the earlier form. First, gift exchange is carried out by individuals rather than by groups, in keeping no doubt with the more individualistic character of our own society. Secondly, it seems to entail only the obilgation to repay, and not the obligation to give and receive as well. The norm of reciprocity thus takes the centre of the stage. Like the total prestation, however, the gift establishes a bond between the partners while failure to repay debases the man who accepted it.

Modern exchange theorists, particularly Blau, have closely followed Mauss in their account of the morality of social exchange. First we have the norm of reciprocity. A fundamental characteristic of social exchange, says Blau, is that 'an individual who supplies rewarding services to another obligates him. To discharge this obligation, the second must furnish benefits to the first in turn' (Blau, 1964, p. 89). Secondly, as with the total prestation, there is a pretence of disinterested generosity. Indeed Blau claims that this is the most crucial respect in which social exchange differs from economic exchange. In social exchange a return is expected but it involves 'diffuse future obligations, nor precisely specified ones, and the nature of the return cannot be bargained about but must be left to the discretion of the one who makes it' (p. 93). The man giving a dinner party is like the Kwakiutl Indian giving a potlatch; he expects to be invited back in his turn but he must leave it to his guest to determine the time and manner of the return.

It follows from this, Blau argues, that social exchange requires individuals to trust each other. 'While the banker who makes a loan to a man who buys a house does not have to trust him, although he hopes he will not have to foreclose the mortgage, the individual who gives another an expensive gift must trust him to reciprocate in proper fashion' (p. 94). In this way we reach another crucial distinction between economic and social exchange. Assuming that men do in fact reciprocate for the gifts they have received (and Blau suggests that self-interest will lead them to do so), social exchange will therefore engender feelings of gratitude and trust. Like the Kula, but quite unlike the economic transaction, it will transform the relationship between the partners, establishing a bond of solidarity between them.

Finally, as is supposed to have happened in the potlatch, failure to make a worthy return leads to loss of face. 'A person who gives others valuable gifts', Blau writes, 'or renders them important services makes a claim for superior status by obligating them to himself . . . if they fail to reciprocate with benefits that are at least as important to him as his are to them, they validate his claim to superior status' (p. 108). At this point Blau is rather vague about what constitutes a 'worthy' or 'equally important' return, but he later gives us a norm of fair exchange which specifies more precisely what is to be returned. It is in fact identical to Homans' rule of distributive justice.

The free gift

These two categories of ceremonial exchange and gift exchange are by no means the only forms of social exchange that have been suggested. Other non-economic modes and morality of exchange seem possible too. Malinowski, in fact, had set out a whole continuum of exchanges ranging from 'real barter' to the other extreme of 'pure gift' for which nothing at all is given or required in return. Similarly, in looking at blood donations in our own society Titmuss suggests that here we have a 'free gift' which carries, 'no explicit right, expectation or moral enforcement of a return gift' (Titmuss, 1970, p. 212).

The most systematic treatment of this kind of gift comes from the anthropologist Marshall Sahlins; and while he was mainly concerned, as was Mauss, with exchange in primitive societies, his account would probably need little modification to make it appropriate to the so-called advanced societies. Like Malinowski, Sahlins presents a continuum of exchange, the different modes of exchange being conditioned by the 'span of social distance' between those involved. Thus, at one extreme, 'the unsociable extreme', we have *negative reciprocity.* This is the attempt to get something for nothing. It is an impersonal form of exchange in which the participants confront each other as opposed interests, each looking to obtain an advantage for himself at the other's expense. The morality is that of *caveat emptor* and the reciprocity, if it exists at all, is purely in defence of self-interest. At the extreme it amounts to straightforward robbery or 'the finesse of a well-conducted horse-raid' but as we move along the continuum we come to barter and the economic transaction 'conducted in the spirit of "what the traffic will bear"' (Sahlins, 1965, p. 149).

As we move on from barter we come to *balanced reciprocity,* the midpoint. It includes cases, as in friendship compacts or peace agreements, where there is a simultaneous exchange of exactly the same types and quantities of goods. But it also seems to include much of what has already gone under the heading of ceremonial exchange or gift exchange. '"Balanced reciprocity" may be more loosely applied to transactions which stipulate returns of commensurate worth or utility within a finite and narrow period' (p. 148).

As with negative reciprocity, the parties confront each other as opposed interests, and while there is a social side to the transaction as well as an economic one, the material side is at least as critical as the social. 'The relations between people are disrupted by a failure to reciprocate within limited time and equivalence leeways' (p. 148). Just as proper reciprocation establishes a bond, failure to do so disrupts it.

Finally we come to *generalized reciprocity,* 'the solidary extreme'. Here the material side of the transaction is repressed by the social. 'Reckoning of debts outstanding cannot be overt and is typically left out of account. This is not to say that handing over things in such form, even to "loved ones", generates no counter-obligation. But the counter is not stipulated by time, quantity, or quality: the expectation of reciprocity is indefinite. It usually works out that the time and worth of reciprocation are not alone conditional on what was given by the donor, but also upon what he will need and when, and likewise what the recipient can afford and when. Receiving goods lays on a diffuse obligation to reciprocate when necessary to the donor and/or possible for the recipient' (p. 147).

This is not perhaps quite the same thing as Titmuss' free gift, but it is certainly rather different from Mauss's total prestation or Blau's social exchange. The crucial point of difference concerns, of course, the morality of the return. *No longer is it a matter of equivalence between the objects exchanged but a matter of the individuals' need.* If balanced reciprocity is typified in our society by the middle-class host who expects his guests to invite him back to a dinner party in their turn, generalized reciprocity is typified by the working-class mother who helps her daughter look after her baby when she is ill and keeps no tally of the debts owed but doubtless expects to be helped herself should she ever need it.

Rational choice and the morality of social exchange

Whereas comparison processes and changing aspirations could easily be incorporated within conventional rational choice theory, it is not at all obvious at first sight that the same can be done with justice and morality. Indeed, if we accept Mauss's account of total prestations, there seems to be virtually no scope for a rational choice approach at all. While the prestations are in theory voluntary, they are (according to Mauss) so clearly regulated and prescribed in practice that no scope for discretion or choice remains. To quote Duesenberry's dictum again: 'Economics is all about how people make choices. Sociology [or in this case anthropology] is all about why they don't have any choices to make.' Thus the occasion for a potlatch, the identity of the guests, the size of the gifts are not matters where the chieftain can do just what he pleases. He is constrained by his culture and, it appears, must act accordingly. True, there seems to be more scope for choice in the Kula; the timing of the expedition and the precise nature of the gift seem to be matters for individual choice. But the overall picture is much the same: 'Although the prestations and counter-prestations take place under a voluntary guise they are in essence strictly obligatory, and their sanction is private or open warfare' (Mauss, 1925, p. 3). Whether the obligations are quite as strict as Mauss suggests I rather doubt, but the essential conclusion is clear enough: if the character of the exchange can be explained in terms of social obligations and prescriptions, there is little work left for the rational choice approach to do. We can, of course, always say that the participants gain utility from conformity with the norms involved, but even the most ardent defender of exchange theory could hardly claim that this has advanced our understanding.

When we turn from total prestations to the social exchanges in modern society that Blau makes his concern, we find fewer obligations and hence, presumably, more scope for choice. True, a man's freedom of action is limited by the norms of reciprocity and of fair exchange, but this need not worry us overmuch. As we shall see later, a system of 'fair prices' can easily enough be integrated with the rational choice theories that we have encountered so far.

What cannot be so easily integrated, however, are the theories of power and status that Blau builds on the norms of reciprocity and fair exchange. As we saw earlier in this chapter, to render important services (according to Blau) is to make a claim for superior status, and failure to make an equivalent or worthy return is to validate that claim. The man who concludes a fair exchange maintains his status; the man who fails to do so, loses it. This theory of status, it is essential to realize, is quite different from the 'economic' theory that Homans had offered earlier. For Homans social approval had been a currency used to purchase social benefits, and the men who could supply a particularly scarce and valuable benefit thus obtained a higher price. 'The capacity to supply a rare service gets the men who actually do supply it a larger amount of social approval than other members of their group get. They are superior to the others and no longer their social equals', Homans wrote (1961, p. 148). There is no mention here of fair exchange. There is no suggestion that the recipients of this rare service failed to make a worthy return. Indeed, the price they were forced to pay may even have been excessive when judged by standards of social justice. All that matters for Homans is that the price actually was higher. The suppliers of the rare service got a larger amount of social approval than did other members of their group, and that was the end of the matter.

The difference between these two theories of status is instructive and reveals some crucial differences between the economic and the sociological approaches to social exchange. In Homans' economic theory social approval is accorded another *in order to obtain his services.* In Blau's sociological theory it is presumably accorded by onlookers (and participants) who *judge the adequacy of the return.* It is not an inducement given by Ego to Alter but a judgement made by a third party. The two are as different as the currency with which a customer buys a commodity and the fine which the courts impose on a customer who takes the goods without paying.

This analogy brings out an important difference between the two theories. The economic theory is *forward-looking.* Bygones are bygones for the economist. Goods for services are handed over with an eye to the future, not to the past. If I reciprocate it is because I want your help again in future, not because I feel grateful for past favours. In contrast, the sociological theory is *backward-looking.* Bygones are of crucial importance. Services are given and judgements made in recognition of past favours, not in expectation of future ones.

This distinction between the forward-looking economic theory and the backward-looking sociological ones is found even more clearly in the case of the two theories of power that Blau unwittingly presents. On the one hand, as we saw earlier, Blau advances an economic theory in which one man's power over another derived from the latter's dependence on him for future benefits. On the other hand, Blau also builds a sociological theory of power on the norm of reciprocity: quite simply, the man who helps another obligates him to reciprocate and thus acquires power over him. The latter is obliged, by way of payment, to accede to the former's requests, and until this reciprocation takes place there is an imbalance of power. In this way Blau is able to talk of 'the power of accumulated obligations', and of the fact that 'by giving orders to others and imposing his will upon them, the ruler or leader cashes in on some of the obligations they owe him for whatever services he has rendered and thus depletes his power' (Blau, 1964, p. 135).

I do not see any prospect of integrating these different theories of power and status, nor do I see any particular need to do so. We must not make Durkheim's classic error of supposing that 'every proved specific difference between causes therefore implies a similar difference between effects' (Durkheim, 1897, p. 146). Different causes can perfectly well give rise to similar effects. A man can look backwards as well as forwards and may comply with another's requests with one eye to his past debts and another to his future loans. It is rather alarming that Blau apparently failed to realize that he had two quite different kinds of theory side by side, but I do not think that any more heinous fault is involved.

Finally, something should be said about the category of free gift or generalized reciprocity. Here we come to something which is different again. By definition these are gifts not given with an eye either to past or to future benefits but given out of a sense of altruism or of a wish to help those in need. It is hard to see how they can be brought within the scope of exchange at all. They certainly do not come within the definition of exchange that Blau first propounded, and neither his economic nor his sociological theories have much to say about them. However, let me reiterate that a rational choice approach can be applied to more phenomena than those that fall within the category of exchange. Providing there is some scope for choice, there is some scope for a rationalist approach. As I remarked earlier, even altruists are faced with the problem of 'scarce means which have alternative uses'.

7. Emergent processes

So far we have dealt almost exclusively with the 'micro-economics' and the 'micro-sociology' of exchange. We have been concerned with face-to-face processes of direct exchange – with the exchange of advice for approval in a work group, the relative power of husband and wife within the family, the exchange of gifts and feasts between Indian chieftains. We thus have a sociology of inter-personal relations or, as Homans calls it, a theory of elementary social behaviour. In contrast we have had no theory of institutions or of the 'emergent processes' (Blau's phrase) that lead to them. Those parts of exchange theory that we have looked at so far, then, offer no challenge to those sociological approaches such as functionalism or Marxism which do attempt to account for the norms, roles and institutions of society.

This distinction is particularly clear if we look at the rational choice theories. They attempt to explain what people will do *given* the existing norms and institutions. They do not attempt to account for the character of those institutions themselves. Thus Downs and Riker treated democratic political institutions as a given, as a part of the context within which the political parties made their choices. They did not concern themselves with the question of *why* elections were held at fixed intervals or *why* each adult resident had one and only one vote. These are not the kinds of questions which the rational choice approach usually tackles.

The same point holds true in the case of the material which we have encountered so far that uses a more sociological approach. Most of this sociological work that we have summarized has been descriptive, describing *what* the morality of social exchange is rather than explaining *why* it has the particular character it does. Even the sociological theories which we have examined (for example, those of power and status) have *assumed* the existence of a norm of reciprocity or of fair exchange. They have not tried to account for the norms themselves.

To be fair, however, the summaries so far have been somewhat selective, and some of our sociological writers do try to account for the norms which they describe. For example, Mauss has a rather curious theory in which he seems to ascribe the norm of reciprocity to a native belief that 'the thing given is not inert. It is alive and often personified, and strives to bring to its original clan and homeland some equivalent to take its place' (Mauss, 1925, p. 10). Even when we remember theories such as this, however, I think it is still true to say that the bulk of exchange theory, whether it is of economic or sociological parentage, has a 'micro' rather than a 'macro' field of operations. The space which I have devoted to it is, I think, a fair reflection of its volume in the literature as a whole.

However, our principal exchange theorists are not content to leave macro-sociology wholly to the functionalists and Marxists, and Blau in particular wishes to develop a theory of institutions and of emergent processes. Indeed, he ways, the construction of such a theory is the central concern of his book. 'The purpose of the intensive analysis of interpersonal relations that occupies much of the first half of the book', he writes, 'is not primarily to investigate the relations between individuals for their own sake, nor is it to search for the psychological roots of human interaction, but it is to derive from this analysis a better understanding of the complex structures of associations among men that develop. It is this fundamental concern with utilizing the analysis of simpler processes for clarifying complex structures that distinguishes the approach here from that of other recent students of interpersonal processes, notably George C. Homans and John W. Thibaut and Harold H. Kelley, from whose perceptive insights the present investigation has otherwise greatly benefited' (Blau, 1964, p. 2).

While Blau's comments on Homans and Thibaut and Kelley are strictly accurate, they are nevertheless somewhat less than just. True these writers' primary concern is with 'elementary social behaviour' or with 'the social psychology of groups' but they also allow themselves occasional ventures into the deeper, if muddier, waters of macro-sociology. Thus Thibaut and Kelley come up with a quasi-functionalist theory of social norms, which they couch in reward–cost terms. And Homans, in a concluding chapter which he likens to a primitive orgy after harvest (his metaphor perhaps reflecting his more enthusiastic attitude towards the enterprise), tries to explain the development and enforcement of social rules. What I propose to do, then, in this chapter is to look at some of these theories concerning the origins and functions of social norms. This will, I think, give a fair reflection of Homans' and of Thibaut and Kelley's interests but will be less than fair to Blau. Blau has a lot to say about emergent processes that I shall not attempt to cover. For example, he examines four types of 'mediating value' and sixteen types of relationship between 'substructure' and 'macrostructure'. But as far as I can detect this is the kind of conceptual scheming and typologizing that one hoped had been abandoned along with Talcott Parsons. It does nothing that I can see to 'clarify complex structures', and I do not apologize for its omission.

The origin of social norms: a rational choice approach

Norms and institutions were presumably created by men, even if they were men who have long been dead, and there is no *a priori* reason to suppose that these men were any the less rational when they were constructing institutions than they were in the rest of their daily lives. True it may be very difficult at this distance of time to discover precisely (or even roughly) why they constructed the institutions that they did. But to say that it is difficult is not to say that it is *in principle* impossible for a rational choice approach.

A position of this kind, or something very like it, seems to be the one that Homans adopts. As a preface to his 'primitive orgy after harvest' he writes: 'If you look long enough for the secret of society you will find it in plain sight: the secret of society is that it was made by men, and there is nothing in society but what men put there' (Homans, 1961, p. 385). And as a preface to his book as a whole he had also written: 'I do not think we need a different kind of explanation for the development and enforcement of rules from what we need for the subject matter of this book, but we may need a more complicated explanation' (p. 3).

As an example of this 'more complicated explanation' I shall take Homans' attempt to account for the norm of output restriction. Originally, says Homans, some members of the work group must have found output restriction rewarding in itself, perhaps because it strengthened their bargaining position vis-à-vis management. However, and this is the crux of the argument, *output restriction is only effective if all the other members of the work group (or at least the great majority) also conform to the norm.* The original proponents of restriction may not get any benefits if they are the only ones to limit output. They must ensure that the others toe the line too, and hence it may be rational for them to institute and enforce a rule to that effect. As Homans put it: 'Restriction gets its results only if a rather large number of members conform to the output norm, and therefore nonconformists deprive the rest of a reward. Accordingly, the members who would have been indifferent to the primary reward are nevertheless apt to conform, for fear of losing the esteem of their fellows; and then restriction of output is well on its way to becoming an institution, taught to new members and even to new generations as one of the laws of life in the factory' (Homans, 1961, pp. 381-2).

In this way the norm of output restriction was originally a rule imposed by some members of the group on others because they found it in their interests that everyone should conform. Presumably the 'moral entrepreneurs' in the group who enforced the norm must have found that the extra benefits of a completely uniform rate of output outweighed the costs of enforcing the norm, and the erstwhile deviants must have found that the benefits of rate-busting were outweighed by the penalties that the moral entrepreneurs now imposed upon them. Given that these assumptions were sound and can be shown to be sound, we have now managed to provide a rational choice explanation for the norm.

Notice, however, that we have not managed to explain why the norm should now come to be *internalized* by these or by any other group members. The rational choice approach can only explain what people *do*. It can explain why people might institute a norm and might then enforce it, but it cannot explain why they should change their values – for this is what internalization amounts to. Values, unlike institutions, must always remain a 'given' in the rational choice approach and to explain how they change we should have to introduce additional psychological mechanisms that have nothing to do with rationality (or even with Skinner's behavioural psychology).

Of course there is nothing to stop our exchange theorists introducing these additional psychological mechanisms, and most of them make some explicit or implicit use of such hallowed slogans as 'what is customary becomes obligatory'. Blau, for example, in an attempt to account for the norm of reciprocity, begins by arguing that people will find it in their interest to reciprocate and hence will do so. After a time, he implies, such customary reciprocation will become obligatory. He writes: 'When people are thrown together, and before common norms or goals or role expectations have crystallized among them, the advantages to be gained from entering into exchange relations furnish incentives for social interaction . . . Eventually, group norms to regulate and limit the exchange transactions emerge, including the fundamental and ubiquitous norm of reciprocity, which makes failure to discharge obligations subject to group sanctions. In contrast to Gouldner, however, it is held here that the norm of reciprocity merely reinforces and stabilizes tendencies inherent in the character of social exchange itself' (Blau, 1964, p. 92).

There is nothing intrinsically absurd in such an argument, although one could wish for a more explicit account of the way in which group norms emerge. Whatever the precise mechanism, however, it is worth noting that the argument must be a very different kind from that used in Homans' example of the norm of output restriction. In Homans' example the norm was needed in order to enable some people to get benefits that would not otherwise have been available to them; in Blau's example the norm of reciprocity is not really 'needed' at all. People will reciprocate *anyway* (at least according to Blau they have important incentives to do so) and on this view the norm is essentially redundant or at best 'reinforces and stabilizes' existing tendencies. It is a kind of codification of existing practice rather than a new rule requiring people to modify their behaviour.

Blau's theory of the norm of reciprocity, then, is partly rationalist (explaining why people should reciprocate in the first place) and partly psychological (claiming that customary practice will become obligatory). However, he also goes further in a non-rationalist direction and develops a kind of sociological or socio-psychological theory of institutionalization that has nothing to do with rationality. We turn to this theory next.

The origin of social norms: a sociological approach

It will be remembered that in his discussion of the morality of social exchange Blau had postulated a norm of fair exchange rather like Homans' rule of distributive justice. It stated that men's rewards should be proportional to their investments. It will also be remembered that Homans' man became angry when he did worse, and guilty when he did better, than he was entitled to according to distributive justice. This anger and guilt were not claimed to be rational responses to injustice but rather seemed to be emotional and spontaneous reactions. They were not oriented to any particular end but seemed to happen involuntarily.

Blau's man seems to behave in a somewhat similar way. If, in a group situation, he gets much less from the leader than he was entitled to according to fair exchange, he is likely to develop opposition ideals; and if he does much better, he is likely to legitimate the leader's authority. In either case he will develop *new* values (of opposition or of willing obedience) that he did not possess previously. Opposition and legitimation are thus emergent processes.

Blau's theory clearly differs from Homans' in its concern with values rather than emotional reactions such as anger. But it also differs in a second crucial (and related) respect. Blau is concerned not with the response of an isolated individual in a single exchange but with the responses of the members of a *group of subordinates*. While anger and guilt may indeed, as Homans' suggests, be the responses of isolated individuals, the legitimation of authority and the development of opposition ideals are essentially the products of group action. Thus Blau writes: 'Social values that legitimate opposition to dominant powers, and thereby solidify it, can emerge only in a collectivity whose members share the experience of being exploited and oppressed, just as social values that legitimate the authority of a superior can develop only in a collectivity of subordinates. Isolated victims of oppression are helpless in their futile anger, but an entire collectivity is not' (Blau, 1964, p. 231).

According to Blau, then, shared experiences of fair or unfair treatment lead to the emergence of new norms and values. These new norms and values should not be regarded as rational responses to the situation. Indeed, it is a contradiction in terms to say that a new value is rationally instituted. Rationality, in the economist's sense, is concerned with choice of *means*, whereas values must surely constitute *ends*. Rather, the emergence of new values must be regarded as the results of non-rational psychological mechanisms. Blau does not elucidate the nature of these mechanisms at all satisfactorily, but he does suggest that they may be those described in Festinger's theory of cognitive dissonance (1957). Thus he seems to argue that accepting another's orders is dissonant with the American emphases on equality and independence and that this dissonance can be reduced or avoided by coming to believe that compliance with these orders 'does not constitute submission to [the leader's] will but is simply part of freely accepted responsibilities' (Blau, 1964, p. 208). To avoid cognitive dissonance we have chosen to believe that our conformity to the demands of the dominant powers is a willing obedience, and for Blau (like Weber) willing obedience is the cornerstone of legitimation.

Put like this the theory has strong rationalistic overtones, and indeed Blau says that these beliefs can be considered 'rationalizations through which individuals adapt to a subordinate position' (1964, p. 208). Instead of a theory that people seek to maximize utility, we now have a theory that people seek to minimize cognitive dissonance. The parallels with rational choice theory are striking. But we should not be misled. This is not the rationality of the economists. Cognitive dissonance theory is not concerned with choices between alternative courses of action but with changes in beliefs and attitudes. And while we might use the language of choice (as I did in the previous paragraph) to describe these changes, we should be clear that our usage is metaphorical.

However, whatever the status of cognitive dissonance theory, it does not in fact do the job that Blau requires of it. In the first place, cognitive consonance could as easily be achieved by abandoning our values of independence and equality as it could be by believing that our obedience is willing. And in the second place it fails to explain why *shared* experiences should be so important (and this after all is the point on which Blau placed most emphasis). Indeed, the theory seems almost more appropriate for the individual case than for the collective one. Blau's argument, therefore, has nothing of the economist's logical rigour. Conclusions are not derived inexorably from premises. Rather, the conclusions are stated first and the premises are sketchily drawn in later.

Let me hasten to add, however, that rigour is not all. For all the rigour of his argument, the economist's conclusions may be derived from faulty premises; and Blau's conclusions, for all his lack of rigour, may nevertheless be sound. Blau's might perhaps best be regarded as a kind of 'black box' theory. The inputs are described (shared experience of exploitation, for example) and so are the outputs (the emergence of opposition ideals). If these descriptions are correct, then there must be some kind of psychological mechanism, explicated or not, going on inside the box. If it has something to do with cognitive dissonance, then so much the better, but it is not vital for us to know at this stage. Let us check up on our description of the inputs and outputs first.

What norms do: a rational choice approach

In addition to these various theories about the origins and emergence of social norms we also get various quasi-functionalist theories about what norms do. They are functionalist in that they look at the *consequences* of social norms rather than at their origins, but they keep within a rationalist framework in that they show how norms improve individuals' rewards (or reduce their costs) rather than, as in the classic functionalist case, showing how they contribute to the survival or equilibrium of the society as a whole. Homans exemplifies this position well when he says: 'We social scientists talk as if "society" were the big thing. But an institution is functional for society only because it is functional for men' (Homans, 1961, p. 384).

One example of this kind of theory comes from Thibaut and Kelley. Their main claim is that social norms have a cost-reducing function and, more particularly, 'serve as substitutes for the exercise of personal influence and produce more economically and efficiently certain consequences otherwise dependent upon personal influence processes' (Thibaut and Kelley, 1959, p. 130). To illustrate their argument Thibaut and Kelley take the case of a husband and wife 'whose problem is that the wife likes to go dancing in the evening and the husband prefers that they go to the movies' (p. 127). They suggest that the options open to each, and the consequential rewards, can be represented by the matrix in figure 14. (This matrix must in fact surely be

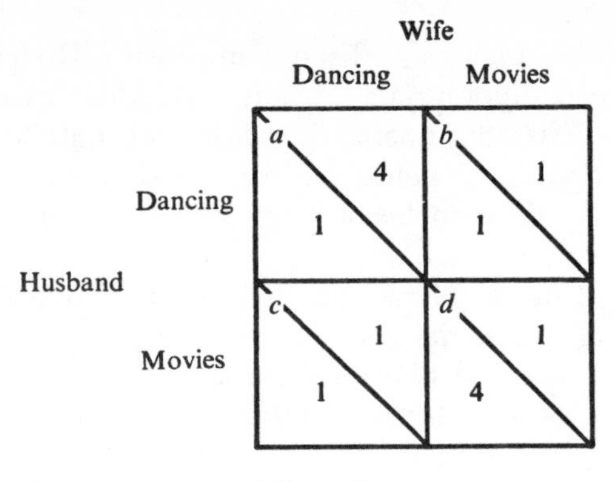

Figure 14

wrong. Since the husband does not like dancing and the wife does not like movies, the entries in the top right-hand cells must be zero, not one.)

Pretty clearly, some kind of cooperation between husband and wife is now called for, or, as Thibaut and Kelley say, some kind of trading is necessary. Now this could be done through the direct exercise of power, since each can affect the other's outcomes through his own choice of behaviour. 'For example, the husband can use his control over the wife's outcomes by promising to go dancing if she will go with him to the movies. Or he can threaten to go to the movies if she fails to cooperate, in which case she will have poor outcomes. Similar opportunities exist for the wife' (p. 127). This kind of bargaining might have the required effect with husband and wife alternating between dancing and movies so that each gets a share of high outcomes. But bargaining itself is a costly activity and the couple clearly lose nothing, and possibly save a lot of time and trouble, if they institute an agreement once and for all to alternate between the two activities. *The norm is thus a rule which has the 'function' of introducing predictability and regularity into the relationship.*

Blau, too, has a quasi-functionalist theory of norms in addition to his various rational and non-rational theories that we looked at earlier. In my view it is by far his best theory. His central point is again very like Thibaut and Kelley's. He argues that some social norms *enable the individuals concerned to achieve better outcomes than would be possible if each simply pursued his own self-interest.* The example he takes is the prisoners' dilemma. Two suspects, let us suppose, are being questioned separately by the police. They are guilty of the crime for which they are suspected, but the police do not have sufficient evidence to convict either unless one or both turns Queen's evidence and confesses. On the other hand the police do have sufficient evidence to convict them both of a lesser offence without more ado. (The two suspects might be Brutus and Charlie. They have successfully disposed of Ahab, leaving no trace of the body, but have been caught redhanded by the police in possession of the stolen treasure.)

The alternatives open to the suspects, therefore, are either to confess to the serious crime or to stay silent. If both confess, both get severe sentences, which are, however, somewhat reduced, since the prisoners have been cooperative and saved the police and the court's time. If only one turns Queen's evidence, the other gets the full sentence, and the informer gets off scot-free as his reward. If neither confesses, neither can be convicted of the serious crime, but they will both certainly be tried and convicted of the lesser offence. We thus get the matrix in figure 15.

How will our two suspects now decide to behave, given of course that they are locked up in separate cells and are not allowed to communicate? Brutus will presumably reason as follows: 'If Charlie confesses to the murder, I am going to get either ten years or eight – ten if I stay silent, but eight if I confess too; clearly I'm better off confessing. But what happens if Charlie keeps quiet? Well this time I either get two years or nothing at all – two years if I stay silent too but nothing if I turn Queen's evidence. Again, then, I'm better off confessing. Whatever Charlie does, it's in my interest to confess.'

Since the matrix is a symmetrical one, Charlie goes through the same process of reasoning too; he too decides to confess; and both thus end up with eight years' imprisonment, the outcome which is in fact the joint worst outcome for the pair. The rational pursuit of self-interest, then, leads them to get a total of sixteen years in jail. Even if they realize that this is what will happen, and they assuredly will, there is no incentive for them to change their decision. There is no point in Brutus' keeping quiet unless he can ensure that Charlie will keep

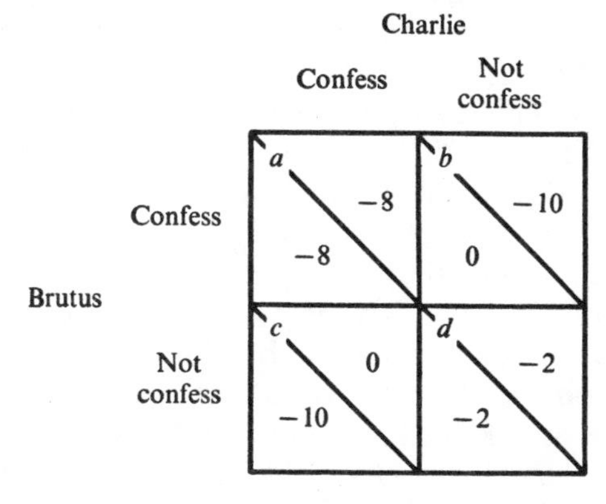

Figure 15

his part of the 'bargain', and he has got absolutely no way of doing this.

The situation changes, however, when we introduce norms and sanctions and the two pirates now obtain incentives to remain silent. If a norm of 'honour among thieves' is enforced by other members of the criminal fraternity, then the two suspects will be faced with a quite different matrix. If confession is punished, we must add an extra penalty in the appropriate cells of the matrix, and if silence is rewarded, we must add extra benefits accordingly. If these rewards and penalties are sufficiently large (a crucial point that Blau fails to mention), we will have transformed the situation from a mixed game (as it is in figure 15) in which there are both common and conflicting interests to a cooperative one. It now becomes rational for the two suspects to say silent (and get the two years' imprisonment) rather than to confess (and end up with eight). As Blau concludes, 'These sanctions convert conduct that otherwise would be irrational into a rational pursuit of self-interest' (1964, p. 258).

While this argument superficially resembles Thibaut and Kelley's theory, there are some crucial differences. True, both emphasize the 'cost-reducing function' of norms, but here the similarity ends. Thibaut and Kelley simply suggest that the norm will eliminate bargaining costs; they do not argue that it will allow the couple to reach a *different* cell of the matrix than the one they would otherwise have reached. Blau on the other hand is not concerned with bargaining costs at all. Indeed, since the pirates are not allowed to communicate, bargaining cannot enter the matter at all. Blau's crucial point is that the norm allows the individuals concerned to reach a 'better' cell of the matrix.

A further difference is that Blau's argument, unlike Thibaut and Kelley's, depends on the presence of a third party who will enforce the norm. Here we no longer have direct exchange but indirect exchange in which Brutus makes a concession to Charlie (and vice versa) in order to avoid punishment from some moral entrepreneur of the criminal community.

Finally we should note that the force of Blau's example, and the distinct conclusions to which it leads, depends on the particular structure of the matrix described. If we label the cells a, b, c, d (as in figure 15, we see that for Brutus $b > d > a > c$ whereas in figure 14 the husband faced a situation in which $c > a = d > b$. These differences are crucial. The peculiar logic of the prisoners' dilemma, and the startling transformation wrought by the introduction of norms, depends entirely on the fact that $b > d > a > c$. Fortunately for mankind not all games are of this kind, although the prisoners' dilemma is not solely an intellectual curiosity. The reader has no doubt already realized that the public goods problem that Olson describes can be represented in the same way. If we take the case of the worker wondering whether to pay his 10p dues to a union which would obtain him £1 wage rise, we can simplify it rather drastically into a two-person game of 'the worker against the rest', giving the matrix in figure 16. As before, b>d>a>c.

In some cases, then, such as those involving public goods or the prisoners' dilemma, norms enable the participants to reach better outcomes than they would otherwise have done. They are (if one insists on using the term) 'functional' for the participants, although not necessarily for the society as a whole. But other norms are clearly not of this kind. The commandment that 'Thou shalt not steal' protects the interests of the property-owners but hardly improves the lot of the propertyless. Homans' argument is surely more appropriate here. The norm is imposed by one group on another because they find it in their interests, and within their power, to do so. Not all norms further the collective good.

What norms do: a sociological approach

Finally I want to look at another quasi-functionalist theory. This is perhaps one of the most famous in exchange theory and comes not from Homans or Blau but from Lévi-Strauss. Lévi-Strauss is concerned with kinship and marriage and attempts to show that 'reciprocity is present behind all marriages'. For example, the incest taboo means that a family cannot retain its own daughters but must give them up to some other group; at the same time it gives the family a right to the daughter of some other group. In this way the exchange of women occurs, each group yielding up women but receiving others in return.

Lévi-Strauss's approach to these exchanges, however, is radically

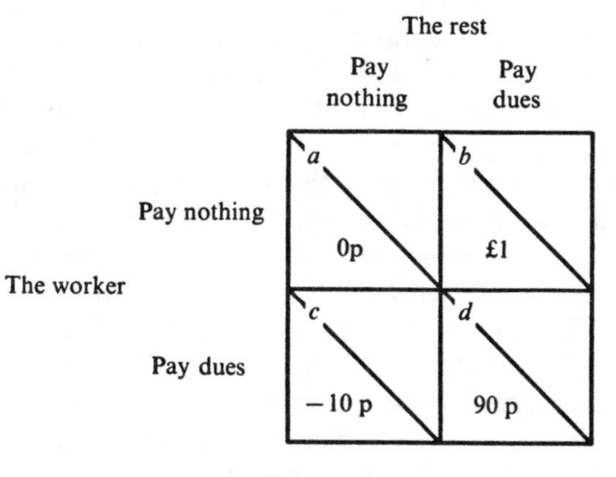

Figure 16

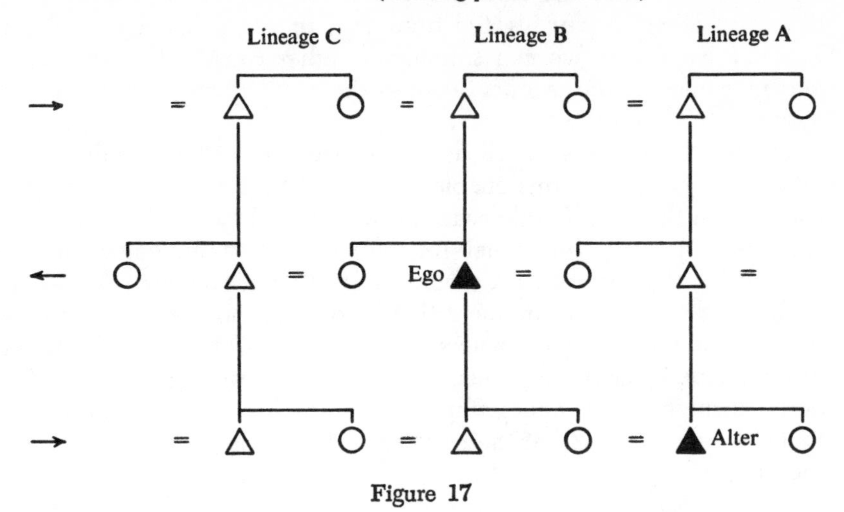

Figure 17

different from anything that we have seen so far. He resolutely sets himself against any 'economic' explanations and claims that 'there is nothing in the exchange of women faintly resembling a reasoned solution to an economic problem (Lévi-Strauss, 1949, p. 139). Instead he seems to suggest that reciprocity is to be understood as a 'formal structure, consciously or unconsciously apprehended by the human mind' (p. 440). Quite what this means I am at a loss to understand, and to attain any degree of comprehension might, I suspect, require us to undertake a detailed study of Lévi-Strauss's brand of structuralism. I do not propose to undertake this study but merely wish to point out that, whatever Lévi-Strauss's account of exchange proves to be, it will be nothing like that of the economist.

Fortunately, some of Lévi-Strauss's remarks about the exchange of women are rather less opaque and repay further study. He first points out that different systems of *unilateral* cross-cousin marriage lead to different kinds of exchange. In the case of *patrilateral* cross-cousin marriage lineage A 'gives' a woman to lineage B in one generation and 'receives' a woman back in the following generation. This Lévi-Strauss calls a pattern of *discontinuous exchange*. In the case of *matrilateral* cross-cousin marriage, on the other hand, things work out rather differently: lineage A invariably gives women to lineage B, lineage B to lineage C, and so on, women being passed round in a circle (reminiscent of valuables in the Kula ring). This form of exchange Lévi-Strauss calls *generalized exchange*.

At first sight this seems a rather remarkable result, but the way in which it is achieved should become clear from the following (highly

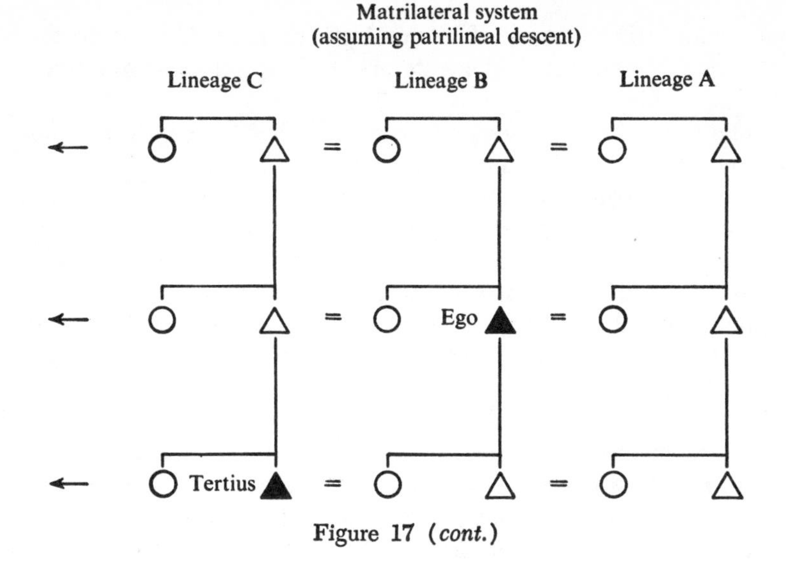

Figure 17 (*cont.*)

schematic) diagram (fig. 17). In the case of patrilateral cross-cousin marriage, Ego marries his father's sister's daughter, who will come, let us say, from lineage A. In due course the daughter of this union will return to her mother's lineage since she in turn is Alter's father's sister's daughter. In this way, if men always marry their fathers' sisters' daughters, a pattern of discontinuous exchange must occur. Lineage B will become alternately a wife-giver to, and a wife-receiver from, lineage A in succeeding generations.

Conversely, in the case of matrilateral cross-cousin marriage, Ego marries his mother's brother's daughter, but in due course the daughter of this union does *not* return to her mother's lineage. Instead, she moves on (as her father's sister did before) to lineage C, since she is now Tertius' mother's brother's daughter. In this way the women of lineage B always marry into lineage C: lineage B is always a wife-giver to lineage C (and a wife-receiver from lineage A).

Having shown how these two systems of cross-cousin marriage give rise to different forms of exchange, Lévi-Strauss goes on to argue that one of the forms, namely generalized exchange, 'allows the realization of a more supple and effective solidarity' within the group (1949, p. 441) than does the other. In typical metaphorical language he writes: '[In the case of marriage with the father's sister's daughter] the integration of the group does not proceed from the participation of every individual and biological family in a collective harmony. It results both mechanically and precariously from the sum of particular ties by which a family is linked with one family or another. Instead of the real unity of a single thread underlying the whole social fabric, there is an artificial unity of bits and pieces, proceeding from the fact that two interconnected elements are each coupled with a third element' (pp. 445-6).

Finally, Lévi-Strauss seems to conclude that their different implications for solidarity account for the relative frequency of the two marriage rules. Patrilateral cross-cousin marriage allows an artificial unity of bits and pieces and accordingly is a less common rule; matrilateral cross-cousin marriage allows the realization of a more supple and effective solidarity and is accordingly more common. (Some cynical commentators, however, have pointed out that neither rule is in fact particularly common and so perhaps the solidarity that they yield is not particularly great either.)

Before I conclude, a number of points are perhaps worth making about this theory. In the first place, it must be clear that Lévi-Strauss is quite right to reject an economic approach to these particular examples of woman-exchange. It would be absurd to suppose that the different lineages consciously choose to bestow their women in such a way as will maximize utility, solidarity or anything else. Rather, the exchanges must be seen as the *unintended* consequences of certain marriage rules and not as intended transactions at all. Secondly, the marriage rules themselves (or rather their prevalence) seem to be explained in *functionalist* terms. As Lévi-Strauss wrote: 'If, then, in the final analysis, marriage with the father's sister's daughter is less frequent than that with the mother's brother's daughter, it is because the latter not only permits but favours a better integration of the group, whereas the former never succeeds in creating anything but a precarious edifice made of juxtaposed materials, subject to no general plan, and its discrete texture is exposed to the same fragility as each of the little local structures of which ultimately it is composed' (p. 448). Here we seem to have the classic functionalism which relates institutions to their consequences for the system as a whole. With Lévi-Strauss we finally leave the individualistic orientation that characterizes virtually the whole of American exchange theory (economic and sociological variants alike) and return to the traditional collectivism of French sociology.

PART II

8. *Rational choice revisited*

The theory of rational choice is one of the main foundations of exchange theory, but it is also a foundation that many critics have claimed to be built on sand. It has in fact come in for more criticism than almost any other aspect of exchange theory, although much of the criticism is in fact misguided and the critics could more profitably have directed their labours towards other parts of the structure.

One main line of criticism simply suggests that ordinary people are not as rational as the theory requires: people, the critics claim, do not consciously weigh up or evaluate alternatives in the way required; they do not usually deliberate for any length of time before making their decisions but more often choose impulsively; they do not usually make decisions on the basis of complete and accurate information about the situation and make little effort to obtain such information. A second main line of criticism (and one that is rather at odds with the first) claims that the theory is in any event tautological: it is true by definition, critics claim, that people maximize utility and as a result the foundations, and the superstructure of exchange theory built upon them must collapse. And a third line of criticism (rather at odds with the second) is that people do not maximize anyway but instead 'satisfice', choosing an alternative which provides a satisfactory outcome but not necessarily the best outcome available.

Of these criticisms the third is usually advanced against the theory of risky choices, and the second against the theory of riskless choice, while the first is applied more indiscriminately. The second and third also have some substance, while the first merely derives from some misapprehensions and ignorance about the theories being criticized. What I shall do, therefore, in this chapter is begin by exposing the fallacies underlying the first set of criticisms; I shall then go on to consider the theory of riskless choice, paying particular attention to the problem of tautology; and I shall conclude with the theory of risky choices and, for light relief, with a postscript devoted to choice under uncertainty.

Some common fallacies

Let us begin with *the fallacy that the rational man must have complete and perfect information.* The fallacy rests on a failure to distinguish between the rationality of a man's beliefs and knowledge and the rationality of what he does given those beliefs. Now it is almost certainly true that no one in the world has completely accurate knowledge, accurate, that is, as defined by the present state of scientific research. Mistaken beliefs are perhaps most obvious to western eyes if we look at primitive peoples: we can have no doubt about the mistake made by the members of cargo cults who believe that, if they build jetties or landing strips like the white man's, and if they make the correct prayers to the white man's god, then ships or aeroplanes will duly arrive bringing them cargo. We are not perhaps quite so good at spotting our own mistakes: most white Englishmen, I suspect, believe that if an unbiassed coin has come down heads twice running, it is likely to come down tails on the third throw. And they would be just as mistaken as the members of the cargo cult.

If rational choice theory required that people should not make mistakes of this kind, it would certainly be doomed to failure. We should find that no men were rational, and the term would be rendered vacuous. However, the rational choice theories that I have presented do not have this requirement at all. They are theories about the way in which people choose *given their beliefs* and they do not themselves venture to say anything about the nature of those beliefs. That is a separate, and extremely important, subject, about which they need make no assumptions.

True, economists frequently suppose, as a convenient approximation, that people have accurate information about certain aspects of their situation (as indeed they do in their theory of price or in their use of indifference curves). But it is essential to realize that this is an *additional* assumption and one that is in no way entailed by the claims that people maximize utility or expected utility. It may make life much easier for us if we can simply assume that people's knowledge is correct, but, provided we can independently discover what information they possess, the theory of rational choice can still apply regardless.

Consider next *the fallacy that it is rational to collect information before making a decision.* Educated people, for example, often go to the bother of acquiring information about the issues of the day, and it is therefore often supposed that their voting decisions must be more rational ones than those of their less educated and less informed compatriots. Again, the person who shops around for food is often supposed to be more rational than the one who always goes to the same (expensive) corner shop. But neither supposition is correct.

First of all, it is essential to realize that the issue of collecting information arises only in situations of uncertainty. If we know, or believe we know, what the outcomes of all courses of action are, we do not need further information anyway. But let us take situations of incomplete information and apply the theory of risky choices to the collection of further information. What we have to do is to consider the benefits of the extra information and compare them with the costs of securing it. The costs are clear enough: we have to spend time and trouble collecting information about the issues of the day, finding out what goods are available in other shops and at what prices. But the benefits are not so immediately apparent: if the extra information which we collect fails to alter our choice, then the extra effort has been wasted (unless we value peace of mind). What we have to do, therefore, is to estimate the probability that a given increment of information will alter our choice and multiply this by the increment in utility that the new choice provides (see Downs, 1957, pp. 214ff). The individual, therefore, who judges that, however much information he collects about the Conservative and Liberal parties and their policies, he will still prefer to vote Labour will quite rationally decide not to collect that information. Since the extra information will not change his vote (or at best will have a very low probability of doing so), it is not rational for him to go to the bother of collecting it. He will get greater utility from spending his time in other ways.

It may be objected to this that many committed partisans do collect political information even though there is no prospect of their changing their sympathies. Are these people to be regarded as irrational? But to answer this question the sociologist needs to obtain more information. If the partisan actually enjoys collecting political information, then it will not be a costly activity but a rewarding activity for him, and hence his behaviour may be quite rational. The ignorant socialist and the informed Tory may not necessarily be following different decision-making procedures but may rather have different preferences for their use of leisure time. The man who avidly reads the political comment in the *Telegraph* and *Spectator* in the run-up to an election is not necessarily any more, or any less, rational than the man who devotes himself to girlie magazines. We may approve or disapprove of their behaviour, but that is a quite separate issue.

Next we have *the fallacy that a quick decision is an irrational one*. This is perhaps the most widespread fallacy of all. How many people are there who doubt that a committee which disposes of a new building programme in minutes and the colour of the common room in hours should be dismissed on the spot for stupidity? Of course they may be stupid, but we cannot infer it from their behaviour alone. And it may be quite rational for them to spend the majority of their time on the minor decision.

Consider first riskless choices. If, as is required by the theory, the individual (or committee) knows what the outcomes of every course of action will be, all he has to do is rank the outcomes and select the best. No doubt in some cases there will be many alternatives and ranking them will take a little time; and in other cases the individual may not have experienced the outcomes before and may need to reflect for some time before he can judge how much utility each will yield. But surely many riskless decisions are straightforward ones where the alternatives are few and the outcomes familiar. It will need only a split second to carry out the operations of ranking and selecting. The vegetarian who immediately rejects a meat dish in a restaurant is not making an impulsive or irrational decision, but is behaving entirely rationally. He may then take much longer to choose between two vegetable curries, but we should suspect that this indicates the difficulty, not the rationality of the choice. Faced with a 'difficult' decision where the alternatives are almost equally preferable, we may need time to make up our minds. Faced with clear-cut alternatives yielding quite different amounts of utility, the rational man has no need for delay.

With risky decisions the situation is rather more complicated, and we shall have to return to some of the more difficult aspects later. But again there must be many simple cases where a quick decision can be reached. If we have to choose between one course of action which has a low probability of reaching our goal, and another which has a high probability, not much time needs to be wasted in thought. As before, we cannot infer whether a decision was a rational one or not from the time taken alone.

Another issue is that of conscious calculation. Some writers such as Homans would suggest that it is *a fallacy that a rational decision must be a conscious one,* but I am not in fact sure that I would agree. The theory, it may be argued, does not specify whether the operations of ranking and selecting alternatives are carried out consciously or unconsciously; all that matters is whether the resulting behaviour is as predicted by the theory.

I am not particularly happy with this argument, however, for it raises a curious puzzle: if people do not consciously follow the principles of utility maximization or expected utility maximization, what are the mechanisms which, perhaps magically, manage to produce the 'right' results? Of course, if evidence is forthcoming which shows that 'conscious and unconscious behavior come out at the same place' (Homans, 1961, p. 80) I shall have to accept that such mechanisms do exist. But no one has yet produced that evidence, and I would not care to rely on its appearance. It seems to me quite plausible that the only decisions which actually do fit the rational choice theory will be conscious decisions, and I do not think that it will be a very great hardship if this proves to be the case. Many decisions are undoubtedly planned consciously, and a theory which applied accurately to these would undoubtedly be of great use.

A final widespread *fallacy is that it is rational only to pursue one's own self-interest.* The many people who act out of a sense of duty or friendship, it is said, cannot be accounted rational and cannot be brought within the scope of rational choice theory; the theory can apply only to the selfish and egoistic.

Of all the fallacies, however, this is the least excusable. Rationality has nothing to do with the *goals* which men pursue but only with the *means* they use to achieve them. When we ask whether someone is behaving rationally we are asking, for example, whether he is choosing the most efficient means to his goal. We are not asking whether he is choosing the 'right' goal. Of course (as in the case of perfect information) we can always make the additional assumption, if we wish, that people actually are egoists and that they do pursue their own self-interest. And economists commonly do make this assumption. But as before we must realize that this is an *additional* assumption and one that is in no way entailed by the claim that people maximize utility or expected utility. To paraphrase my earlier remarks: 'It may make life much easier for us if we can simply assume that people pursue their own self-interest but, *provided we can independently discover what their actual goals are,* the theory of rational choice can still apply regardless.' This raises a complicated set of issues connected with the question of tautology, and it is to this that we turn next.

Riskless choice and tautology

The central principle of the theory of riskless choice is, of course, that people choose the alternative which ranks highest in their preferences (or that they value most, or that lies above their CL_{alt}, depending on which terminology one prefers). But, it is often objected, we only know what people 'really' prefer by observing their actual behaviour. Preference and choice cannot be defined or measured independently of one another, and hence the proposition must be a tautology. It can have no explanatory power.

Put like this the criticism is much too facile and will not do at all. We are not at liberty to re-define the terms in someone else's theory or to state *ex cathedra* what they 'really' mean. If we are to refute a theory we must examine the version formulated by its proponents, not some straw men of our own construction. Some theorists choose to define their terms in bizarre and idiosyncratic ways, but the theories are theirs, and they are entitled to formulate them as they will. If

Homans, Blau, or Thibaut and Kelley can define the terms of their propositions independently, and can obtain valid measures for them, then the propositions cannot be tautologies whatever else we may think of them.

The need for careful attention to the theorists' own versions of their propositions is all the more important since the principle of utility maximization, and the notion of utility in particular, has had a long and chequered history and has been formulated in many slightly different ways both by economists and by exchange theorists. One of the earliest versions held by economists treated utility as *the subjective benefit or satisfaction which an individual derived from the use of some commodity. The magnitude of this subjective satisfaction, it was claimed, could be assessed on a cardinal scale by asking individuals to carry out introspective experiments.* This position, long since abandoned by economists, is essentially the same as the one now put forward by Thibaut and Kelley. They write: 'By rewards, we refer to the pleasures, satisfactions, and gratifications the person enjoys. . . . By costs, we refer to any factors that operate to inhibit or deter the performance of a sequence of behavior. . . . Thus cost is high when great physical or mental effort is required, when embarrassment or anxiety accompany the action, or when there are conflicting forces or competing response tendencies of any sort' (Thibaut and Kelley, 1959, p. 12). Defined like this in terms of *subjective* feelings of pleasure and pain, it is quite clear that reward and cost are defined independently of behaviour and choice, and the proposition cannot conceivably be said to be true by definition.

A much more serious matter, however, is whether we can obtain valid measures of reward and cost, thus defined. And on this Thibaut and Kelley are of little help. They merely say: 'The scaling operation [required] would be a very ambitious enterprise and would present a number of technical difficulties. However, the present enterprise is in the theoretical consequences of such an operation (real or imaginary) rather than in its technical properties or even its feasibility' (p. 13). This is a quite extraordinary statement. If the scaling operation is not feasible, then many of Thibaut and Kelley's assertions simply become untestable, and, while it is perfectly respectable (and indeed fruitful) in science to have theoretical systems which contain 'unobservables' which cannot be directly measured, it is absolutely essential that there be *some* inferences from the theoretical system which *are* directly testable. If this is the position which Thibaut and Kelley intend to take, they should make it absolutely clear which these testable inferences are.

However, Thibaut and Kelley are unduly defensive about the feasibility of measuring subjective pleasure and pain. It is not immediately apparent why subjects should not be asked to introspect and to report their judgements to investigators. These techniques have already been used, apparently with great success, by psychologists to obtain subjective measures of loudness or of brightness (see Stevens, 1968) and I do not see *a priori* why they should not be able to yield subjective judgements of utility as well. It is also worth noting, perhaps, that economists did not abandon introspective techniques of measuring utility because they had tried them experimentally and found them wanting. Instead (rather remarkably for a subject which claims to be a science) they abandoned them, without empirical trial, when they found *cardinal* measures were not needed for the theory of riskless choice, conveniently forgetting that they are absolutely essential for the theory of risky choices.

In any event, the issue of whether cardinal or ordinal measures are needed is quite separate from the issue of whether introspective measures of subjective utility are feasible. Economists are undoubtedly correct in pointing out that only ordinal scales are required for the theory of riskless choice: the theory (in whatever formulation one chooses) merely claims that the individual selects the alternative which yields him *more* utility than any of the others – it does not matter by how much it exceeds them. And economists might well be correct if they suggested that cardinal scales based on introspection will be unsound (a matter to which we shall have to return). But I see no reason to suppose that ordinal scales of subjective utility will be noticeably difficult to obtain. And I therefore see no reason for rejecting Thibaut and Kelley's formulation out of hand as either tautological or untestable.

After abandoning cardinal utility the economists reformulated the theory of choice in terms of *ordinal preferences* (and this was the way in which I presented it in chapter 2). It is this formulation which Blau presents. The notion of preference, however, is just as tricky as its predecessor utility. The OED defines 'to prefer' as 'to choose rather, to like more' which seems to leave both behavioural and subjective interpretations equally open. And it is true to say, I think, that economists themselves are divided about the interpretation to be used. Some treat preference in terms of liking and are prepared to ask subjects to report their relative (subjective) liking for different alternatives. This I assume to be the position that Blau would take, and it is one which (apart from the emphasis on liking rather than gratification) comes very close to Thibaut and Kelley's.

Other economists, however, reject introspection and subjective data altogether and adopt a purely behaviourist position. They seem to define 'to prefer' as 'to choose rather' and accordingly talk of revealed preference, of preference, that is, as revealed by the actual choices made. On this view the proposition that people choose the alternative which comes highest in their preferences is most certainly a tautology, and the naive observer might expect the whole superstructure of economic theory (not to mention exchange theory) to collapse as a result. It does not seem to do so, however, and therefore we may take heart for exchange theory as well.

Behavioural economists first of all point out that the theory of choice still has the testable inference that people will choose transitively: that is, if they choose A rather than B and B rather than C, then they will choose A rather than C. The rational man simply becomes the man who chooses transitively. Secondly, and rather more importantly, the economist can combine the (now tautological) principle of utility maximization with assumptions about what it is that gives people utility to yield eminently testable hypotheses. Thus he assumes that the consumer prefers more goods to less, other things being equal, and that the entrepreneur prefers more profit to less. He can accordingly conclude that they will *choose* more goods and more profit respectively. For the behavioural economist it is this kind of assumption about people's choice behaviour that becomes the foundation, and on it he can build exactly the same superstructure of price theory as the one we looked at in chapter 3.

Remarkably, none of the main exchange theorists seem willing to follow the economists in making utility maximization a tautology. This is all the more surprising since some of them, such as Homans, seem as chary as the economists of using introspective data and seem equally inclined towards a behaviourist position. True, Homans does not wish to assume that people are necessarily self-interested, but there is nothing in a behaviourist approach which requires this particular assumption. We can just as easily assume that people prefer *less* to more as we can assume the converse. Instead he begins by defining value as 'degree of reinforcement' (which he leaves unexplained). Next, as a good behaviourist, he proposes to measure men's values 'in just the same way that we measure the pigeon's'. He writes: 'We cannot ask the pigeon how hungry it feels or how much it wants grain. What the experimenter actually does is this. First, he knows from his experience with other pigeons that grain will reinforce the animal's activity, that grain is a reinforcer. Second, he weighs the pigeon or counts the hours since it was last fed. In either case he examines the pigeon's past history of reinforcement: the value of grain to the pigeon is greater, the thinner the poor thing is or the longer it has gone without food. Then value and quantity have been independently measured, and the proposition is no tautology but a real proposition, abundantly capable of support with evidence' (Homans, 1961, p. 42). So it is, but the proposition Homans now seems to be testing could be better described as the proposition that 'the longer someone has gone without a reward, the more activity he will put out to get it' – an entirely reasonable proposition but not the one that Homans uses in the bulk of his book.

Short of such idiosyncratic strategems as Homans' the two main procedures that I have already outlined seem to be the most likely ones to commend themselves. Either we define the independent variable (value, utility, preference or whatever we choose to call it) in *subjective* terms and rely on introspective judgements on the part of the subject to yield us measures. Or alternatively we adopt a behaviourist position like the modern economist, abandon utility maximization as a tautology, and replace it with specific assumptions about people's choice behaviour. Either alternative seems to me entirely reasonable, although, not being a behaviourist, my preference is for the former.

It is one thing to say that we have obtained non-tautological formulations, however, but quite another to show that the propositions thus formulated are actually sound. We have not, I fear, quite finished with riskless choice yet. Whichever of the two formulations we adopt, some tests will be necessary. In the case of the second, behaviourist, alternative, of course the test will have to wait for the specific assumptions about people's choice behaviour to be made. And since it will vary from one theory to another (depending on whether the theory deals with entrepreneurs, political parties, pirates or gourmets), no general points can be made now. In the case of the former, 'subjectivist', alternative, however, a general test can be made. Thus in one experiment (Bass et al., 1972) subjects were asked to report their subjective preferences for various soft drinks such as Pepsi, Coke and 7-Up. The investigators then kindly made crates of the different drinks available and allowed the subjects regular opportunities to drink a bottle. Not surprisingly, perhaps, they did indeed tend to choose the brand for which they had expressed top preference: half the time they chose the brand which they had said they liked most, and the remainder of the time they tended to choose rather similar brands. For such a simple experiment this may not sound a very impressive result, but at least the result is in the right direction, and for this we should be thankful.

Risky choices and computational problems

From the problem of tautology we now go to almost the exactly opposite problem: excessive difficulty. To maximize expected utility, it is claimed, involves mathematical operations that are really too difficult for the ordinary person (Simon, 1955). And on the face of it this is not an unreasonable suggestion. To maximize expected utility the individual has to consider each of the possible outcomes of a given course of action, assess the utility of each, multiply the utility by the probability of the outcome's occurrence, sum the products, and compare this sum of products with the sum of products of the other courses of action.

Fortunately, however, in many cases we do not have to go through this whole rigmarole. There will surely be some cases where the individual is faced with alternative courses of action whose outcomes give identical utility but where the probabilities of achieving the outcomes differ. Here no multiplication or summation is needed at all. To follow the expected utility rule all the individual has to do is to rank the probability of success. And it is difficult to believe that individuals do not follow this rule. If we want to complain about shoddy goods, we will write to the person who we think is most likely to do something about it – to the manufacturer or the Consumers' Association – and we will not waste time writing to, say, our M.P.

More commonly, perhaps, both probabilities and utilities will differ, and here the rule becomes somewhat more complicated. But again we may find cases where it is not impossibly complicated, as for example where we have a choice between a certainty and a fifty–fifty gamble. Thus a potential emigrant may effectively have a choice between a certainty – carrying on as he is with his known and familiar way of life – and the gamble of going abroad where things might turn out better or might turn out worse. Now if the potential emigrant has no grounds for supposing that things are more likely to turn out better abroad than worse, he can disregard the probabilities altogether and concentrate instead on the 'gains' and 'losses' of emigration. By the gains I mean the *difference* between his present utility if he remains where he is and the utility he would get abroad if things turn out well; and by the losses I mean the difference between his present utility and the utility he would get if things turned out badly. The expected utility principle now simply says that he should compare these two differences and emigrate if the gains are greater or stay at home if they are smaller. If he is already pretty miserable at home, so that the losses could only be very small, this comparison will not be a particularly difficult one to carry out, and he will presumably judge that the 'risk is worth it' and emigrate.

Notice, however, that the comparison requires something stronger than the ordinal measures of utility which are all that we required for the theory or riskless choice. It is not enough to know that we prefer riches to poverty and poverty to starvation. We also need to know about the *strength* of our preferences. Is our preference for riches over poverty stronger than our preference for poverty over starvation? And for this we need something approaching a cardinal (or as it would now be called an interval) scale of utility.

A full interval scale allows us to say that one difference is twice another, and so on. In the present, simpler, case we do not need anything quite this strong but instead a scale which permits a *ranking* of differences. And this, I think, is quite feasible (although there is no escaping the fact that the higher the level of measurement we require the less likely we are to get it). Thus in one experiment I asked subjects (sociology graduate students) to rank a series of university lecturing posts in order of preference, yielding the familiar ordinal scale. I then presented them with a number of *pairs* of posts and asked them to grade their strength of preference for the one over the other member of the pair. 'Consider your liking for the jobs in the following pairs', I instructed the subjects. 'Then state how big the difference is (in terms of your own personal liking) between the two members of each pair.' The subjects duly complied.

On its own, however, all this tells us is that the subjects were pleasant and cooperative people who were prepared to carry out whatever strange and bizarre tasks the experimenter assigned them. To know whether we have actually obtained the desired level of measurement we have to show that there are *empirical* operations that can be performed isomorphic with the mathematical operations that a scale of that level allows. For example, if our scale tells us that one stone is twice the weight of another, there is an obvious empirical operation – taking two of the lighter stones and balancing the heavy one against them in a pair of scales – which gives empirical content to the notion. In the case of our present measure of utility there is an equally obvious check. We can face the subjects with choices between certainties and fifty–fifty gambles and see if our scale predicts their choices accurately. Fortunately for us, it appears that it did (Heath, 1974b).

When we move on from fifty–fifty gambles the situation becomes more complex still. For example, we might be faced with the decision whether or not to have a minor operation which has a good chance of success but where there is a slight possibility (as there always is) of things going badly wrong under the anaesthetic. The possible gains of a perfect recovery may thus be substantial but not as great as the possible losses of being incapacitated (or worse) by the operation. On the other hand the losses are a great deal less likely to occur than the gains.

In this kind of situation we cannot simply ignore the probabilities as we did before. If we are to follow the expected utility rule we really do have to multiply probabilities and utilities, sum the products, and so on. And to do this we have to have full interval scales for both probability and utility. *Without these scales the operation is not so much too difficult for the ordinary person to carry out as illegitimate to carry out.* We are not entitled to multiply one ordinal scale by another or even one ordinal scale by an interval scale; and if we do we will obtain only arbitrary results. Admittedly there is no compelling reason for ordinary people to be aware of the theory of measurement and to obey it. People can if they wish (and they sometimes do with probabilities) assign numbers on no sound basis, multiply them, sum their products, and so on. But it strains my credulity to believe that they customarily do so with utility. I suspect that many people are indeed aware of the fact that they face a dilemma when the gains outweigh the losses but the losses are more likely to occur.

Whether the desired levels of measurement are obtainable, and whether people then actually follow the expected utility rule, is an empirical matter which has not yet been satisfactorily resolved. As in the case of riskless choice, two main methods have been used. One (favoured by psychologists) relies on the subjects to report their introspective judgements; the other (favoured by economists) is a behavioural one and relies on the observation of actual choices.

The former method (which supposedly yields the even stronger ratio scale of measurement) essentially takes the form of asking subjects to assign numbers to various items proportional to the strength of their liking for them (see Stevens, 1968). So if a subject likes one job, or one soft drink, twice as much as another, he simply assigns a number twice as large to it. Again subjects have duly been cooperative and carried out this kind of task, but unfortunately no experimenter yet seems to have carried out the requisite checks to see if the resulting scale actually predicts the result of complex decisions.

The second method does not require subjects to assign numbers but to make choices involving various gambles. The basis of the method (although in practice it is rather more complicated) is this. The subject is offered a choice between, say, a certain ten pence and a fifty–fifty chance of getting twenty pence or nothing. If he chooses the certainty, the 'prize' in the gamble is successively increased by small steps until at some point the subject becomes indifferent between the certainty and the gamble. Being good behaviourists we do not *ask* the subject whether or not he is indifferent but instead infer that he is indifferent when, in a series of trials, involving identical alternatives, he chooses the certainty half the time and the gamble half the time too.

Now suppose that the subject turns out to be indifferent between a certain ten pence and a fifty–fifty gamble between twenty-five pence or nothing. We can accordingly conclude (on the assumption that the subject is following the expected utility rule) that he finds the difference in utility between ten pence and nothing to be the same as that between ten pence and twenty-five. We can now continue the experiment, give the subject choices between a certain twenty-five pence and a gamble between ten and, say, fifty pence, increase the prize until we find the amount at which the subject is indifferent between the gamble and the certainty, and consequently find another interval equal to that between ten and twenty-five pence. And in this way a whole series of equal intervals can be constructed. (For the full method see Davidson, Suppes and Siegel, 1957).

This is an extremely ingenious and elegant method, although it is apparently flawed by the fact that it assumes the truth of the expected utility rule – the very thing that we are trying to test! We seem to be lifting ourselves up by our own bootstraps, assuming the truth of one principle in order to obtain a measure which will then allow us to test the original principle itself. Fortunately, however, such acts of levitation are not as difficult to perform in science as they are in the ordinary world. If we now carry out *additional* checks and find that these are confirmed, we will gain confidence both in our level of measurement and in our assumptions that subjects maximize expected utility. If of course the checks fail, we shall not know whether it is the level of measurement or the expected utility rule which is at fault (or indeed whether it is our experimental procedure), but we can be sure that something is wrong.

The kinds of checks I have in mind are these. Suppose we have found, using our procedure, that there are equal intervals according to one particular subject's set of choices between a, b, c, d and e. All we now have to do is to give him choices between a certainty of getting c and a fifty–fifty gamble between a and e. If the subject is not indifferent between them, we can abandon our pretensions to have constructed an interval scale.

Remarkably, this simple check has not been carried out. And those weaker checks that have been carried out did not yield particularly encouraging results. What the outcome of the full check will be we cannot of course tell yet, but I think we have to take the possibility seriously that people may not have interval scales of utility and consequently may not be able to follow the expected utility principle in situations involving complicated choices.

What, then, are the alternative decision procedures that people might follow? One possibility that is often canvassed is that people may instead 'satisfice'. Stripped of its jargon the principle of satisficing states: 'Continue searching for new alternatives until you have found one which guarantees you a satisfactory outcome, not necessarily the best possible outcome.' This rule requires no interval judgements but simply the judgement whether the utility from some outcome lies above, equals, or falls below some comparison level. It seems a splendid rule for someone going shopping who has to decide whether to go to the bother of visiting another supermarket which might possibly have cheaper lines than the one he is in at the moment. More generally it is appropriate where the uncertainty is due to lack of knowledge and where it can be removed by successive searches until a satisfactory outcome has been found. Unfortunately, however, not all cases are of this kind. The person going in for his operation knows that there is a possibility that things will go wrong. However much information he collects he cannot get rid of this unpalatable fact and he cannot *guarantee* himself a satisfactory outcome. He has a high probability of obtaining a modest benefit and a low probability of obtaining a very nasty result. To tell him to satisfice would be met with a rude reply.

My own hypothesis is that, faced with 'impossible' decisions of this kind, people resort to a variety of supplementary rules or procedures for coping with the situation (see Heath, 1974b). Most commonly, I suspect, they will either attempt to delegate the decision to someone else such as the doctor, or alternatively they will drift until the decision is taken for them by events themselves. These procedures cannot be judged either rational or irrational, for just as the individual has no rational way of reaching a decision in the first place, so the sociologist has no way of judging its rationality. To drift, therefore, in a state of indecision may not be indicative of a weak-minded or irrational individual as it commonly supposed but may be indicative of a situation where rational decision-making is impossible.

Uncertainty revisited

Finally, let us take a quick look at game theory and uncertainty. As I mentioned in chapter 2, game theorists do not claim that people actually follow minimax or mixed strategy rules. These are simply the things they *ought* to do (in the specified situations) if they are to behave rationally. However, there is no harm in seeing what people actually do, and for believers in human rationality there are some comforting results. In laboratory experiments involving two-person zero-sum games with a saddle-point subjects do seem to adopt the minimax strategy eventually, or at least they did so when the experimenter (truthfully) told them that they would be playing against a rational opponent (Lieberman, 1960).

A major difficulty with game theory, however, is likely to be finding situations in the real world where the appropriate conditions actually hold. People may indeed minimax when required to do so, but if they are rarely faced with that requirement the theory becomes (at least for explanatory purposes) rather uninteresting. One study which demonstrates this point rather neatly (if unintentionally) is the one mentioned earlier by Davenport on Jamaican fishing. Davenport was concerned with a game played between a fishing village and the sea. In the simplest case the fishermen had two options open to them: they could either set their pots out at sea, where the better-quality fish were to be caught, or they could set them closer to shore behind some protecting sandbanks. The sea for its part could either stay calm or could produce strong currents which would damage or destroy the pots placed beyond the banks (but leave those closer to shore unharmed). Given the prices of the various quality fish, the costs of equipment, and so on, Davenport was able to derive the matrix in figure 18 (Davenport, 1960, p. 10).

It can be seen that there is no saddle-point in this matrix and that the minimax strategy is therefore inappropriate. Instead a mixed strategy is called for, and the correct computations (which I shall not try to explain) show that the fishermen should set their pots inside the banks 81 per cent of the time and outside 19 per cent, while the sea should produce a strong current 30 per cent of the time and should remain calm for the remainder. Astonishingly, in actual practice the fishermen seemed to set 79 per cent of their pots inside the banks, and the sea obligingly produced a strong current 25 per cent of the time.

Aside from the amazing accuracy of the results, the most surprising thing is Davenport's temerity in supposing that this was a situation in which game theory could be used. The assumption that it is a zero-sum game could conceivably be defended, for every fish caught by the fishermen is one lost to the sea. But it is hardly a two-person game, for there were many individual fishermen and no sign that they got together to agree on a common 'fishing village' strategy. Some of the

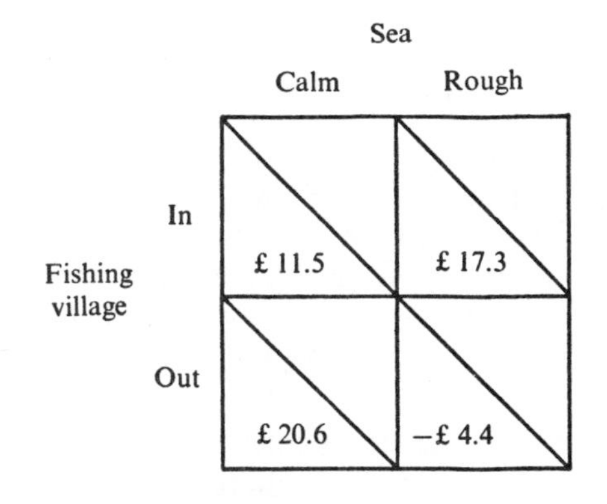

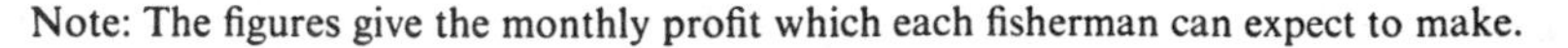
Note: The figures give the monthly profit which each fisherman can expect to make.

Figure 18

fishermen in fact seemed to have set *none* of their pots out at sea, and it is doubtful if many individuals set their pots out in the prescribed ratio. It seems to be a simple coincidence that the aggregate of all the individual decisions happened to give the predicted figure.

But the most astounding assumption of all is that the sea was a rational opponent choosing his strategy so as to minimize the number of fish caught. On any commonsense view the sea must be taken as a random actor, his periods of calm and storm in no way influenced by his expectations of the fishermen's behaviour (see Read and Read, 1970). But given this revised assumption the rational thing for the fishermen to do is not to minimax at all but to maximize expected utility. As I described in chapter 2, it is irrational to minimax against an irrational opponent.

9. *Rational choice theory applied*

It is now time to move from the theoretical discussion of chapter 8 to some practical applications of rational choice theory. There are numerous examples in the works of Homans and Thibaut and Kelley, but on the whole I find them rather dull. What I propose to do instead is to look at a number of examples from other writers who have used, or who could have used, a rational choice approach. I shall begin with an example from the social psychologists Latané and Darley (1970).

Bystander intervention in emergencies

Latané and Darley start with the puzzle provided by such incidents as the Kitty Genovese murder. Kitty Genovese was set upon by a maniac as she returned home from work at three o'clock one morning. Thirty-eight of her neighbours came to their windows when she cried out in terror, but none came to her assistance or even telephoned the police even though the murderer took half an hour to finish the job. Why?

Latané and Darley suggest that the explanation may lie in the very fact that so surprises us: the number of onlookers present. They then investigated this in various experimental situations and found that the likelihood that a bystander would intervene in an emergency did indeed vary with the number of others present. For example, the investigators staged various incidents during what purported to be conventional laboratory experiments, pouring smoke into the room where the unsuspecting subjects were seated or arranging for a stooge in a nearby room to shriek out and fall to the ground with a loud thump. As anticipated, they found that the real subject was more likely to do something about the supposed emergency – going and reporting it or investigating it in some way – if he was the only person present.

Latané and Darley suggest a number of possible explanations for this finding. The one which concerns us most deals with the rewards and costs of intervention. They suggest: 'Perhaps most importantly, the presence of other people can reduce the cost of not acting. If only one bystander is present at an emergency, he carries all the responsibility for dealing with it; he will feel all of the guilt for not acting; he will bear all of any blame others may level for non-intervention. If others are present, the onus of responsibility is diffused, and the individual may be more likely to resolve his conflict between intervening and not intervening in favor of the latter alternative' (Latané and Darley, 1970, p. 21).

The structure of this explanation is worth some examination, for it is an excellent example of the kind of thing that is feasible for the sociologist using the theory of rational choice. It begins with the assumption that people find blame a cost and hence will prefer to have less rather than more of it. If we wish to adopt a behaviourist stance we could make this the simple proposition that, *ceteris paribus*, people will choose the course of action that yields least blame. Next the argument deals with the situational factors that determine the relative amount of blame received, namely that the fewer others are present the more blame non-intervention will incur. Latané and Darley do not in fact test either of these main claims, but it is clear that both are contingent propositions and can be tested quite independently of the behaviour which they are intended to explain. In particular, we can observe whether people avoid blame in situations quite different from those involving emergencies. As I suggest in the previous chapter, therefore, we can advance testable theories even if we treat utility maximization as a tautology.

A number of further points about the argument are worth noting. First, men's values or preferences are treated as a constant: what varies, and what gives the argument its explanatory interest, is the situation – the number of other people present. In this the argument is identical to the typical economic explanation but unlike the many sociological arguments which look to the differences in men's values to explain the differences in their behaviour.

Second, the argument does not assume that men's *only* end is to avoid blame. Indeed, Latané and Darley explicitly allow that there may be many other aspects of the situation which men will find rewarding or costly and which will affect what they finally do. *All that is assumed is that the extra blame in the situations where there are fewer bystanders will sometimes tip the balance between intervention and non-intervention.*

Third, and consequently, Latané and Darley are not entitled to draw any conclusions about the absolute number of individuals who will intervence in any given situation. All that their argument allows them to infer is that the *probability* of a given individual's intervening will be higher when there are few bystanders than when there are many. They cannot deduce whether or not he actually will intervene in either of the situations, and to do so they would need to know about all the other rewards and costs that entered the individual's calculations. This would be a pretty formidable enterprise and one that would hardly be worthwhile.

While Latané and Darley's explanation uses a rational choice approach it makes no use of the conventional economic apparatus of indifference curves and the like that we discussed in chapter 2. This may be no bad thing. Indifference curves are merely one technique among many that can be used, and a lot can be done without them. A number of situations can be found, however, for which indifference curve analysis is ideally suited (although not always employed by the original author), and I propose to turn next to some examples.

Income and fertility

A rational choice approach has often been used in the study of fertility, and it lends itself well to indifference curves. We start with the assumption (an entirely reasonable one) that it costs money to bring up a family and hence that children compete with other uses of income such as consumer durables or holidays abroad. We can thus draw the customary indifference map with number of children on one axis, consumer durables on the other, and a financial budget constraint line. From this it follows clearly enough that a fall in income will reduce fertility and, as Becker (1960) has suggested, a rise in income will increase it (see fig. 19). When there is less money to go round, we can expect parents to cancel plans for a new car and *pari passu,* for a new child; and when there is more money available both consumption of durables and number of children can increase.

Examples where income-changes have had the predicted effects on fertility and where the assumptions of the theory seem to hold reasonably well can easily be found. Thus the Factory Acts of the nineteenth century reduced the hours and ages at which children could work, thus effectively reducing family income. True, this would have been mit-

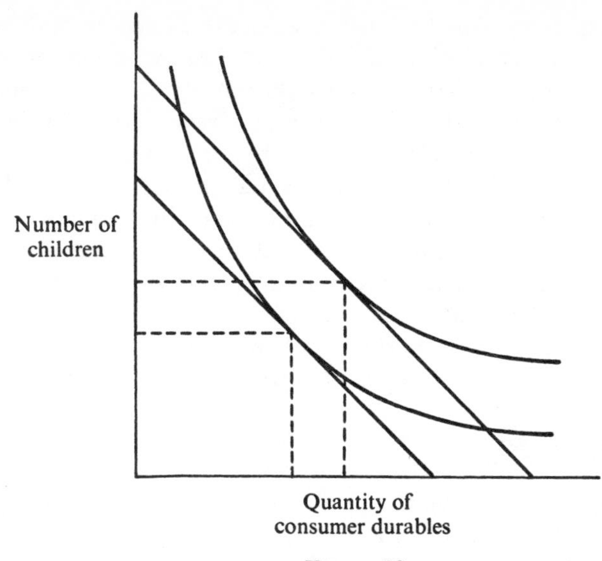

Figure 19

igated somewhat by the increased employment for adults that was released, but this would not have been distributed proportionately to family size: single and childless adults would have benefited just as much as those with families. As predicted, in the decade following these Acts the birth rate seems to have fallen quite substantially (although for a rigorous test of the theory one would need to know whether the fall was largely confined to the urban working-class areas where the theory could be expected to apply most strongly).

There is one very important point to note about this type of theory, a point which has often proved of difficulty to the non-economist. *It does not require that parents rear children in order to send them out to work and secure an income from them.* Parents may get all kinds of emotional and spiritual satisfactions from having children just as they may get all kinds of satisfactions from buying works of art or going on foreign holidays. All the theory says is that if family income falls, or is expected to fall, there will be less to spend and consumption will have to fall. And one way in which expenditure can be reduced in future is by planning to have fewer children. (Another, incidentally, would be to have 'poorer quality' children.)

Similar arguments to these (although not of course using the apparatus of indifference curves) were also advanced by Banks (1954) to account for the decline of middle-class fertility later in the nineteenth century. Banks's is a rather subtle argument and his literary presentation leads him into a certain amount of imprecision. Basically, however, he seems to be arguing that the cost of preparing children for middle-class professional careers was rising in the second half of the nineteenth century as educational qualifications became more important. On its own, of course, this would not entail a fall in fertility, since incomes were also rising. But with the Great Depression incomes stopped rising and middle-class families found it harder to maintain their relative status and style of life. What we can do therefore is to draw an indifference map with number of children on one axis and *relative* style of life measured on the other. The Great Depression is now represented by a shift in the budget constraint line, showing that the cost of maintaining a given relative (but not absolute) standard of living had increased. Fertility falls accordingly, and will be accentuated by any additional increases in the cost of educating children.

'From Stone to Steel'

Another example where indifference curves can easily be applied comes from Salisbury's study *From Stone to Steel* (1962). Salisbury described among other things how the introduction of steel axes in place of the original stone ones among Siane tribesmen in the New Guinea highlands enabled the men to complete their customary tasks of house construction and fence building in considerably less time than before with the result that a great deal more time could now be spent on activities such as political discussion or preparation for rituals. As before, we can draw a hypothetical indifference map indicating the Siane tribesmen's preferences for, say, political intrigue and housing. It seems a reasonable set of assumptions that they will prefer bigger and better-constructed houses to smaller and poorer ones, that they will prefer more elaborate and better-planned intrigues to small-scale ones, and that they will have a diminishing marginal rate of substitution between the two. This all yields the familiar indifference map such as that shown in figure 20. The equivalent of the budget constraint line can now be given by a *time constraint* line. The Siane tribesman can either spend all his time on house building, yielding OA worth of housing, or all his time on politics, yielding OB worth of intrigue, or divide up his time between the two, yielding some combination given by the time constraint line.

The introduction of steel for stone axes can now be simply described. Essentially it means that there is a shift in the time constraint line, since more housing units can be obtained for any given expenditure of time. Perhaps if the individual devoted all his time to house construction he could now obtain OCs worth of housing and we would thus have the new constraint line BC. Our tribesman can now move to a higher indifference curve and, given the map drawn in figure 20, he will move to point Q, reallocating his time so as to get bigger and

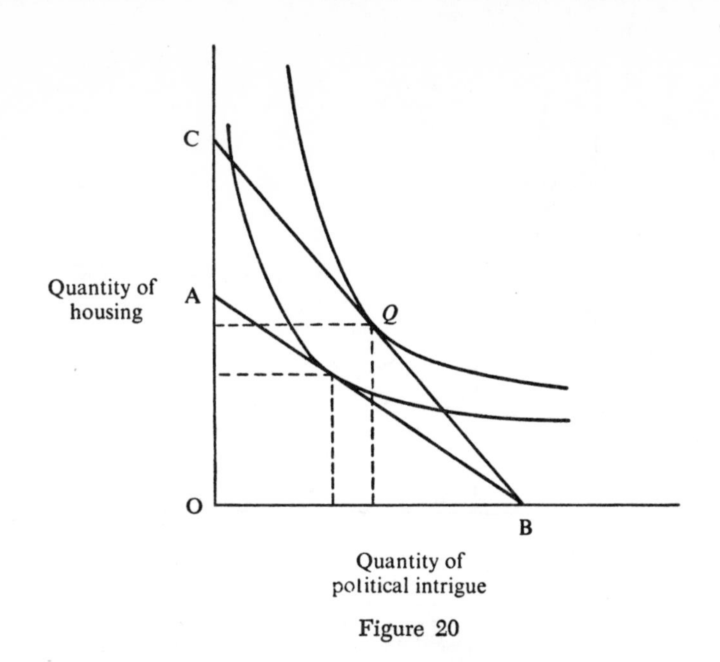

Figure 20

better intrigues as well as better housing. Just as in chapter 2 a fall in the price of cummerbunds led to an increase in the consumption of zabaglione, so a fall in the 'price' of housing has led to an increase in the consumption of intrigue.

While this may all be sound enough, it may not be immediately apparent how it improves on Salisbury's simpler account. Doubtless it shows that indifference curve analysis can be applied to the behaviour of Siane tribesmen in a non-monetary economy as well as to white Europeans, but have we done any more than put the old argument in a new, more complicated language? I think that in fact we have. Most importantly, the economic analysis forces us to spell out our assumptions and demonstrates, in a way that the original verbal presentation did not, that a number of quite different possibilities exist. Depending on the precise nature of the indifference map, a fall in the 'price' of housing could lead to an increased allocation of time to intrigue, to the same allocation of time as before, *or even to an increased allocation of time for housing.* Keeping all our assumptions intact we can also draw the indifference map in figure 21, which shows that the individual reduces his political intrigue as house-building becomes easier. This kind of result might be more common than we imagine. Thus the adolescent who leaves school and begins to earn a wage finds that legitimate leisure pursuits are now effectively cheaper, while delinquency (on which no money needs to be spent) retains the same 'price'. Given his particular preferences, then, it is quite feasible that the adolescent will cut down on his delinquent activities and devote

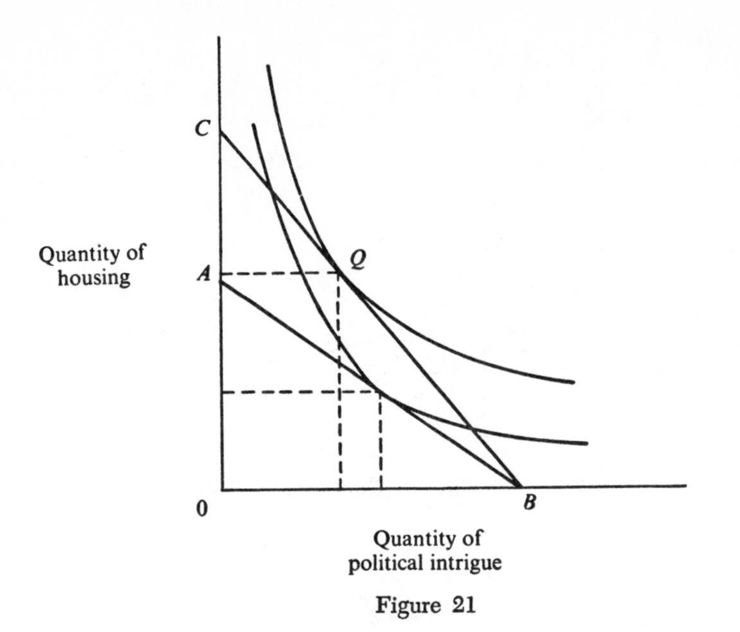

Figure 21

himself more to legitimate pursuits. We do not need to impute changed values or a resolved identity crisis to account for the changed behaviour. The values may have stayed exactly the same, but the new opportunities have encouraged law-abiding behaviour.

Changing values

As with the Latané and Darley example, then, all these applications of indifference curve analysis have taken values and preferences to be constant and have explained the differences in behaviour in terms of situational factors – the introduction of steel axes, factory legislation, educational reforms or the Great Depression. As I have said, this is precisely the character of the classic economic explanation. But there is no reason in principle to restrict ourselves to explanations of this kind. The rational choice approach can easily enough hold situational factors constant and explain differences in behaviour in terms of values, or it can indeed vary both together. Thus we might find that the introduction of steel axes leads to different responses in different societies. In one, where there is a harsh climate and the people place a high priority on housing, the increased time made available by the new axes might be devoted wholly to building works. In another, sunnier society, it might all go on political intrigue.

The introduction of values as a variable is likely to be particularly important in cases where we wish to make cross-cultural comparisons or where we wish to make long-term historical comparisons. In the case of fertility it may be reasonable enough to assume that values remain constant in the short run and that the Factory Acts led to a short-run decline in fertility. But it is patently clear that in the long run increasing income has not led to continually increasing fertility, and changing values present themselves as the most plausible explanation.

Now it is easy enough in theory to incorporate different values into the analysis. All we have to do is to redraw the indifference map. But it is not nearly such an easy matter in practice. So long as the only assumptions that we needed to make in drawing our map were that the individual preferred more of the commodities in question to less and that he had a diminishing marginal rate of substitution between the two, it would in many cases (although not in that of fertility) be quite feasible to obtain independent behavioural evidence for them. But once we wish to know more about the precise character and location of the indifference map, the amount of information needed increases alarmingly and it becomes quite impracticable to collect it behaviourally. Like it or not, we are forced to go back to the reports of our subjects on their subjective preferences. Even so, it is a formidable undertaking to construct a complete indifference map. Thus one attempt to utilize indifference maps in anthropological research required each subject to make 1,176 judgements (Roberts et al., 1971). The investigators were merely trying to get students from different cultures to give their preferences for different combinations of shirts and shoes. The quantities involved went from nought to six pairs of shoes and from nought to six shirts, giving 49 possible combinations in all. But to construct the complete map the subjects had to compare each possible combination with every other possible combination, and it is this that entails the 1,176 comparisons.

Whatever the theoretical rigour that indifference curves introduce, then, they are unlikely to be widely used in empirical research. We simply cannot ask each subject one thousand questions, or even one hundred questions, and we shall have to employ some simpler techniques if the rational choice approach is to be applied. The solution is clear enough, however. We must restrict ourselves to examples like the Latané and Darley one. *In these the crucial thing is to vary only one thing at a time.* We must compare situations where variation involves only a single extra reward or cost; or we must compare groups of people whose values differ in one single respect. Provided we can properly assume that 'other things are equal', these comparisons will place no great demands on our capacities for data collection, and we will be able to predict how the rates of behaviour in the two situations or in the two groups will differ.

Once we alter more than one thing at a time, however, we will be in difficulty. Suppose for example that in real life, as opposed to the experimental laboratory, situations where there are few bystanders present are also ones where help is going to be very much more costly to provide: we may need to walk much further to find a telephone or wait much longer till the ambulance arrives. Intervention will thus be accompanied by extra *dis*incentives as well as by the incentive of avoiding the extra blame. And we will thus no longer be able to make confident predictions based on our knowledge that people dislike blame. *We will need to know whether the extra blame outweighs the extra effort involved, and this means knowing the individual's preferences for combinations of blame and effort.* Our problems of data collection have returned. They are not of course insuperable, but we do well to avoid them.

Crime and detection

So far we have applied only the theory of riskless choice, and this is all right so long as problems of risk can properly be assigned to the category of 'other things being equal'. No doubt bystander intervention in emergencies entails all kinds of risk, but the Latané and Darley argument is not affected so long as the risks are the same whether there are many or few bystanders present. Sometimes, however, we will surely want to compare situations involving varying amounts of risk. Can our rational choice approach be applied here or do the difficulties discussed in the last chapter render our efforts futile?

The proper response, I think, is guarded optimism. True, if the argument of the previous chapter was sound, there may be many situations where the individual will find it impossible to make a rational decision. But while this may prevent our predicting individual behaviour, we may still find aggregate predictions permissible. This apparent paradox will, I hope, be resolved if we take the particular example of crime detection and punishment.

Crime provides a classic test case for the application of rational choice theory in general and the theory of risky choice in particular. (For another, rather different, rational choice theory of crime see G. S. Becker (1968).) The demand that rising crime rates be met by harsher penalties is often premissed on a rational model of man: harsher penalties will increase the possible cost of crime to the criminal and make it less likely to pay. To the criminal, moreover, a life of crime clearly involves decision-making under risk and uncertainty: there is always a possibility, not a certainty, of being caught, and so possible losses must be weighed up against possible gains.

In many cases, however, the decision will be what I have termed an 'impossible' one. For most crimes the probability of being caught is objectively very low. It is only really in the case of murder that one is unlikely to get away with it. But if one is caught the penalty may be very serious indeed and on its own would surely outweigh the gains of a successful robbery. The criminal may thus be faced with a low probability of obtaining a really unpleasant outcome (five years in prison, say) and a high probability of a fairly pleasant one. Short of multiplying utilities and probabilities he has no way of reaching a rational decision, and even then it will be an arbitrary result if the right levels of measurement are not available. To increase the penalty from five years to life imprisonment, or to increase the probability of being caught from one in fifty, to say, one in ten will have no material effect on the decision. It is still an 'impossible' one. *All that would really work would be to increase the probability of detection so much that it actually became the most likely outcome.* This would make the decisions unambiguous enough. Consideration both of costs and benefits and of probabilities now point in the same direction: don't commit crime.

I suspect that this analysis will fit the professional criminal rather well. He probably has a shrewd idea of the objective probabilities of being caught and an equally shrewd dislike of prison. When we look at the population as a whole, however, we are likely to find much more variation in their subjective assessments both of the gains and losses and of the probabilities. A surprisingly large number of people actually seem to believe that 'people who break the law are almost always caught and punished' (Jensen, 1969). And there must be many people for whom the penalties (fines for the wealthy or prison for the homeless) are not particularly serious. As a result, well-publicized shifts in the probability of detection or in the severity of the penalty may change the decision in a relatively large number of cases from a 'possible' one to an 'impossible' one, or vice versa, with corresponding effects on the crime rate.

In aggregate, then, we would expect to find a correlation (although not perhaps a very good one) between the crime rate and the probability of detection or the severity of the penalty. Our expectation is partially borne out. For example Tittle (1969) found that the greater the certainty of detection for a particular type of offence in a given area, the smaller was the number of offences reported there. However, he also found that the more severe were the penalties the *greater* was the number of offences. Harsh penalties seemed to encourage crime, not deter it. If such an extraordinary conclusion were sound, we would here have a formidable challenge to rational choice theory. As Tittle points out, however, the direction of causation may be in quite the reverse direction. A rising crime rate may stimulate the authorities to increase the penalties, while a high probability of detection may reflect the fact that the crime rate in a particular area is low, thus giving the police more time to track offenders.

What is needed, then, is not a correlational study but a 'natural experiment' in which the probability of detection or the severity of the sentences has actually been changed. Fortunately for us (although not for the participants) one notable example of this is available. In September 1944 the Germans arrested the whole of the Danish police force and for the remainder of the German occupation the task of policing was carried out by an improvised and unarmed watch corps. This corps, observers claimed at the time, was all but wholly ineffectual except when the criminal was caught red-handed. The immediate result of this was a rapid rise in the crime rate, particularly in the number of robberies, and the payouts by insurance companies rose ten-fold. The increase was not general, however. Hardly surprisingly, there was no increase in crimes like embezzlement and fraud where the offender's identity could be discovered even in the absence of an effective police force. Rather more surprisingly the number of murders and sex offences showed no change (Andenaes, 1952).

There are various possible ways of accounting for the latter finding, but one possibility that I would wish to take very seriously is that these are offences committed on impulse or under the influence of drink and hence are ones to which rational choice theory cannot apply. While the extent of impulsive (or compulsive) behaviour is often grossly exaggerated, there can be little doubt that it does occur sometimes. And while the application of rational choice theory is very wide, I doubt if it is universal. Indeed, it would be rather puzzling if 'rational choice' theory could be applied equally well to the drunk and the sober, to the man 'who has lost control of himself' as well as to the man 'who is in full possession of his faculties'.

A final, and perhaps most surprising, result of the Danish 'experiment' was the failure of the harsher penalties imposed on those who were caught to stem the rise in the crime rate. As Tittle had found in his correlational studies, the size of the penalty did not seem to act as a deterrent. This finding, which is also familiar to us from studies of the death penalty, provides a serious challenge to the rational choice theory after all. The analysis of 'impossible' decisions, however, suggests one possible answer. If the penalty is *already* a harsh one (so that, leaving probabilities aside, it already outweighs the potential gains from the crime), increasing it merely leaves the decision as an impossible one. And exactly the same non-rational rules and procedures can be used as before to reach a conclusion. It is only if the penalty is changed from a relatively mild one (relative, that is, to the potential gains) to a relatively harsh one that any major change in the character of the decision is effected. Of course, we cannot know *a priori* how the Danish criminals rated the existing penalties, but it is surely quite plausible that they found them relatively distasteful.

This concludes our survey of applications. It is far from exhaustive but rather is intended to illustrate the kind of thing that can be done and the kind of problems that arise. Many other applications could have been described (in the field of labour mobility and job choice, for example), but I doubt if they would have raised new issues. In most of them the crucial problem will be that of data collection. As we saw in chapter 8, criticisms of rational choice theory are often based on elementary fallacies, and there is little evidence that people are actually irrational in their decision-making. The problem is obtaining *independent* evidence of people's preferences, evidence, that is, which is independent of the behaviour to be explained. We can always *postulate* preferences which, if true, would account for the behaviour under discussion, but postulations are not the same as explanations.

10. *Exchange and power again*

The theory of exchange, like many of the rational choice theories, is deceptively simple. As we saw in chapter 3, it follows inevitably from the theory of choice: if each individual chooses the course of action that yields him the most-preferred outcome of those available, then an exchange will take place only if it yields the most-preferred outcome available to *both* parties. If we hold the theory of choice to be sound, then the theory of exchange must also be sound. And if we hold the theory of choice to be a tautology, then the theory of exchange must be tautological too. In either case the actual application of the theory requires assumptions and independent evidence about men's preferences (revealed or otherwise) and about the alternatives open.

While this may all be well enough in principle, there are again likely to be some serious problems in practice. To account for the occurrence of a particular exchange is not quite such an easy matter as many writers have supposed, and there are some distinguished examples of naivete to be found. My favourite one comes from Merton's and Gouldner's discussions of the political machine.

Social exchange and the political machine

In his paper on manifest and latent functions Merton had claimed that the political machine, among other things, recognized that 'the voter is a person living in a specific neighborhood, with specific personal problems and personal wants' and accordingly met some of these personal wants that were not adequately met by legitimate social institutions (Merton, 1957, p. 74). In particular, Merton claimed, the legitimate institutions provided welfare benefits to the ordinary person only after detailed legal investigations of his eligibility, these investigations robbing the client of his self-respect. In contrast the precinct captain of the political machine dispensed benefits without any formal investigation. His relationship to the 'clients' was a more personal one and enabled them to retain their dignity and self-respect.

In this way Merton looks at one side of the transaction and shows why people should prefer to approach the precinct captain rather than the formal welfare agencies. For ordinary people, then, transactions with the political machine are the most attractive ones available. Incidentally, Merton seems to suppose that this is a functionalist account, but if this is so then functionalism is simply another name for rational choice theory. Indeed, Merton sometimes uses explicitly economic language in formulating his arguments, as for example when he concludes: 'Finally, and in many respects, most importantly, is the basic similarity, if not near-identity, of the economic role of "legitimate" business and of "illegitimate" business. *Both are in some degree concerned with the provision of goods and services for which there is an economic demand*' (Merton, 1957, p. 79).

However, while Merton may look at the demand for the machine's services, Gouldner rightly points out that he has provided 'no explicit analysis . . . of the feedback through which the social structure or groups, whose needs are satisfied by the political machine, in turn "reciprocate" and repay the machine for the services received from it' (Gouldner, 1960, p. 163). To account for the transaction, then, we have to show what is in it for *both* sides, for the machine as well as for the ordinary people.

Gouldner thinks that this job is easy to complete. 'In this case', he writes, 'the patterns of reciprocity, implied in the notion of "corruption" of the machine, are well known and fully documented' (p. 163). There seems to be no need for further investigation. But if Merton has missed half the explanation, Gouldner has missed a large part of it too. It is not enough to show that the machine gets some benefits in return. We also have to show (as Merton was of course aware) that the benefits are better than those that could be obtained elsewhere or by other courses of action. In other words, it is not enough to know that the machine gets votes and illegal favours in return for welfare benefits. *We also need to show that this bargain is a better one, taking into account the costs of providing the benefits, than could be obtained by, say, legitimate politics.* True, the votes may be more numerous and reliable than those that a conventional political campaign would have obtained, but then the costs are no doubt higher too. To provide benefits that can compete with those of the legitimate welfare agencies is presumably quite a large and expensive task.

To account for the transactions between machine and client, then, we have to show why it is that conventional politics (and the other main options open) provide a poorer bargain than do machine politics, and this is not going to be such an easy matter after all. Indeed, if it were so straightforward, why would we ever have conventional politics at all? What we have to do is to show what the special features are of American political life that make corruption so attractive. Moreover, when we apply this more rigorous analysis to the problem, we can see that Merton's account of the other side of the transaction is inadequate too. Merton may have looked at the benefits – the retention of self-respect – but he has ignored the costs. Welfare agencies may investigate one's private affairs, but they do not ask one to turn out and vote or to perform corrupt favours. So is a transaction with the machine necessarily so much better after all?

In answering these questions fully we would run into serious problems of data collection once again. However, some important points can still be made. Thus we can say that the transaction will take place only if the following conditions hold: (1) the contributions which the client provides the machine must cost him *less* than the self-respect which he would forfeit to the official welfare agency; (2) the contributions provided by the client must be *more* valuable to the machine than those it would obtain from an equal expenditure on legitimate political campaigns. Just as the gourmet in chapter 3 was not willing to pay more than £2 for his zabaglione, so the client is not willing to 'pay' anything more in utility than self-respect. And just as the restaurateur is not willing to accept a price below 50p, so the political machine is not willing to accept a return lower than the one it can get through conventional politics. As before, the alternatives available set limits to the exchange.

Our knowledge of the alternatives available should also set limits to our imagination. On the facts given us by Merton we cannot plausibly expect the machine's clients to make great efforts in its service. I may be unduly cynical but I would guess that most demands by the machine would be met by a resolve to swallow one's pride and go to the formal welfare agencies. Nor could we expect the machine to go to great effort on behalf of ordinary people in a one-party area where it had an overwhelming majority. As we saw earlier, the expected utility of a vote depends on the probability that it will make a difference to the outcome of an election. Even if the spoils of office are very great, there is no point in spending more money than is necessary to obtain them.

A thorough analysis of exchange, then, has provided us with new checks and predictions against which to test the original account. Whereas Merton and Gouldner accounted for the transaction by showing in a rather half-hearted way what benefits were in it for each side, we have been able to show that the participants' preferences must satisfy a strict system of ordering. We can predict that corruption will be more likely (because more profitable) where elections are closely fought than in one-party seats. Competition will improve the service to the consumer and will make greater efforts to buy his vote worthwhile. So perhaps America is a more corrupt society because it is more competitive.

These checks and predictions may not, of course, be supported by empirical investigation. Indeed, I doubt if they would be. Their failure, however, should throw doubt not so much on the basic theory of exchange itself (although this is a possibility) as on the original assumptions made by Merton and Gouldner. It is these assumptions which actually give the theory its bite and it is these assumptions which we must abandon if the theory fails. For example, the political machine may in practice not only allow clients to retain their self-respect but may also give them benefits which are simply not available from the official agencies. Or it may use sanctions such as physical coercion which are more effective than those of conventional politics. And this could change the clients' calculations completely. They might find that it paid them to do considerably more in return than had hitherto been allowed.

Virtually all other accounts of actual exchanges make much the same errors as Merton and Gouldner. Either the writer looks at one side of the exchange only (as did Merton) or (as did Gouldner) he ignores the alternatives open. Often, indeed, writers seem content to indicate what is being exchanged (votes for favours, for example, or scientific papers for recognition, or help with the children in return for assistance in old age) and then 'account' for the exchange by indicating the norms involved. But the facts that there are norms requiring one to enter a particular exchange by no means allows us to ignore the alternatives open. The existence of norms does not make the rational choice approach to exchange redundant. At most it means that the alternatives to the exchange are sanctions from others or guilt feelings from oneself. These alternatives, however, are not in principle different from any others, although they may be rather harder to establish empirically. Blame and guilt can be weighed in the balance like anything else, and even the most saintly can be tempted to deviance if the gains are sufficiently rewarding. If the avoidance of blame or guilt are the *only* reasons for exchange, it may not take particularly attractive alternatives to stimulate deviance. Indeed, one of the great merits of the rational approach is that it forces us to abandon the notion of man as a 'cultural dope', blindly following the norms and prescriptions of his culture. Instead it forces us to recognize man as a decision-maker who decides whether or not to conform in the light of the options available to him.

Family power structure

Like the theory of exchange, the theory of power follows logically from the theory of choice. As we saw in chapter 3 the basic idea is simply the one that the less satisfactory are the alternatives to a particular supplier, the more dependent one is on him and the higher the price that he will be able to obtain if he wishes. If we hold the theory of choice to be sound, then the theory of power must be sound too. And if we hold the theory of choice to be tautological, then so is the theory of power. In either case the theory only becomes interesting when we make assumptions about men's preferences or values and about the alternatives available to them.

In practice, most applications go beyond the theory as I have stated it. They do not deal solely with men's *ability* to secure a higher price but with the actual rate of exchange itself. They assume that individuals will take advantage of their bargaining power and thus obtain an improved bargain. In this way, as I pointed out earlier, we do not have to measure power itself but can deal instead solely with the overt rate of exchange. We can thus replace a 'dispositional' concept with an 'observable' one. However, this gain is achieved at the expense of introducing some extra assumptions, assumptions which could of course be false. After all, the individual may not realize that he is in a strong bargaining position, or he may not have the wit to take advantage of it. Alternatively, it may be objected, he may not *wish* to take advantage of it. He may be fond of the other person or feel an obligation to help him.

Strictly speaking, however, this last objection involves a rather different kind of point, and it does not really upset the theory. If a powerful man is fond of his subordinate, his affection reduces his power. It means that he gets additional utility from the transaction over and above that gained from the goods and services received. It makes this particular transaction more attractive to him than similar ones with other people. And it thus makes him more dependent on it. Where a powerful man is fond of his subordinate, then, *both* partners are relatively dependent on the relationship and *both* have some power.

It may sound from this that we can squeeze anything into our rational choice framework, although at the expense of making the approach vacuous. But this would be unfair. We can in fact make the additional prediction that there will be more variation in the rate of exchange where the partners are fond of each other than there will be where the partners have a more 'businesslike' attitude. Their fondness makes the exchange relatively attractive and thus makes the limits to the rate of exchange relatively wide. Where it will settle down we have no way of knowing, but we do know that there is a relatively wide range over it which it *could* settle down.

Applications of the theory of power are numerous if unsophisticated. As well as the examples given by Blau and Homans the basic notions have been used by Anderson (1971) to account for the relative power of fathers over their sons; by Bailey (1969) to account for the relative power of political leaders; by Sharp (1952) to account for the changes in sex, age and kinship roles among the Yir Yoront. No doubt there are many more examples too, but the case where the theory has been most rigorously applied is that of family power structure. It is this that I propose to examine.

The starting-point was a study by Blood and Wolfe (1960) of nine hundred families in the Detroit metropolitan area. One of the investigators' main concerns was the distribution of power between husband and wife, and to measure this they asked the wife who made the final decision about such things as the job which the husband should take, whether the wife should work, where they should go on holiday, and so on. They then tested an 'ideological' theory and a 'resource' theory. Essentially, the ideological theory stated that the distribution of power would depend on the norms held by the groups or sub-culture to which the family belonged, Catholic, immigrant and ill-educated groups supposedly espousing more patriarchal norms than other groups. This theory received virtually no support from the data. When other relevant variables were controlled the fathers in Catholic families were found to have no more power than those in non-Catholic families, those in immigrant families to have no more power than those in native families, and those who were ill-educated actually to have *less* power than those who were better educated.

In contrast the resource theory received considerable support from the data. It stated: 'the sources of power in so intimate a relationship as a marriage must be sought in the comparative resources which the husband and wife bring to the marriage. . . . A resource may be defined as anything that one partner may make available to the other, helping the latter satisfy his needs or attain his goals. The balance of power will be on the side of that partner who contributes the greater resources to the marriage' (Blood and Wolfe, 1960, p. 12). Blood and Wolfe then took resources to be income, education, and participation in the community, and relative access to these did indeed predict the distribution of power with some accuracy (see for example table 1).

As it stands, the resource theory is not by any means identical to the rational choice theory of power which I have described. Blood and Wolfe do not explicitly mention the *alternatives* open to each of the partners but deal simply with the *amounts* contributed. And this is really very different. For example, a husband can contribute a very large income and the wife nothing, but if by law the wife is able to secure a painless divorce and sufficient alimony from her (now) ex-husband to maintain her in the style of life to which she is accustomed, she has no *financial* reason to give in to his demands. (She may of course have other reasons, but let us deal for the moment with the theory that relative financial contributions to the marriage are the crucial factors.) On the rational choice theory, then, the wife does not necessarily have to go out to work in order to secure greater power within the family. Legal reforms or institutional reforms could be just as effective if they improved the alternatives open to her. Reforms which entitle the wife to a half-share in the family property in the case of divorce, or which entitle her to the same rate of pay as men, increase her bargaining power whether or not she actually chooses to avail herself of the new opportunities.

A revised theory of family power which actually takes account of the alternatives available to the spouses has in fact been put forward by Heer (1963). 'In the revised theory, the greater the difference between the value to the wife of the resources contributed by the

Table 1. *Comparative work participation*

	Wife not employed			Wife employed		
	Husband working overtime	Husband working full-time	Husband not working	Husband working overtime	Husband working full-time	Husband not working
Husband's mean power	5.62	5.28	4.88	4.50	4.46	2.67

husband and the value to the wife of the resources which she might earn outside the existing marriage, the greater the power of her husband, and vice versa' (p. 138). This theory, Heer claims, fits all the empirical data for which Blood and Wolfe could account (a point, incidentally, disputed by Blood and Wolfe). Thus it accounts, as did the earlier one, for the finding that the husband's power varies directly with his income: 'Women who marry a successful man have made a relatively good "catch" and are quick to recognize that the husband they have is probably better than any other they might obtain. Consequently, such a woman would be wary of contradicting her husband if he really felt strongly about something. Women who marry unsuccessful men might begin to wonder if they had made such a good choice after all and would not be afraid of endangering the relationship by insisting on their own way' (p. 138).

The revised theory also accounts, Heer claims, for the finding that mothers of small children have less power than wives with no children or than mothers with older children: 'The mother of small children has less power than before or afterwards precisely because the return she might expect under some alternative to her present marriage is rather meagre. If she seeks a divorce, she will have the problem of bringing up small children without a father. In addition her bargaining power in the remarriage market is probably not very high' (p. 138). The resource theory, however, does not account for this nearly so well. Is not the wife who is bringing up small children helping her spouse to 'satisfy his needs or attain his goals'? So might she not be contributing to the marriage as much as, or more than, before?

While, from a theoretical point of view, Heer's is undoubtedly a considerable improvement on Blood and Wolfe's, there are a number of important objections which, rightly or wrongly, can be advanced against it (and indeed against most applications of the rational choice theory of power). Two main criticisms which have been advanced by Blood himself are, first, that the theory is overly materialistic, requiring people to be interested only in the economic and monetary aspects of a marriage, and, second, that it is overly calculative, requiring the spouses to take the possibility of divorce or separation explicitly into their calculations (Blood, 1963).

Let us examine the issue of materialism first. It is certainly true that the theory assumes that people *do* value material welfare and that the wife, if she is unable to get such a good standard of living after divorce as she had before, will therefore be more committed to her present marriage and more willing to make concessions than she would otherwise have been. If it now transpires that wives in general, or some particular category of wife, are actually indifferent to material welfare and do not care how much money they or their families have, then this particular version of the theory will undoubtedly have to be discarded. We could then replace it with a theory that assumed wives to be concerned about the emotional support and companionship which their husbands gave them, and we could predict that the husband's power would vary with his kindness. We would still have a rational choice theory of power, but since our assumptions about men's, or rather women's, values have changed, our predictions must change too.

Suppose, however, that it transpires that wives value material welfare (as originally assumed) and that they value support and companionship *as well.* (And this, surely, is the most likely 'discovery' that empirical investigation would reach.) Would this in any way undermine Heer's theory? Of course it would not. If it happens that husbands are all the same as regards the emotional support which they offer their wives, then Heer's predictions are totally unaffected. *The wives may in fact get far more satisfaction from this emotional support than they get from their husbands' financial contributions, but this will not alter the fact that some wives are more dependent financially on their husbands than are others and hence have less power.* As we saw in the Latané and Darley example, we can happily allow that people have other values than those specified in the theory. All that we require is that they can be dealt with under the heading of *ceteris paribus.*

Difficulties arise, therefore, if other things are *not* equal – if, for example, there is an inverse correlation between husbands' emotional contributions and their financial ones. If people who earn large sums of money are relatively short on good humour and tolerance (as they probably are), the investigator will have to watch his step more carefully. In particular he will have to control for good humour or companionship or whatever it is that is causing the trouble when he sets out to test his theory. This may cause serious problems, but note that they will be *practical* ones, not theoretical ones.

Consider, next, the criticism that the theory is overly calculative. According to one investigation (Burgess and Cottrell, 1939) only 37 per cent of couples had ever considered separation, so how can the availability of alternatives outside marriage be relevant to family power structure? But this objection betrays a misunderstanding of the theory. The theory states that the actual rate of exchange will settle down somewhere within the limits set by the alternatives available elsewhere. As we have seen before, it cannot determine precisely where it will settle down nor does it specify how the husband and wife will arrive at a 'price'. The couple may if they wish engage in a bargaining battle in which the threat of divorce is used to keep the other's demands in check (rather like the threat of a strike or a lockout in the case of industrial negotiation). But they do not have to do this. They could simply follow the norms and expectations held by peers or kin. They need only consider divorce or separation if they happen to be getting a worse 'bargain' than they could get elsewhere, taking into account of course the not insignificant financial and emotional costs that the process of separation involves.

The theory of power is therefore calculative insofar as it assumes that people take note of the way in which other husbands treat *their* wives. If people are oblivious of what is going on around them, then no rational choice theory can really get off the ground. But it is only if the alternatives look more attractive than one's own marriage that divorce would get serious consideration. Other people can surely dismiss the possibility from their minds.

A more serious objection than either of these two is the factual one that Blood and Wolfe's findings have not always been replicated elsewhere. In Yugoslavia and Greece, for example, it seems to be the poorly paid and poorly educated husband who is more powerful, much as was predicted by the 'ideological' not the 'resource' theory (see Buric and Zecovic, 1967; Safilios-Rothschild, 1967). The husband in the weakest economic situation seems to have most power, so surely we must introduce norms or ideology into our explanation.

Unfortunately there is not sufficient evidence available for us to know precisely what should go into the explanation at all. For example, one possibility which would enable us to eschew norms and ideology altogether is this: the wives of the wealthy and educated middle classes might have much better access to the divorce courts (and so to alimony) than their lower-class counterparts. The penalties of separation may thus be rather smaller and their power correspondingly greater.

However, there is no reason in principle why we should eschew norms and ideology in our rational choice explanation. As I suggested earlier, provided we can get empirical support for our assumptions, we do not have to restrict ourselves to material values alone. There will almost certainly be practical problems of data collection, but the theoretical issues will be easy enough to resolve. Thus the norms of male dominance espoused by lower-class sub-cultures could be regarded as a kind of restrictive agreement or cartel operated by men and maintaining their power. To whatever 'supplier' the 'consumer' goes she is faced by the same price and, short of organizing a rival cartel or doing without altogether (or, more effectively, by doing both as in the *Lysistrata*), she has no option but to submit. Moreover, even if a particular husband were willing to adopt a more egalitarian relationship, pressure from other members of the cartel may force him to maintain the 'price'. As one of Bott's informants told her, 'A lot of men wouldn't mind helping their wives if the curtains were drawn so people couldn't see' (Bott, 1957, p. 70).

The cartel argument will only work of course if the upper-class and the lower-class marriage markets can be kept separate. If lower-class wives had access to an upper-class marriage market in which no cartel was operated, class differentials in marital power could be eliminated. Fortunately for the theory, however (and unfortunately for lower-class wives), there does seem to be considerable structuring of the marriage market along class lines. There is undoubtedly a considerable amount of class homogany, and while this may partly reflect the preferences of those involved it must also reflect the actual opportunities for social contact.

Even if the cartel argument fails, there are plenty of other possibilities that a rational choice approach can offer. Thus, quite simply, it may be that there are class differences in what people *want* from marriage. The difficulty will not be to think up possible theories but to test them. However, this leads on to the most substantial difficulty of all, namely that of measuring the distribution of power itself. As I suggested earlier, what we want is not so much a measure of power as a measure of price – of the actual rate of exchange. And this, I fear, is likely to prove rather difficult in the context of marriage. Most of the studies, like Blood's and Wolfe's, deal with 'who makes the final decision', and this can perhaps be regarded as a measure of the amount exchanged. But much more is exchanged in a marriage than compliance. Bringing in wages, helping with domestic chores or looking after the children, putting up shelves and mending fuses all need to be included too. The task of measuring these individually, let alone combining them into a single index to give the rate of exchange, is depressingly daunting. The only hope that I can offer is to pass the buck to the respondent himself. After all, some respondents have to compare these rates of exchange if the theory is to have any merit, and so I think the best thing we can do is perhaps to ask them, for example, whether they are getting as much out of their marriage as their acquaintances get.

The problems of measurement are not, however, 'mere' technical ones to be ignored by the theorist and simply handed over to a competent investigator. As we saw in the case of expected utility, the judgements which the respondent can make determine which theory it is possible for him to follow. Similarly in the present case. If the subjects cannot make comparisons about the overall rates of exchange, they cannot be following the theory. We shall have to look elsewhere for our explanations of marital power.

How pessimistic we should be I do not know. On the negative side it must be said that in marital relationships above all others we must expect to find 'multiplex' bonds where a host of different incommensurable items are involved. It must also be said that in investigations of transitivity it is precisely in examples such as these where multi-dimensional items have to be ranked that most 'mistakes' occur. On the positive side, however, it is worth noting that economic goods and services are often multi-dimensional too. It is not obvious, for example, that motor-cars are any easier to rank than husbands. Is it any more feasible to combine reliability, economy, safety, power and appearance into a single index than it is to combine kindness, dependability, looks, wealth, faithfulness or any of the other desirable characteristics of a spouse? Yet if economic theories work well enough with cars, as they seem to do, perhaps it is not altogether vain to hope that they will apply to husbands too.

11. *The theory of price*

With the theory of price we come to the most ambitious attempt by exchange theorists to apply not merely an 'economic approach' but rather a fully fledged economic theory to social exchange. Here we have a theory that was originally intended to apply to the exchange of goods and services in a market economy where money provided the medium of exchange. And we are now trying to apply it to the exchange of social valuables in apparently non-market and non-economic sectors of our own or of primitive societies. A great deal of (rather fruitless) debate has occurred particularly in economic anthropology about the legitimacy of such attempts at extrapolation, and we are certainly warned to tread carefully through what has so far proved something of a morass. (For a useful collection of papers on this debate see LeClair and Schneider, 1968.)

I may, I hope, help our journey somewhat if we begin by distinguishing between two different classes of assumption. On the one hand there are those assumptions about the nature of a market economy which the economist takes for granted and does not usually mention explicitly. On the other hand there are those which the economist does recognize explicitly and is prepared to modify. Thus in the theory of price under perfect competition the economist explicitly assumes that there are a large number of buyers and sellers and that none has such a large market share that he can independently have a significant effect on the volume of transaction. But the economist is perfectly well aware that this assumption will not always hold, and he has accordingly developed theories of imperfect competition and so on where the assumption is relaxed. This kind of explicit assumption should therefore cause us little trouble. If the original assumptions do not apply well to social markets, we will be able to borrow alternative ones which do the job better. More troublesome, perhaps, will be the taken-for-granted assumptions about the institutional structure of a capitalist market economy, and it is with these that I propose to start.

The institutional assumptions

The main institutional assumptions are, I think, the following. First, it is assumed that private property is legally recognized and that individuals have the right to dispose of their property for a financial consideration. Second, it is assumed that the individual is free to enter into contracts with whomever he wishes and, third, that contracts freely entered into will be enforced by the legal authorities. Fourth, and finally, it is assumed that the individuals concerned are free to negotiate the precise rate of exchange and can set the price at any level which is mutually agreeable. There are perhaps other assumptions that I too have taken for granted, but I think that these are the main ones with which we need be concerned. The crucial questions are, therefore, whether they can be applied to social markets and, if not, whether appropriate modifications can be made to the theory of price.

Consider, first, the institution of private property or, rather, since it is more important for us, the assumption that the individual has the right to dispose of items for a financial consideration. Now it is certainly true, and I doubt if any exchange theorist would forget, that these rights are not the same in all countries or societies or apply equally to all goods and services within them. In some societies, for example, land is held in trust and cannot be alienated. In others people have the right to bestow their daughters in marriage and are entitled to receive a bridewealth payment in return. In our own society certain classes of person have the right to bestow jobs, titles or peerages on others but are not entitled to any financial remuneration for themselves. On the other hand there are no restrictions on the non-pecuniary returns that can be made: political services to the party, or indeed to the Prime Minister, are entirely permissible and so are academic contributions to the work of the department or of the professor. In our society at least there is a vast array of personal services which individuals have a perfect right to dispose of where they will. It seems to be only financial or sexual 'corruption' that our morality proscribes.

Whether the theory of price (or indeed the theories of exchange and power) can be applied depends therefore on the nature of the rights and proscriptions involved and, additionally, on the degree of their enforcement. After all, professors may be required to give jobs to the best applicants, but the criteria for recognizing merit are so many and so vague that an infraction could scarcely be recognized and much less punished. To establish the precise nature of these rights may be a matter of some ethnographic difficulty (as for example in the case of the brideprice debates in anthropology) but in principle the matter is clear enough, and exchange theorists would hardly be tempted to apply their theories where the institutions are known to be inappropriate.

Nor should there be much difficulty in principle with freedom of contract. Legal and normative restrictions on the classes of individual with whom one can enter into transactions are well known in caste or racist societies, and for many transactions there will be similar restrictions in our own society. Thus the head of department can appoint only a properly qualified candidate, that is one with a degree, and cannot hand out jobs to all and sundry. The Prime Minister cannot confer a peerage on a foreign national. Nor can one get engaged to one's sister. Again, however, I doubt if these restrictions should worry us, for we would hardly be tempted to infringe them.

The enforcement of contracts in principle poses few problems either, although there may be considerable variety in the nature and degree of enforcement. Thus in some societies marriage contracts are as formally recognized and as powerfully sanctioned as any in the society. In other cases there may be no legal sanctions but the transactions may be informally recognized and the norm of reciprocity (a kind of functional equivalent of the law of contract) will be applied and enforced. Thus the member of a baby-sitting ring who defaults on her obligations cannot be taken to court, but informal sanctions will doubtless be applied. True, informal sanctions do not always carry the same weight as legal ones, and the individual may choose to break them and risk the consequences. But infractions of the law are not exactly uncommon either, and so at worst we will have a difference of degree between the economic and the social exchange.

More serious will be cases akin to Sahlins' negative reciprocity where there are no norms to regulate the exchange or where the norms are not or cannot be enforced. What this does is to introduce a very important degree of uncertainty into the transaction. The participants now have to consider not only the value of what is exchanged but also the probability of getting a return. The problems should not, however, be quite so great for the sociologists as they are for the participants. In the first place the sociologist can reasonably predict that the greater the uncertainty the lower will be the volume of transactions and the higher will be the price. (For some further predictions and evidence see Anderson, 1971.) And in the second place we may here find that game theory comes into its own. The absence of norms (and hence the absence of intervention by third parties) clearly makes for a two-person situation and Sahlins' description of negative reciprocity fits uncommonly well with the zero–sum assumption.

Much the most troublesome of the institutional assumptions, however, is that of the freedom to negotiate a price. If Mauss and Blau are correct, this freedom is simply not present in social exchange. As we saw in chapter 6, Blau holds that the crucial respect in which social exchange differs from economic exchange is that 'the nature of the return cannot be bargained about' (Blau, 1964, p. 93). The price must be left to the recipient and cannot be specified in advance. And as I suggested earlier, it is little short of perverse that Blau suggests such an apparently major divergence between social and economic exchange and yet still attempts to apply the economic theory of price to social markets without any serious consideration of the need for modifications. It can hardly be accidental that one *can* bargain and negotiate in economic markets; and one would hardly expect to remove this freedom without finding some consequential changes.

One change that would surely occur is a great increase in uncertainty. As in cases where the law of contract (or its equivalent) does not hold, participants would be much less sure than they would otherwise have been about what return they would receive. On its own, however, this would not make a market system wholly inoperable. Even if participants cannot stipulate openly what price they require, there are various other ways in which they can at least drop broad hints. One obvious thing to do is simply to refuse to enter into a transaction if the erstwhile price had been too low and to hope that one's partner gets the message. And doubtless there are other techniques that the Trobriand Islanders, for example, could teach us.

Nevertheless, this would surely be an extraordinary way of proceeding in an economic market and one that could be expected only where, in Sahlins' words, 'the material side of the transaction is repressed by the social' (1965, p. 147). Responses to shifts in supply or demand would surely be slow and inefficient and we would expect to find relatively large numbers of buyers or sellers to be left unsatisfied. It would surely endure only so long as the participants rated the losses through inefficiency to be less than the loss of honour they would suffer if once they broke the rule and stipulated the return in advance. It might accordingly be a rather fragile system, liable to swift disruption if social controls are weakened or if there is pressure on the material side.

An illuminating example of the breakdown of this system comes from Radford's study of a prisoner-of-war camp. Radford reports that gifts of cigarettes (presumably with the usual but unspecified expectation of receiving a return in due course) soon ceased in the camp and that cigarettes became a regular currency. 'Very soon after capture people realised that it was both undesirable and unnecessary, in view of the limited size and the equality of supplies, to give away or to accept gifts of cigarettes or food. "Goodwill" developed into trading as a more equitable means of maximising individual satisfaction' (Radford, 1945, pp. 190–1).

Our provisional conclusion, then, must be that a proscription on bargaining is an inefficient method of conducting a market system and one that might not long survive if the goods and services exchanged increased in value. It would not necessarily preclude the operation of a price system, but we would not expect it to work particularly well, and we would accordingly expect the theory of price to yield poor predictions.

Two considerations, however, suggest that something may be rescued from the disaster wreaked by the proscription on bargaining. In the first place, the proscription may not be quite so universal as Blau and Mauss imply. True enough 'if a person gives a dinner party, he expects his guests to reciprocate at some future date. But he can hardly bargain with them about the kind of party to which they should invite him, although he expects them not simply to ask him for a quick lunch if he had invited them to a formal dinner' (Blau, 1964, p. 93). Dinner parties, however, are surely prime examples of the material side of the transaction being repressed by the social. But there must be many social exchanges where this is not the case. In arranged marriages, for example, where considerable amounts of wealth may be given as brideprice or dowry, open negotiations do seem to occur. In politics the parties make the most open (and outrageous) promises about the things they will do in return for our votes, and I doubt if the deals carried out between politicians leave a great deal to the beneficiary's discretion. And in the family it cannot be unknown to discuss the division of labour rather than to leave it all to one's partner's intuitions. Social exchange is not all of a piece and we may find that the 'most basic and crucial distinction' between it and economic exchange turns out to be a continuum and not a dichotomy.

A second consideration which may alter our provisional conclusion is the existence of norms of fair exchange. Indeed, I doubt if the proscription on negotiation will ever occur as an isolated institution. Rather it will tend to be associated with norms that remove some of the discretion from the recipient and specify what return is to be made.

In ceremonial exchanges such as the Kula or the potlatch an 'equivalent' return must be made, as we saw in chapter 6, and for the more conventional exchanges of our own time there is no shortage of postulated rules. It is really only with Titmuss' free gift that the recipient is left with untrammelled discretion, and it is hard to see that this category can be brought within the compass of social exchange. Elsewhere discretion is more (or less) closely circumscribed.

The most straightforward cases are ones where 'distributive justice', 'fair exchange' or 'balanced reciprocity' apply. Here, broadly speaking, the value of what is returned should be equal (or proportional) to the value of what was given, and we thus have (in the pure case) a straightforward example of fixed exchange rates. The *timing* of the return may be unspecified but the *value* is clearly specified by the culture if not by the donor. Of course if the culture is rigorously obeyed we cannot have prices fluctuating with changes in supply and demand, but this most certainly does not mean that economic theory will become inoperable. Fixed exchange rates can easily be incorporated into the theory and instead of fluctuating prices it will simply predict a fluctuating volume of transactions.

The consequence of fixed exchange rates can be seen easily enough in figure 22. In addition to the conventional supply and demand curves we can add a horizontal line giving the 'fair price'. From this we can read off that consumers will be willing to purchase quantity OA at the fair price while sellers will be willing to provide the (larger) quantity OB. If we have a case where, as in Blau's work groups, the

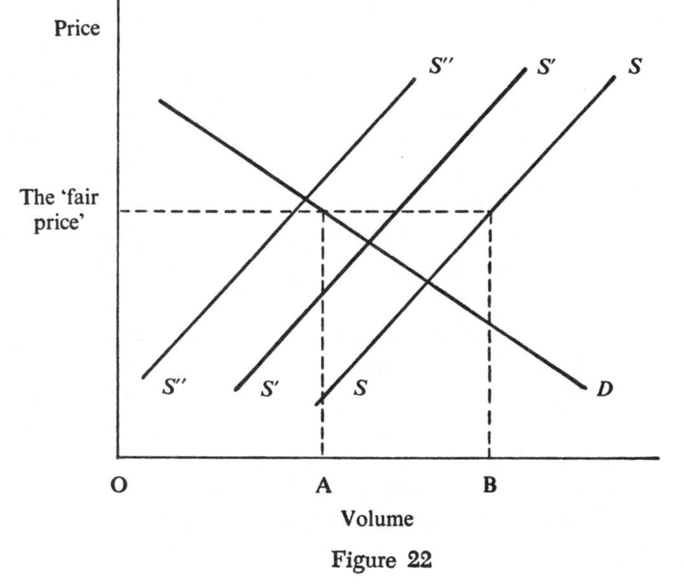

Figure 22

initiative is taken by 'consumers' asking for advice with their work, we can predict that the actual volume of transactions will be given by OA, leaving a number of unsatisfied sellers. The recruitment of some new workers, shifting the demand curve to the right, will simply increase the volume of transactions, and the promotion of some workers to a different group, shifting the curve to the left, will decrease the volume. We should note, however, that the changes may be rather 'sticky' under this system. A small shift in the supply curve (to S′S′) will have no effect on the volume of transactions, and will merely reduce the number of unsatisfied sellers. It will take a larger shift (say to S″S″) before the volume is actually reduced.

We can take our economic analysis further than this, too, if we wish. So far we have assumed that the norm of fair exchange is invariably obeyed, but this is not an assumption that can be altogether realistic nor one that fits in well with an economic approach. If people obey the norm, they presumably do so either out of fear of their consciences or fear of the sanctions imposed on transgressors. Either way we would expect that a sufficiently large temptation might induce people to overcome their scruples and engage in 'black market' transactions. The temptation might need to be very large in some cases and very small in others, but I do not think that we can seriously contend that the norms of social exchange are so well internalized or so well enforced that no one can ever be tempted into transgressions. We are led to predict, therefore, that a fixed rate of exchange and some unsatisfied sellers may lead to a black market with prices *below* the prescribed one while, conversely, a fixed rate and unsatisfied buyers may lead to a black market with prices *above* that prescribed. Of course, whether the black market actually does emerge or not will depend on a large range of factors such as the number of unsatisfied buyers or sellers, the value they place on conformity, the likelihood of being caught, and so on. We would be foolish to venture anything stronger than the possibility of a black market, therefore, but even possibilities should be of interest to the investigator.

Few sociological investigators have paid any attention either to price or volume fluctuations, and certainly none have looked at black markets. The work of Radford, however, on the economics of a prisoner-at-war camp may again be instructive. After cigarettes became the standard currency in the camp an Exchange and Mart notice-board was established and later an 'official' restaurant and shop were opened. Finally paper money backed by food (the BMk – Bully Mark) was introduced and an attempt was made at a planned economy with fixed prices. Prices were fixed partly from market data and partly on the advice of the Medical Officer. The Exchange and Mart noticeboards came under official control, and advertisements which exceeded a 5 per cent departure from the recommended price were liable to be crossed out by authority.

The planned economy not only had the blessing of the M.O. (who was concerned that people might sell too much, to the detriment of their health); public opinion too was strongly in favour of just and stable prices. The morality of social exchange seemed to prevail, once again, and the scheme was at first a success. It could not, however, cope with large changes in supply. In August 1944 the supply of food and cigarette parcels was halved, and, the demand for cigarettes being relatively inelastic, a new price structure was required if supply and demand were to balance. Addicted smokers were presumably relatively long on food and short on cigarettes (although of course absolutely short on both) and must have been willing to pay more for their cigarettes and less for their food than the recommended prices allowed. As Radford reports, 'when the price level fell with the August cuts and the price structure changed, the recommended scale was too rigid . . . The scale was moved up and down and several times, slowly following the inflationary and deflationary waves, but it was rarely adjusted to changes in the price structure. More and more advertisements were crossed off the board, and black market sales at unauthorised prices increased: eventually public opinion turned against the recommended scale and authority gave up the struggle. In the last few weeks, with unparalleled deflation, prices fell with alarming rapidity, no scales existed, and supply and demand, alone and unmellowed, determined prices' (Radford, 1945, pp. 198-9).

Norms of fair exchange, then, may be all very well in stable conditions, but morality may not always triumph over market forces and it may prove vulnerable to external shocks. If nothing else, our economic approach may demonstrate the contingent character of morality. Even if a norm of fair exchange survives, however, it should be clear that economic analysis can be applied. Fixed exchange rates need cause us no difficulty.

But will it be so straightforward when we move from Blau's 'fair exchange' to Sahlins' 'generalized' reciprocity where 'the time and worth of reciprocation are not alone conditional on what was given by the donor, but also upon what he will need and when, and likewise what the recipient can afford and when' (Sahlins, 1965, p. 147)? This will certainly not be a case of fixed exchange rates. Indeed, in a pure case of generalized reciprocity we can hardly talk of price at all. While there may be flows of goods and services in each direction, the ratio between them may reflect neither market forces nor just prices but individual need. Price represents the quantity of goods or services that one must surrender in order to obtain, or to repay, a given benefit, but in generalized reciprocity payment may not be required for specific benefits.

Even an economy or society run on the lines of 'from each according to his ability, to each according to his need' is not immune from changes in supply and demand, however, and it must show some response to such changes. On its own morality will not eliminate scarcity. What we can expect, therefore, is that changes in supply and demand will, as in the case of a system of just prices, lead to changes in the volume of transactions. If the number of one's dependents is increased, one's ability to meet their individual needs must be reduced. At best one could reallocate one's time and labour so as to meet the increased needs in full; at worst no such reallocation would prove possible and each dependent would receive less pro rata. Doubtless the intermediate case would be the most common, and I would confidently predict, for example, that parents with larger families (controlling for social class and so on) would spend more time in total on their children but less time on each individually.

The specific assumptions

We can now at last leave the institutional assumptions and return to the formal theory of price under perfect competition which we met in chapter 3. There it will be remembered we assumed that there were homogenous commodities, perfect knowledge on the part of buyers and sellers, and a large number of participants in the market. From these assumptions it followed that there would be a single price reigning in the market and that this price would also be given by the intersection of the supply and demand curves. We also assumed that the demand curve would slope down from the left to right, while the supply curve would slope up, and from this we can see that a fall in supply (that is, a shift of the supply curve leftwards) will increase price and reduce the volume of transactions. These conclusions all follow logically from the assumptions, and the crucial questions are therefore: (1) how far are these assumptions accurate descriptions of the social world and (2) how far will inaccuracies in these assumptions (if such are found) damage our predictions?

As it happens, the most casual glance at the assumptions of homogeneous commodities, perfect knowledge, and large numbers of buyers and sellers must reveal a woeful gap between the formal theory and the real world of work groups, marriage markets or political negotiation. The work group which Blau describes in *The Dynamics of Bureaucracy* (1955) and which formed the basis for a great deal of his theorizing contained a mere fifteen workers. The quality of the advice provided by the experts must surely have varied considerably, and while the small numbers involved may have increased the knowledge possessed, the fact that the workers (law enforcement agents) had to spend a lot of their time in the field and away from the office must surely have decreased it. This can hardly be fertile ground for the theory of perfect competition.

As I suggested at the beginning of this chapter, however, economists too have to deal with cases where their assumptions do not hold up, and they have various modifications which can help us over our difficulties. Thus product differentiation is almost as familiar from the housing market as it is from the marriage market and need cause us little difficulty. It will mean, most obviously, that there will be no one reigning 'house price' in the market and that (as in the theory of power) there will be a bargaining area within which the price must fall. This, however, need not affect our conclusion about the general *direction* of price changes that will be brought about by changes in supply or demand. Just as in the theory of power a change in the alternatives available alters the size of the bargaining area and hence the average rate of exchange, so too changes in demand or supply affect the alternatives available and the average rate of exchange. Indeed, the theories of power and price become practically indistinguishable.

Again, lack of knowledge need cause us little difficulty. Perfect knowledge was needed in order to yield a single, unique price reigning in the market. In its absence there will be scope for discrimination with sellers charging different prices to different buyers, and we can accordingly expect a variety of prices to occur. But again there is no reason why it should affect our conclusions about the *directions* of price changes.

Finally, consider the consequences of having a small number of buyers and sellers in the market. This again is highly familiar in conventional economic markets, and economists have accordingly developed theories of oligopoly and monopoly to deal with cases where there are few sellers (or only one). True, the theory of oligopoly is one of the less satisfactory in economics, and different versions reach different conclusions. The crucial problem with oligopoly is that the behaviour of one individual *does* have a significant effect on the situation facing the others, and hence each must take into account the others' likely reactions in reaching his own decision. The situation in fact becomes that of an n-person non-zero–sum game, and such games, unlike the two-person zero–sum one, have proved rather intractable.

We would be foolish therefore to venture any precise predictions about the level of price and output that will occur when there are few sellers (and even more so when there are few buyers as well).

Nevertheless, whatever the problems of the theory of oligopoly, it gives no reason to suppose that an increase in demand will *lower* price or that a fall will raise it. The only condition that would lead us to abandon our general conclusions about the direction of price changes would be the discovery that the supply or demand curves sloped in quite different directions from the ones we had postulated. Such a discovery is quite conceivable, if unlikely, although once made it will be easy enough to revise our predictions.

What then are the main conclusions to be drawn from this discussion of the assumptions (institutional and otherwise) which lie behind the theory of price? The first, and perhaps most important, is that we must be careful to check the ethnographical data. We must find out what can be exchanged, whether just prices exist, what character the demand and supply curves have. Depending on what we find, we may have to make modifications to the theory of price under perfect competition that we outlined in chapter 3. If we find norms of fair exchange, then we should expect to find that changes in supply or demand lead simply to changes in the volume of transactions; but if there are no such norms we may hope to find price fluctuations too. If contracts cannot be enforced, we should expect a reduced volume of transactions. If the return must be left to the recipient's discretion, we should expect price to be rather 'sticky'. None of the possible findings so far mentioned, however, lead to the demise of the economic approach. That would occur only if social life was so circumscribed by rules and obligations that *no* area of choice remained to the recipients. If there were not only obligations to give, to receive and to return but also obligations which specified how much should be given and how often, and how much should be returned and when, then I think the economic approach would have nothing to offer. But situations of this kind are, I suspect, as rare in social life as those to which the theory of perfect competition can apply in an unadulterated form.

As a final attempt to convince the sceptics, let me give an actual example where the theory seems to work in a straightforward and simple fashion. The Sebei of Uganda, it appears, exchange cattle and other goods for wives. They bargain openly about the brideprice, with the groom's family trying to make it as small as possible and the bride's to make it as large as possible. A just price does not seem to be enforced, and accordingly price fluctuates with supply and demand. Thus when British pacification and disease control led to a long-term increase in the cattle population, there was a steady shift in the demand curve and a corresponding climb in brideprice. Again, some areas among the Sebei are devoted largely to crops and have little livestock available, while others (in the east) have relatively small human population and relatively large herds. As we would expect, there is a flow of women from the areas which are relatively poor in cattle to those which are relatively rich, and no doubt there is a higher incidence of polygyny in the latter too. At reigning prices the inhabitants of the eastern areas can presumably afford more women and, as the Sebei themselves say, women will therefore tend to marry to the east (Goldschmidt, 1969). Nor let me add, are the Sebei an isolated example. Similar phenomena occur in the New Guinea highlands (Salisbury, 1962) and, closer to home, in rural Ireland too (Arensberg and Kimball, 1940).

12. *Problems in the theory of groups*

Up to now we have been extremely fortunate, for we have always been able to assume that the economists have formulated theories that were logically if not empirically watertight. We have had to worry about the realism of the assumptions and the problems of measurement, but we have been able to take it for granted that the economists' conclusions followed logically from their assumptions. It was only unfortunate sociologists such as Blau who seemed to get into logical difficulties.

We should not become too complacent, however. It is sometimes claimed that a major advantage of introducing economic reasoning into sociology is the added rigour that will result, but I fear that the grounds for this claim are insubstantial. When we turn to the theory of groups we find that economists such as Olson or Downs are as capable as any sociologist of perpetrating *non sequiturs*, and we are advised to pay as much attention to the logic of the argument as we do to the realism of its assumptions. The explanation of this apparent paradox is, I suspect, fairly simple. Economic theories of exchange and price have been with us for a very long time, and the versions which we meet in textbooks are the products of a long history of theorizing. The theories of Downs and Olson, however, are largely breaking new ground and raise novel problems for the economist. The mere fact of using an economic approach did not guarantee the authors success and I fear that it will not guarantee ours either.

It would be tedious and unnecessary, in view of the excellent critiques available elsewhere (for example, Barry, 1970) to go through all the confusions and *non sequiturs* present in the writings of Olson, Downs and Riker one by one. In my exposition of the theories in chapter 4 I tried as far as possible to give a coherent account of the basic elements of the theories, omitting many of the (often unnecessary) complications. Doubtless I have been no more able to avoid inaccuracies and *non sequiturs* than my predecessors, but rather than subject the theories to a detailed logical analysis I would prefer to restrict myself to a few of the more important logical and empirical issues.

Public goods and self-interest

One of Olson's major, and most startling, conclusions was that rational self-interested individuals would not act to achieve their common or group interests in the absence of special conditions such as selective incentives. Social scientists from Marx onwards, Olson claims, have fallen into the trap of supposing that groups with shared interests will organize together in order to further those interests; but their supposition could not be further from the truth. Shared interests alone will not suffice to produce group action.

Olson's argument undoubtedly reveals the alarming naiveté of many early sociologists and political scientists (and doubtless of many contemporaries too). But has not Olson's concern for rigour been overcome somewhat by a desire to shock? Does his conclusion follow quite so inevitably from his assumptions as he would have us believe?

The basis of Olson's argument is that the rational, self-interested individual will consider the expected utility of his contribution to the provision of a public good and will compare it with the alternative uses to which it might be put. And this is sound enough if we grant the assumptions of rationality and self-interest. It is also sound enough to conclude that our rational, self-interested individual will not contribute 10p to a union that would secure a £1 wage rise if there is only a one in hundred chance that the 10p would make all the difference between the union's success and failure. He is better off keeping his money and spending it on something else. The union accordingly will not be formed.

In this particular example, however, we have the benefit of some *specific* assumptions about the size of the contribution required, the probability that it will make a difference, and the size of the ultimate benefit that would be forthcoming. In the absence of these assumptions we cannot deduce whether or not the union will form. We may think it pretty implausible that the costs, benefits and probabilities involved could ever be such as to make it rational to join a trade union in the absence of selective incentives. And no doubt we would be right. But we should be quite clear that we have had to smuggle in some 'reasonable' assumptions in order to reach our conclusion. It simply does not follow from Olson's original assumptions that rational, self-interested men will *never* act to achieve their common interests in the absence of selective incentives. The only *general* results we are able to get (and they are results eminently worth getting) are that, other things being equal, individuals will be less likely to participate in collective action where the good is a public one than they will where it is a private one, and, secondly, that in the case of a public good the larger the number of people whose contributions are needed, the less likely they are to make those contributions. These are by no means unimportant or uninteresting conclusions and one wonders whether Olson's apparent desire for stronger ones is anything more than a foolish attempt at sensationalism.

A second, rather more important, issue concerns the assumptions themselves from which Olson starts. Like Downs, and indeed like many economists, he assumes that individuals are motivated by self-interest alone. 'Erotic incentives, psychological incentives, moral incentives and so on' are all excluded (Olson, 1965, p. 61n). These restrictions greatly irritate sociologists and are one of the main features that distinguish the work of Olson, Downs and company from that of Homans and Blau. Thus Homans (writing before Olson) said that 'we are out to rehabilitate the "economic man". The trouble with him was not that he was economic, that he used his resources to some advantage, but that he was antisocial and materialistic, interested only in money and material goods and ready to sacrifice even his old mother to get them. What was wrong with him were his values: he was only allowed a limited range of values; but the new economic man is not so limited' (Homans, 1961, p. 79). Similarly Blau, in criticizing Downs's assumption of self-interested behaviour, wrote: 'First, political actions do not rest exclusively on the rational calculation of advantage but sometimes are largely expressive manifestations of people's feelings and values. To be sure, such expressive action is by no means devoid of rewards. However, second, the rewards obtained in political life are not confined to those that the government supplies and that consequently are contingent on election victory but include many directly derived from political participation' (Blau, 1964, p. 236).

The issues involved here should be fairly familiar now from the discussion they received when we examined the theory of power. Nevertheless, they are so important that it is worth going over them again quickly and examining Olson's rationale for his position. First of all there can be little doubt that most people, *other things being equal*, do prefer more monetary, social and political advantage to less. We can therefore retain our conclusion that, other things being equal, individuals will be less likely to participate in collective action where the good is a public one than they will where it is a private one. The crucial problem, however, is whether other things really will be equal. Typically, the sociologist assumes that they will not. Behaviour may be motivated by morality as well as by self-interest, and it may be precisely in the case of public goods that morality is most important. Olson, on the other hand, thinks otherwise and guesses that morality can be ignored. Moral incentives are not needed since 'most organized pressure groups are explicitly working for gains for themselves, not for gains for other groups, and in such cases it is hardly plausible to ascribe group action to any moral code' (Olson, 1965, p. 61n).

There can be little doubt that the sociologist is right and that Olson is wrong. Indeed, I find it quite amazing that a man who exposes the naiveté of others so well should make statements of such breathtaking naiveté as that contained in the above quotation. I have not carried out any count of organized pressure groups, and I very much doubt if Olson has either, but a large number of 'altruistic' pressure groups most certainly exist. The Child Poverty Action Group, Help the Aged, the Royal Society for the Prevention of Cruelty to Animals, the National Society for the Prevention of Cruelty to Children are the merest beginning to the list. By no stretch of the imagination are they working for material gains for themselves; conceivably they are working for social gains; but much more plausibly the gains are moral. We shall be extremely fortunate if we do not have to introduce morality in order to account for the formation of these groups.

A second objection which Olson advances against the use of moral incentives is the familiar one that they render the theory untestable. 'It is not possible to get empirical proof of the motivation behind any person's action; it is not possible definitely to say whether a given individual acted for moral reasons or for other reasons in some particular case', Olson claims (1965, p. 61n). Now it may be true that we cannot say *definitely*, that we cannot *prove* empirically, what someone's reasons were for a particular action, but then I doubt if there are many things that can be proved empirically. It would be quite far-fetched to go from this to the conclusion that we cannot say *anything* about a person's motivation. It is about as sensible as saying that, since nature has not seen fit to draw a line down the side of men's heads, we cannot say anything about the back of one's head or the front.

A third, and rather more interesting objection, comes from Barry. The introduction of moral incentives, he claims, 'leaves no scope for an economic model to come between the premises and the phenomenon to be explained' (Barry, 1970, p. 16). This would of course be true if people were motivated *solely* by moral considerations, but this is as implausible as the counter-claim that people are *never* motivated by moral considerations. Surely there is work for both the 'moral' and the 'economic' arguments. The relative importance of each will no doubt vary from topic to topic, but that is an empirical matter and not one to be settled *a priori.*

The assumption of self-interest can and should, therefore, be modified. The addition of moral incentives makes the formation of 'altruistic' groups more easily explicable and it in no way undermines the main general results of the theory. It remains true, whether we allow for morality or not, that groups seeking private goods will be more likely to form, other things being equal, than those that seek public goods; and it remains true that in the case of a public good the larger the number of people whose contributions are needed, the less likely are those contributions to be provided (other things, as ever, being equal). As indeed Olson recognizes, the moral incentive is simply analogous to the selective incentive: it merely provide an *additional* reason for making a contribution.

Political parties and integrity

Compared with Downs, Olson is a model of rigorous thinking. *Non sequiturs* and *ad hoc* assumptions abound in *An Economic Theory of Democracy,* and it would be pointless to enumerate them all. As in the case of Durkheim's *Suicide* the importance of the book derives more from its advocacy of a new approach than from its detailed explanations, and whatever the flaws by which it is marred it remains one of the most important contributions to post-war political science.

Nevertheless, some of Downs's muddles are rather illuminating and demonstrate once again the importance of allowing economic man a wider range of values. Downs, it will be remembered, argues that the two political parties will gradually converge when voters are equally distributed along the left–right continuum, and he goes to some lengths to prevent them from finally adopting identical positions. Abstention by extremists is one of his main weapons here, and he argues that it will provide an incentive for the parties to stay apart. As Barry has pointed out, however, the argument will not do. 'Suppose', he writes, 'that a bloc of those electors on the left threaten to abstain unless the party which is infinitesimally to the left of the median (the point which splits the electorate in half) moves to, say, the forty-ninth centile. Unless the right-wing extremists have issued an ultimatum too, this is an invitation to electoral suicide. For obviously, if everyone does vote, a party cannot win at the forty-ninth centile so long as the other party stays at the half-way mark or (even more effective) moves up to just to the right of the forty-ninth centile. On the contrary, the only thing to do would be move to a point midway in the electorate *excluding* the "extremists". Thus, if 10% of the left-wing voters threatened to abstain, the equilibrium position of the parties would be at the 55th centile!' (Barry, 1970, p. 112). Abstention by extremists does not seem so rational after all.

Nevertheless, parties do seem to stay a little distance apart even in societies such as our own where the voters seem to be massed at the centre of the spectrum; and where (as in Ulster) the voters seem to be massed bimodally near the extremes, the parties do appear to be poles apart in ideology too. Can this be explained by a rational choice model or is political behaviour inaccessible to this kind of analysis?

Various expedients could no doubt be tried, but the one to which I am most inclined is to allow the parties additional values. Let us suppose, for example, that the members of our political parties were not only engaged in the pursuit of office but were also committed to various ideologies or principles. Furthermore, let us assume that they derive utility from remaining true to these principles. If they deviate from their original positions they lose 'integrity', and the more they deviate the more they lose.

The drawbacks of this kind of additional assumption should be fairly clear. To make a precise prediction about the position on the spectrum where a particular party will end up we will need to know how it 'trades off' integrity and office (assuming that it cannot simultaneously obtain office and remain true to its principles). Some parties (such as those on the extreme left) seem to place such a high value on their ideological purity that even a small compromise would have to guarantee them office if it was to be acceptable. Other parties, of a more pragmatic character, seem much more willing to abandon their principles in the pursuit of office. Clearly, if this is the case, we cannot predict where on the continuum the two parties will end up unless we know (or assume) something about their willingness to compromise. By introducing additional goals for our parties to pursue we may have gained in realism but our model has lost in determinacy.

Nevertheless, we have made some other gains too. In the first place we have given the parties an incentive to stay apart. Movement along the continuum now entails costs (in lost integrity) as well as gains (in extra votes) and so the parties at some point *may* stop converging. More usefully we can now explain why the parties should remain further apart ideologically when there is a bimodal distribution of voters with voters polarized at the two extremes (as in figure 11) than they will when the voters are concentrated in the centre of the spectrum (as in figure 10). Downs had explained this in terms of abstention by extremists, but as we have just seen this argument will not work. Abstention by extremists on one side (unless matched by equal abstentions on the other) will be counterproductive. However, in the revised model parties weigh up the gains and losses of convergence, and it is easy to see that the gains of a given movement centrewards will be greater where the voters are massed in the centre. A given shift will bring more votes than it will in the bimodal situation and hence will be more likely to outweigh the costs of lost ideological purity. It will after all be rational for parties to move closer together in Britain than they will in Ulster and we have thus achieved the reassuring result of bringing our model into line with real life. (Note that, in order to obtain these results, it is not sufficient merely to assume that the parties have ideological preferences. Just as it is rational for a left-wing elector to vote for a middle-of-the-road party in order to prevent the worse fate of a right-wing party winning, so it may be rational for a left-wing party to take up a middle-of-the-road position. To keep the parties apart we have to assume that they derive utility from remaining true to their principles.)

The sceptical reader may rightly say at this point that all we have been doing is tinkering around with the model in order to bring its predictions into line with what we knew all along to be the case. We have not been deriving new or novel predictions and then testing them systematically against the data. At best we have simply shown that the known facts are susceptible to a rational choice explanation, and while this may not be altogether uninteresting it is certainly not as impressive as the generation of new predictions. Still, as we shall see in the next section, novel predictions have been derived and tested. The rational choice theorist is by no means condemned to *ex post facto* analyses.

Coalition formation and ideology

As we saw in chapter 4 the conventional theory of coalition formation as advanced by Riker and others predicts that minimum winning coalitions will form. It also predicts, more boldly, that of these minimum winning coalitions the one with the smallest surplus of seats will actually form. This is indeed a novel and surprising prediction. That there will be no surplus *parties* in the winning coalition is easily understood, but the prediction that there will be the minimum possible surplus of *seats* does not square so readily with common sense. The prediction has, however, had a systematic test and its fate is instructive.

The test was carried out by Taylor and Laver (1973). They collected data on the possible and actual coalitions which could or did form in twelve western European democracies during the period 1945-71. They also obtained expert judgements from a number of specialists on the ideological positions of the various parties. This information is not of course needed to test Riker's theory but it is, as we shall see, highly relevant for various other theories with which Taylor and Laver wished to contrast Riker's. (The countries which Taylor and Laver used were

Austria, Belgium, Denmark – for which post-1960 data only were used – Finland, Germany, Iceland, Ireland, Italy, Luxembourg, the Netherlands, Norway and Sweden. Countries such as Britain which had not had any experience of coalition government were excluded as of course were non-democratic countries such as Spain and Portugal. The major notable omission is that of France. There were a variety of reasons for this omission, of which perhaps the most compelling was the difficulty of obtaining a reliable measure of parties' positions on the ideological spectrum.)

Table 2 gives the basic data relevant to Riker's theory. It shows the number of elections that took place, the number of governments that formed, the number of governments that were 'winning' coalitions (winning solely in the sense that they had a majority of the seats in Parliament) and so on. As can be seen, there were in fact quite a number of non-winning – i.e. minority – governments, and this is certainly a result that our model had not predicted. The model does hold up reasonably well, however, when we turn to the number of *minimum* winning coalitions. In five countries the majority of governments were minimum winning coalitions, and in four more countries where minority government was common we find that winning coalitions, when they did occur, were invariably minimum winning ones. This leaves three countries – Finland, Italy and the Netherlands – where the theory (and common sense) did remarkably badly. These countries represent a puzzle to which we shall have to return.

Next let us turn to Riker's size principle. This predicts that the coalition which forms will be the one with the smallest surplus of seats – a novel prediction but, alas, one that at first glance receives remarkably little support from the data. Of the 132 governments which formed, a mere 13 were the ones predicted by the size principle, whereas 57 had been minimum winning coalitions. However, as Taylor and Laver point out, this may not be a fair comparison. The size principle is a relatively 'strong' theory, making very specific predictions: in most cases there would be a single specific coalition that it would predict. There might on the other hand be a large number of coalitions that would all qualify as minimum winning ones and so by chance alone we would expect more of those that actually formed to come from this category. What we have to consider, therefore, is whether the actual results are significantly better than those that might have occurred by chance. The required significance levels are also given in table 2, and they confirm the impression obtained by our first glance. The size principle fares extremely poorly.

There could be a number of reasons for this failure. For example, it could be that people just are not rational in politics, perhaps because the decisions involved are 'impossible' ones. Still, I would doubt

Table 2. *Types of coalition in 12 European countries: 1945–71*

	Austria	Belgium	Denmark	Finland	Germany	Iceland	Ireland	Italy	Luxem-bourg	Nether-lands	Norway	Sweden
Number of elections	6	7	5	8	4	9	4	6	7	8	3	7
Number of governments formed	9	12	5	24	5	11	4	25	10	12	6	9
Number of 'winning coalitions'	7 (0.250)	11 (0.050)	1	16 (0.100)	5 (0.250)	8	2	11	10 (0.050)	11 (0.100)	2	3
Number of 'minimum winning coalitions'	7 (0.050)	11 (0.001)		5 (0.250)	5 (0.025)	7 (0.050)	2 (0.050)	1	9 (0.001)	4 (0.010)	2 (0.100)	3 (0.250)
Number of coalition governments with the smallest surplus of seats	0 (0.250)	3 (0.250)	0	1	1	4 (0.025)	1 (0.250)	0	0	1	2 (0.010)	0
Number of 'minimal connected winning coalitions'	7 (0.005)	5 (0.050)	1 (0.250)	4 (0.010)	4 (0.010)	3	1 (0.250)	8 (0.001)	9 (0.001)	3 (0.010)	2 (0.025)	3 (0.100)

Notes: Data for Denmark cover the period 1960-71 only. Significance levels are given in brackets. Levels above 0.250 are omitted.

if there is usually a great deal of doubt about the number of seats parties have or about other relevant matters, and so I am much more inclined to look to the assumptions of the theory for the cause of the trouble. Thus it could well be that the spoils of office are not distributed proportionately to the strength of the parties within the coalition. Alternatively, or additionally, it could be that there is more to political life than the pursuit of office. As I suggested in the case of Downs's theory, parties may be committed to various ideologies or principles. In forming a coalition they will have to compromise these principles and the more disparate the parties the greater the compromises involved. Again, then, trade-offs may be required. A particular party may have the option of going in with a much larger, but ideologically similar, party, in which case it might get only a few cabinet posts but at least see policies enacted with which it is fairly sympathetic; or alternatively it may have the option of going in with a slightly weaker, but ideologically dissimilar, party with whom it would need to make greater compromises of principle. As before, we shall need to have some detailed knowledge about preferences before specific predictions can be made.

Nevertheless, there are some general results which are intuitively very appealing although rather hard to prove. For example, if there were a number of potential winning coalitions each with equal ideological spread, we would expect the one with the barest majority to form. And if there were a number of minimum winning coalitions, each with parties of equal size, we would expect the one with the smallest ideological spread to form. Plausible though this may sound, however, it is not obvious how it can be proved. True enough, it is straightforward when there are only three parties, but it becomes extremely complicated when there are four or more.

Let us take the simple case involving three parties first. Suppose they are distributed along the ideological spectrum as in figure 23. Suppose too that they are of equal size and that the ideological position that the coalition takes up is the mean of those of its component members. It is easy enough to see that on these assumptions coalition BC is the most likely to form. If AB forms, it will take up ideological position alpha; if BC forms, it will take up position gamma. Party A clearly prefers alpha and party C prefers gamma, so all depends on party B. Since it is nearer on the spectrum to gamma than it is to

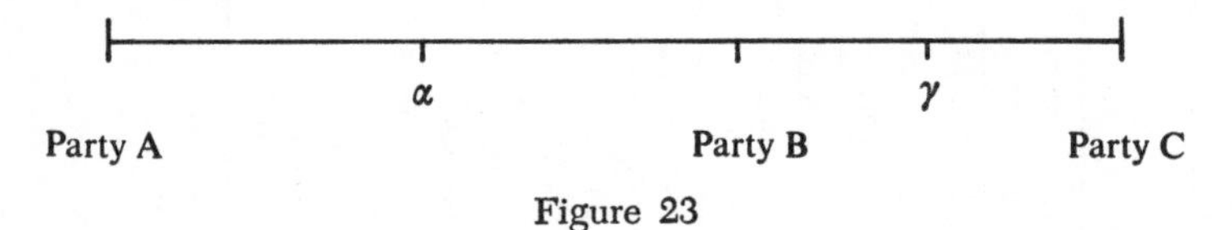

Figure 23

alpha, it will prefer coalition BC which will therefore now obtain a majority and win.

But suppose we now add a fourth party, as in figure 24. There are now two possible winning coalitions, namely ABC and BCD, that are in serious contention. (ABD and ACD can be ruled out straightaway: the other two coalitions are clearly preferable to a majority of their members.) As before, party A clearly prefers the former coalition and party D the latter, so all depends on B and C. But this time B prefers ABC with its mean position of alpha, and C prefers BCD, ideologically positioned at gamma. We seem to have reached an impasse and it could be that this will be the kind of situation that will lead to minority government. Alternatively, the parties might attempt to compromise on non-ideological issues. Thus party A might offer to give some of its seats in the cabinet to C in order to entice him into the coalition, and equally D might try to buy off B. Since D is closer to BCD's mean position than A is to ABC's, we could perhaps assume that he will be prepared to make greater non-ideological concessions than will A and hence that BCD – the coalition with the smallest ideological spread – will be most likely one to form.

This, I hope, gives some indication of the problems involved. As can be seen, it is rather difficult to obtain results even when we assume that the parties are all equally strong and so forth. If we complicate matters and allow for inequalities in size, predictions become even harder to come by. Nevertheless, I do not think that we should abandon this line of theorizing and revert to the simpler (although more unrealistic) models where determinate results are easier to obtain. In the first place, of course, we saw that the simpler model advanced by Riker may have given determinate 'results', but they were results which received singularly little support from the data. Occam's razor is an excellent instrument but we must not use it to shave away recalcitrant data.

In the second place there is a strong empirical case for the inclusion of ideology in our models. Thus Taylor and Laver tested the hypothesis that the coalitions which formed would contain only ideologically 'adjacent' members. (The full hypothesis was that 'minimal connected winning' coalitions would form: a coalition is *connected* in the sense that the members are adjacent on a one-dimensional ideological ordering and it is *minimal* in the sense that the coalition could

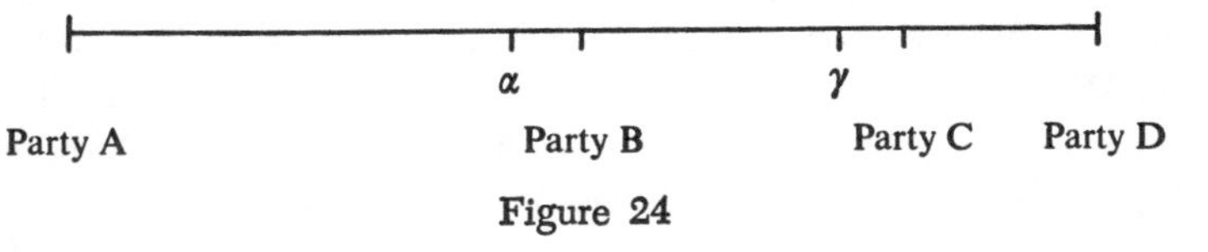

Figure 24

lose no member without ceasing to be both connected and winning.) As can be seen from table 2, this hypothesis performs impressively well in general and in particular does well in two of the countries, Finland and Italy, where the earlier predictions fared badly. If proof were needed, this would demonstrate clearly enough the importance of ideological position in coalition formation.

And finally, in the third place, the difficulty of deriving determinate predictions may in itself shed some light on the process of coalition formation. As I have suggested before, if matters are difficult for the sociologist, they may be difficult for the ordinary members of society too. Situations where complicated trade-offs are required between principles and power will doubtless be ones where internecine conflicts within the parties are most likely and where the outcomes will most depend on 'chance' factors such as the absence of a principal figure, giving his opponents opportunity to organize. Indeed, given the prevalence of such factors, one may suppose that the theories tested have performed uncommonly well. At least they have shown that there is more to politics than chance alone.

13. Rights, deserts and need

We now move a second time from the rational choice theories of exchange to the sociology and psychology of exchange. As we saw in chapter 5, a major emphasis of the exchange theorists is on comparison processes. Thibaut and Kelley pointed out that men's satisfaction or sense of grievance depends not simply on the *absolute* quantity of rewards – of praise or money – that they get but on the *relative* amounts. On this view a crucial question which men ask themselves is whether they are getting as much as other people like themselves are getting or as they themselves got in the past. Relativities become a central issue.

It is only a short step from this to questions of justice and fairness, and as we saw, it is a step that Homans makes. The question now becomes not so much 'Did I get as much as I *expected* to given the amounts which other people like me are getting?' but 'Did I get as much as I *ought* to have got?' As Homans puts it, 'when two men are in a social, or exchange, relation with each other, each is both giving reward to the other and receiving reward from him, and the question for each man then becomes: Did he get as much reward from the other, less the cost to himself in getting that reward, as he had the *right* to expect? And did the others get from him, at a certain cost to the other, no more reward than he had the *right* to expect?' (Homans, 1961, p. 74; my emphases).

This concern with rights (and duties), with justice and fairness, pervades much of exchange theory from Mauss to the present day, and of course they are some of the central concerns not only of exchange theory and of sociology but of intellectual discourse in general. The omission of justice would thus be the omission of one of the most distinctive and salient features of human life. A theory of rational egoists may suit the economists' purposes well enough – I am not qualified to judge its success in that field – but it does not look too convincing to the sociologist. As Rawls has suggested: 'a person who lacks a sense of justice, and who would never act as justice requires except as self-interest and expendiency prompt, not only is without ties of friendship, affection, and mutual trust, but is incapable of experiencing resentment and indignation. . . . [He] lacks certain fundamental attitudes and capacities included under the notion of humanity' (Rawls, 1972, p. 488). The sociologist does well, therefore, it would seem, to broaden his model of man to include these 'fundamental attitudes and capacities'.

Homans' decision to include a sense of justice in his model of man cannot, therefore, be faulted. The precise conception of justice that is to be included, however, will surely be a much more contentious matter. There has for centuries been (unresolved) argument among philosophers about the meaning of justice, and it would surely be surprising if this dissensus were not repeated among ordinary men and women too. If there were universal agreement among our respondents on the standards of justice that should be followed it would be the most remarkable piece of good fortune for the sociologist. It is not, I think, one which we should expect.

Our exchange theorists, however, exhibit remarkably little awareness of the likelihood of dissensus. Blau talks of the norm of reciprocity and the norm of fair exchange as if they were cultural universals about which there was no room for argument. For Blau, the norm of reciprocity is 'a basic principle underlying the conception of exchange' (1964, p. 89), while notions of fairness or justice are merely 'common norms . . . that stipulate fair rates of exchange between social benefits and the returns individuals deserve for the investments made to produce these benefits' (p. 155).

To be fair, Blau is the least sophisticated of our writers in this respect. Homans, for example, does allow that there may be some problems. Though both men in an exchange relationship will make comparisons, says Homans, 'there is no guarantee that they make it in the same way, that each appraises the rewards, costs, and investments

– both his own and the other's – on something like a scale of values identical with that of the other. Person may feel that distributive justice has been done when Other does not. Other, for instance, may appraise his costs in time lost from doing his own work at a higher value than Person does, and so feel angry that Person is exploiting him, while Person remains unconscious of any guilt' (Homans, 1961, p. 76). Nevertheless, even Homans sees the disagreement to be limited to the estimation of the rewards, costs and investments involved. The general rule itself – the rule that rewards should be proportional to costs and net reward, or profits, to investments – is not made a matter of serious dispute. Indeed, he goes so far as to claim that 'men are alike in holding the notion of proportionality between investment and profit that lies at the heart of distributive justice. The trouble is that they differ in their ideas of what legitimately constitutes investment, reward, and cost' (p. 246). Homans' man thus seems to inhabit a world where there is little in the way of philosophical dispute about the general meaning or conception of justice but where discussion has progressed to (or perhaps never got beyond) questions of whether, for example, responsibility is to be counted as a reward or a cost. Perhaps this world is also the world of ordinary men and women in Britain and America today, but it is not something that I would wish to take for granted at the moment.

The matter is not so very different when we turn to writers like Sahlins. True, Sahlins allows for a range of different principles, namely those of negative, balanced and generalized reciprocity, but even these are not really competing principles, at least in Sahlins' eyes. He does not seem to be arguing that some people organize their transactions along the lines of balanced reciprocity while others hold that, say, generalized reciprocity is the appropriate mode. Rather, he is arguing that, in primitive societies at least, generalized reciprocity is the rule among or in dealings with close kin, balanced reciprocity with fellow members of one's tribe or clan, and negative reciprocity with strangers or enemies. They are thus claimed to be principles which are employed in different contexts, not ones which are arguably appropriate to identical circumstances.

If we look at philosophical writings, however, as I think we should, we find a very different picture. We do not find different principles merely suggested for different circumstances but also a vigorous competition between different principles of justice themselves. True, sociologists and philosophers are engaged in somewhat different enterprises; broadly speaking, philosophers are trying to adjudicate on the proper meaning of justice whereas the sociologist is trying to discover what are the conceptions of justice held by lay members of society. He is not, in the way that the philosopher is, attempting to decide whether these conceptions are coherent or acceptable as they stand. He is simply trying to find out what they are. Nevertheless the starting-point of a great deal of philosophy, most notably of course, ordinary language philosophy, is with the more sociological question of what concepts such as justice mean in ordinary, everyday usage. The philosopher's methods of investigation are admittedly very different from those which the sociologist might use. Typically he does not go into the field and obtain samples of ordinary people's speech for linguistic analysis but prefers to stay at home and rely on his commonsense knowledge of the English language and its usage. Doutbless this will yield only an understanding of the way in which the upper classes conceive of justice, but even this will be something to be starting with. The data are ones which the sociologist should not despise.

Now it would be quite wrong to give the impression that philosophers are anything like agreed on the different meanings of justice which they have isolated. Nevertheless, there do seem to be three main usages which they have isolated. These are, first, justice as respect for the established *rights* of others; second, justice as the distribution of benefits according to *deserts;* and third, justice as the distribution of benefits according to *need.* These, I would argue, are quite distinct conceptions of justice (following Miller, 1974, on whom I largely rely). They are conceptions which are frequently in conflict with one another and thus have conflicting implications for behaviour. And yet all three are conceptions which are widely held by the very same people. The real world, I suggest, so far from exhibiting the extraordinary consensus of the sociologist, is more correctly characterized by dissensus and doubt.

First of all, however, let us examine the three conceptions of justice to which I have just referred. All involve rather tricky problems of definition and one has to tread carefully. The problem is particularly acute because we often use the three terms to refer to a general moral or normative entitlement as well as to specific kinds of moral claim. Thus we sometimes say that someone has a right to something, or that he deserves it, or that he needs it when all we wish to say is that he has some kind of moral claim upon it. We use the terms simply as synonyms for 'ought'. But at other times we use them to indicate *different* kinds of moral claim, and by saying that someone *deserves* a benefit we wish to indicate a different kind of claim from that implied when we say that he *needs* it. It is with this kind of specific claim that we are concerned here.

Let us begin, with rights. The classic case occurs when an explicit promise is made. If I promise to perform a favour for a neighbour – perhaps promising to feed his cat when he is away one weekend – then most people would agree that it makes sense to say that I now have a duty, by virtue of that promise, to feed the cat and that my neighbour accordingly has the right that I should do so. If I fail to turn up with the cat-food, perhaps because it is raining and I cannot face going out, my neighbour will justifiably feel angry. My verbal promise has given him a legitimate expectation that he would return to find his cat well fed and he will have a legitimate sense of grievance if it is not.

This is a fairly clear-cut case, and there would be few people, I suspect, who would deny that promises create rights. However, rights may also be created without explicit verbal promises being made. The man in the Kula ring who makes a gift of soulava to his guest surely bids him goodbye with a legitimate expectation of a return of mwali in due course. No words or promises need be uttered to this effect. But both parties know what the rules of the Kula are and know that a man who accepts a gift thereby incurs an obligation to make a return. To accept the gift is an unspoken, but perfectly understood, acceptance of the obligation to make a return. More generally, we can see that the existence of rights depends on the existence of a body of law or of agreed rules. To discover what the rights are we have to carry out an empirical enquiry to discover what rules are maintained in the society in question. We have to discover where the society stands on the law of contract, the morality of social exchange, and so on. If there is no norm of reciprocity, then we can accept gifts with impunity and failure to reciprocate cannot on this score be accounted unjust; but if there is one, acceptance of a gift creates rights and duties and justice will demand that they be upheld.

Consider, next, desert. This is more a matter of giving people what their own personal behaviour or personal qualities merit. Thus suppose that, when I go to feed my neighbours' cat, I find that it has just come off worst in a fight and has a badly lacerated ear. I therefore decide, let us say, to take it along to the vet and as a result spend the morning sitting in a waiting room when I would much rather have spent it at home. It now makes very good sense to say that I *deserve* some special thanks or gratitude from my neighbour. My special efforts on his behalf deserve a recompense. It would not, however, make quite such good sense to say that I have a *right* to a recompense, at least not according to the definition of rights that I have given. After all, it was my own free choice to take the cat along to the vet. I was not obliged to do so and nothing that my neighbour had said compelled me to. Indeed, he may have preferred that the cat be left untreated since he did not trust the skill of the local vet to whom I had taken it.

The crucial point, then, is that it is my special kindness which deserves a return. As Miller puts it: 'Desert is a matter of fitting forms of treatment to the specific qualities and actions of individuals and in particular good desert (i.e. deserving benefit as opposed to punishment) is a matter of fitting desired forms of treatment to qualities and action which are generally held in high regard' (Miller, 1974, p. 114). Of course, what is 'held in high regard' may vary from society to society or even from individual to individual. Few, I suspect, would deny that *voluntary* actions on another's behalf meet the criterion, but there would be much more dispute when innate or ascribed characteristics such as birth or rank are held to deserve returns. And as we see that more and more attributes, desirable and undesirable, are determined by our genes or our environment, so the criterion of desert is likely to lose its justificatory power.

Finally, we come to the principle of need, and this at first seems straightforward enough. Thus we might well have said that, although my neighbour had no right to expect it, it was certainly just that I should have his cat treated. If so, we would have been employing the principle of need. The cat needs treatment and it is only just that I, being the only person in a position to see that he gets it, should take it upon myself to go to the vet. (True, we may not wish to extend the principle of justice to our dealings with animals and may prefer to restrict it to dealings with their owners. But nothing hangs on the distinction in this particular case.)

It can easily be seen that need, rather like desert, relates to the personal qualities or situation of the individual in question. In the one case I deserved a recompense by virtue of personal kindness; in the other the cat needs treatment by virtue of its personal plight. The crucial difference between the two cases, however, is that desert relates to desirable and admirable qualities while need relates to some lack or deprivation. To quote Miller again: 'No one wishes to have [needs] or admires others for having them' (Miller, 1974, p. 116).

However, while it is clear enough that a need is some kind of lack, it is much less clear precisely what is to count as a need. Clearly, not all things that we lack are needs. If my house lacks a toilet, few would dispute my need. If it lacks a garage, many would. And if it lacks gold-plated taps, everybody would. What I would suggest, therefore, is that a need is some lack which must be made good before someone is able to be a fully participating member of society, able to exercise his rights and perform his duties satisfactorily. This, I think, takes care of the major needs which we recognize, namely those of health and education, housing and income. Thus, the man who can barely read or write or who has a large family on a low income may be in no position to perform his obligations as a parent; the man who is disabled or homeless is in no position to exercise his rights as a citizen. This formulation also takes care of the fact that needs change over time. As society becomes more complex, so, for example, does literacy become more important and its absence a greater handicap. The Trobriand Islander can perform his obligations in the Kula ring without the ability to read and write. But how can the illiterate Englishman send presents to his kin at Christmas?

These, then, are the main principles of justice which can be distinguished. As they stand, they are not of course inconsistent. I can quite properly subscribe to all three at once, holding that my promise gave my neighbour rights, that his cat needed help, and that my special kindness deserved some recognition. But when it comes to particular cases, I will be fortunate indeed if I am not faced with a dilemma. Thus I may quite properly hold that a workman deserves to lose his job, since he was caught pilfering from his workmates. But I may also hold that he ought to be allowed to keep his job since he has a large family to support. Again, I may hold that my colleague has a right to my help, since I promised it to him, but I may feel that he does not deserve it since he himself has never helped anyone else.

In a particular situation, then, the three principles may give quite different answers. Considerations of desert may lead me one way and of need another (and self-interest perhaps in yet a third). The principles thus compete in the sense that I cannot in practice follow them all simultaneously. I must either decide which one is to have priority or more sensibly, I must weigh one principle against another. I must consider how much importance I attach to the needs of the man in question and balance this against the man's deserts. That I will make these trade-offs in a way identical to how other people make them is hardly to be expected.

We are now in a position to return to the sociological discussions of justice. We can see, first of all, that each of the three principles figures prominently in the literature. Thus Mauss, in his discussion of the morality of the total prestation or of the gift is principally engaged in documenting the rules which accord rights and duties to the participants. Not once in *The Gift* does he mention desert or related concepts. Scarcely ever does he mention need. The obligation to give is not, as Mauss describes it, an obligation to give to those in need but an obligation to give to those (such as Kula partners) who stand in specified relationships to the giver. Nor is the obligation to make a return an obligation to give to people the return they deserve for their earlier contributions. These ways of describing the obligations are quite foreign to Mauss (and, I suspect, to the peoples with whom he is concerned). The language which he uses is much more that of the law of contract. Indeed, contract is one of his most commonly used words. The obligations to give, to receive, and to return constitute a 'form of contract', and there is thus 'a series of rights and duties about consuming and repaying existing side by side with rights and duties about giving and receiving' (Mauss, 1925, p. 11).

With Homans and Blau the situation is quite different. Their conception of 'distributive justice' or of 'fair exchange' is much more akin to the principle of desert. When Homans talks of the proportionality of rewards, costs and investments it is hard not to see in costs and investments the 'qualities and actions' that deserve a return. And when he distinguishes between 'good costs' and 'bad costs' it is hard not to see the distinction between those personal qualities which are admirable (and hence deserving of a reward) and those which are not. Thus the fact that Homans' ledger clerks incurred the 'good costs' of doing responsible work entitled them, in their own eyes at least, to extra rewards; the fact that the cash posters incurred the 'bad' costs of boring work did not. Whatever Homans' personal morality may happen to be, he certainly seems to see around him the morality of desert.

Finally, there can be little doubt that Sahlins' category of generalized reciprocity involves the principle of need (although, as Sahlins describes it, it can hardly be regarded as a pure type). When he says that 'the time and worth of reciprocation are not alone conditional on what was given by the donor, but also upon what he will need and when, and likewise what the recipient can afford and when' (Sahlins, 1965, p. 147), he puts the matter beyond doubt.

Nor can there be much doubt that all three conceptions of social justice are widely held in our own society. I do not in fact know of any systematic evidence that promises create legitimate expectations, but it is hardly likely to be the kind of contentious issue that warrants serious sociological investigation. There is, moreover, plenty of evidence that a request for a favour creates an obligation to make a return, that the obligation is greater if the person 'went out of his way' to do the favour, and that we should volunteer favours unasked to those who are in need of them (Muir and Weinstein, 1962; Heath, 1974a). Nor are these merely empty platitudes to which we happily pay lip-service but which we speedily abandon when there is any conflict with our personal self-interest. There is plenty of experimental evidence that, in minor matters at least, people are prepared to act upon these principles of justice. Thus in one notable study Adams and Jacobsen hired students to proofread galley pages and exposed them to three different conditions of inequity. They led some of the students to believe that they were unqualified to earn the standard proofreaders' rate of thirty cents per page but told them that they were nevertheless going to be paid at that rate. They led a second set of students to believe that they too were unqualified to earn the standard rate but told them that they were therefore to be paid at the lesser rate of twenty cents per page. And they led a third set to believe that they actually *were* qualified to get the thirty cents and they duly paid them that amount. The first group thus presumably believed that they were being paid more than they deserved while the other two groups believed that their rewards were in line with their deserts. The result of the experiment was then as follows. Instead of going on their way rejoicing (as one might have expected of rational egoists), the first group actually worked harder and produced better-quality work than did either of the other two groups. They increased their contributions so that their rewards were brought more into line with their deserts (Adams and Jacobsen, 1964).

Rather more surprising, perhaps, have been the results of experiments on helping behaviour. In one American experiment on the New York subway – hardly a propitious place to expect assistance when in need – a stooge pretended to collapse in the carriage shortly after the train had left the station. In some cases the stooge appeared sober and carried a black cane (the cane condition); in others he smelled of liquor and carried a liquor bottle wrapped tightly in a brown bag (the drunk condition). Two confederates were of course on hand to watch the reactions of bystanders. They saw that help came quickly under the cane condition. In 59 of the 65 trials help was voluntarily offered by one of the fellow passengers (and often by several) within seventy seconds of the original incident. Even under the drunk condition the stooge received spontaneous help on 19 of the 38 trials (although it was rather slower in coming). Moreover, when help was slow in forthcoming, many of the passengers showed the signs of people troubled by their consciences. Many women, for example, made comments such as 'It's for men to help him' or 'I wish I could help him – I'm not strong enough', 'I never saw this kind of thing before – I don't know where to look', 'You feel so bad that you don't know what to do.' True, we do not know the precise motives of those who did go to help the victim, but the responsibility to help those in need is surely the likeliest candidate (Piliavin et al., 1969).

The interesting question, therefore, is not whether people are in general willing to assent to these three principles of justice or even sometimes to act upon them. Instead, the interesting questions arise when there is a conflict between expediency and justice or between the different principles of justice themselves. Do claims of need take priority over the claims of desert, or must one principle be traded off against another? If they must be traded, what is the rate of exchange (or, more technically, the marginal rate of substitution)?

It would be surprising in the extreme if any simple answers could be given to these questions. Nevertheless, some headway can be made.

First of all, taking Sahlins' lead (although slightly modifying his position), we might reasonably suggest that considerations of expediency receive greatest weight in dealings with the 'out-group', that is with strangers or aliens, and that considerations of justice receive more weight in dealings with the 'in-group', that is with kin, friends or compatriots. As in simpler societies our morality tends to be context-specific. We may have extended our notion of what constitutes the in-group, but we are still far from realizing a 'universal brotherhood of man' in which justice governs all our dealings. 'Charity begins at home' is not merely a prescription of what we ought to do; it is also a description of common practice around the world.

However, while most societies seem to be alike in discriminating between members of the in-group and of the out-group, between family members and non-family members, and so on, there also seem to be substantial differences *between* societies and cultures in their application of the different principles of justice. Thus Miller has suggested, very plausibly, that a concern with rights will be greatest in a traditional or feudal society where there is little possibility of social mobility and little concern with individual autonomy or independence. The principle of respect for established rights is the most conservative of our principles of justice and flourishes accordingly. Criteria of desert, on the other hand, will tend to flourish 'in a liberal society where people are regarded as rational independent atoms held together in a society by a "social contract" from which all must benefit' (Barry, 1965, p. 112). It is no accident that it is the American writers and students of American society who have been the main advocates of a desert-oriented principle of distributive justice. In an open, mobile society where individual success depends, at least partly, on competition in a free labour market, desert offers the most fruitful source of legitimation to those who have succeeded. Success can be ascribed to effort and ability, and failure to incompetence and laziness. Both can accordingly be justified. To be sure, this is not to say that the workings of a free labour market will inevitably ensure that rewards will be proportional to deserts. Exogenous factors over which a man has no control – a poor harvest, a technical advance which makes his skills redundant, an act of God – may prevent him from realizing his just deserts. Indeed, it is tempting to suggest (although I know of no relevant evidence) that the more common are such acts of God the less popular the criterion of desert will prove to be. It would follow from this that the greater the *justificatory* potential of distributive justice, the less its *explanatory* potential (since men's rewards can straightforwardly be explained in market terms without any recourse to principles of justice). Conversely, the greater its explanatory potential (where the workings of the market and of justice are most at variance with each other), the less compelling will the participants themselves find it.

Finally, if the maintenance of existing rights is the most conservative form of justice, distribution according to need is the most radical. If the criterion of desert serves to justify inequalities of outcome, the criterion of need is equally redistributive in its implications. We would not, accordingly, expect it to flourish in inegalitarian or even in market societies. It will prove most popular, I suggest, in places like the family where each member in turn passes through periods or situations of need; it will prove least popular among privileged groups which are able to protect themselves from the vicissitudes of fortune. Indeed, there is some sketchy evidence that the criterion of need flourishes more in working-class communities (where, for example, the threat of unemployment is more indiscriminate in its victims) than in the more secure and ordered middle-class communities.

14. Gifts, favours and donations

The different principles of justice by no means exhaust the morality of social exchange. As we saw earlier, Mauss describes an obligation to give and to receive as well as an obligation to return; Blau emphasizes a proscription on bargaining as well as a norm of reciprocity; and both deal with the status implications of unequal exchange. These different phenomena, we may suspect, will prove to be no more universal than Homans' rule of distributive justice. The gift is no unitary institution.

The differences *within* social exchange (as well as the differences *between* social and economic exchange) have of course been clearly enough recognized by the anthropologists. Mauss drew his distinction between the total prestation and gift exchange (although he seemed to see them as occurring in different types of society rather than as coexisting in one and the same society); Malinowski and Sahlins have drawn their continua ranging, in Malinowski's case, from the pure gift to trade and, in Sahlins', from negative to generalized reciprocity. And similar distinctions could doubtless be drawn within our own society too. Beginning with Titmuss' free gift which constitutes a 'form of creative altruism' we could trace a continuum culminating in self-interested market transactions, coercion or even theft.

I am not convinced, however, that the construction of such continua is our best strategy. They have come in for considerable criticism from anthropologists, largely on the grounds that their underlying dimensions (usually those of motivation or 'sidedness') are hard to establish if not factually incorrect. I suggest that we start instead, as in the previous chapter, with the distinctions made in ordinary speech and that we attempt to elucidate the meanings and institutions associated with each rather than the degree of altruism or self-interest involved. Ordinary speech, moreover, yields us some distinctive categories with easily recognizable differences in meaning. Thus we have different words to describe a present, a favour, a donation, a bribe, an offering, alms, a bequest, and no doubt more. And it is clear enough that, for example, the paradigm of an offering is a gift to the church, that alms are given to the poor, a bequest in one's will, a donation to charity, and a present at Christmas. The term 'gift' itself is equally clearly a generic one, as recourse to the Oxford English Dictionary will show. Almost all the words in our list can be defined, and are so by the OED, as gifts. Interestingly, the term 'gift' itself is defined as 'The thing given. 1. Something, the property in which is voluntarily transferred to another without the expectation of an equivalent.' The editors of OED thus seem to accept Mauss's dictum that the gift is 'in theory voluntary, disinterested, and spontaneous' but they lack the sociological sophistication to suspect that it is in practice 'obligatory and interested'. What I propose to do in this chapter, therefore, is to move on from the dictionary definitions to consider the nature of the obligations involved in some of the main classes of gift. I shall begin with presents and then move on to favours and donations. These three categories are not of course exhaustive, but they cover, I suggest, the most frequent forms of social exchange in our own society.

The present: a modern total prestation

Broadly speaking, we can distinguish two different kinds of present (doubtless with mixed cases in between). Thus on the one hand there is the 'institutionalized' present given at Christmas, birthdays or weddings; on the other there is the 'unexpected' present given on no set occasion but purely at the discretion of the donor. The distinction between the two types lies, of course, in the obligation to give. The wedding present or the Christmas present, like Mauss's total prestation, is obligatory. They must be given on well-known ritual occasions and, particularly in the case of the wedding present, by a clearly specified set of people: all guests who are invited are expected to bring a present, however small, and failure to do so would be regarded as a signal lapse in good manners.

Moreover, with presents, whether institutionalized or not, the obligation to receive is equally clear. Indeed, in one piece of research this turned out to be the strongest of all the obligations connected with gift-exchange, far overshadowing the norm of reciprocity (Heath, 1974a). Indeed, in the case of presents the norm of reciprocity slips into the background. This again is clearest in the case of weddings: the bride and the groom must write their 'thank you letters' but they certainly make no return of equivalent value. True, they in their turn will be expected to give presents at their friends' weddings, but this is not regarded by the participants themselves as a reciprocation. It is not the norm of reciprocity which requires them to 'return' wedding presents to their friends but the demands of the original obligation to give. Similarly the bride's father might be said by the sociologist to reciprocate when he provides food and drink at the reception, but I doubt if lay members of the society would describe it as such. Instead they would surely say that the bride's father is expected to provide the reception as his part of the proceedings. He too is obliged to give. If this produces an actual pattern of reciprocity or exchange, then that is an interesting consequence of the institutions surrounding the wedding: it is not the consequence of the norm of reciprocity. We must not make the (common) error of supposing that all examples of reciprocity in social life can be ascribed to the *norm* of reciprocity. For a norm to exist it must, by definition, be socially recognized and sanctioned by the participants themselves; patterns of reciprocity in contrast can easily be unintended and unrecognized (as in the case of cross-cousin marriage).

Despite the unimportance of the norm of reciprocity, then, the institutionalized present is much like the total prestation in its emphasis on the obligations to give and to receive. As with the total prestation, too, the morality seems to be that of rights and obligations, rather than of desert or need. Thus we would be very critical of the parent who failed to give his child a present at Christmas 'because he did not deserve one'. Desert is not a relevant consideration. Conversely, we still make every effort to find a present 'for the man who has everything'. That he does not need one is not a relevant consideration either.

There are other interesting parallels with the total prestation, too. Typically, the objects given will be material ones, often luxuries, possibly money, but never services. They will be given and received, as often as not, by groups, 'moral persons': thus at weddings the presents are given by families or couples, and the bride and groom are joint recipients. The presents, too, have values which are 'emotional as well as material': while the present is frequently a 'useful' object, it is also a symbol of friendship and affection. True, the symbolic aspect is most emphasized in the spontaneous gift, but I doubt if it ever entirely loses its symbolic significance even in the most ritualized forms. Correspondingly, to accept a present is thus to accept friendship and to refuse one is to reject it. As in the situation that Lévi-Strauss describes when two customers at the same table in a cheap restaurant exchange their wine: 'The little bottle may contain exactly one glassful, yet the contents will be poured out, not into the owner's glass, but into his neighbour's. And his neighbour will immediately make a corresponding gesture of reciprocity. . . . [This] substitutes a social relationship for spatial juxtaposition. But it is also more than that. The partner who was entitled to maintain his reserve is persuaded to give it up. Wine offered calls for wine returned, cordiality requires cordiality. The relationship of indifference can never be restored once it has been ended by one of the table-companions. From now on the relationship can only be cordial or hostile' (Lévi-Strauss, 1949, pp. 58–9).

Again, Mauss's account still holds true in that 'the form usually taken is that of the gift generously offered'. The solemnity which Mauss and Malinowski noted is paralleled in the care with which we wrap our presents in distinctive and colourful paper. Overt bargaining is equally proscribed, although it is worth noting that we often ask people directly what they would like for 'their' presents, while we also sometimes let it be known what we ourselves would like (most noticeably with wedding lists). Perhaps it betrays our more materialistic attitude, but when large sums of money are to be spent on presents we are not quite so willing to leave the nature of the gift wholly to the discretion of the donor.

But even if there are numerous parallels with Mauss, there are also important points of divergence (whether because our modern presents are different from simpler societies' prestations, or because Mauss's account of the latter was itself inaccurate, I hesitate to assert). First, I am doubtful that the accompanying behaviour always is 'formal pretence and social deception'. I would not deny that deception will sometimes be present, and no doubt pretence and deception reach their acme in the business gift (see Shurmer, 1971), but I cannot believe that we can generalize so boldly about our own society as Mauss did about simpler ones. A common institution, we should note, will tolerate many different forms of individual motivation and meaning: the cynical 'golden handshake' is not the only possibility. Sometimes, *pace* sociologists, things really are what they seem.

There is, however, a second and more important respect in which I would wish to diverge from Mauss's account. This concerns the role of status and honour. Mauss and his successors have argued unambiguously that face is lost for ever if a worthy return is not made while an excessive return establishes a counter-claim to superiority. Lévi-Strauss indeed goes so far as to argue that 'The exchange of gifts at Christmas, for a month each year, practised by all social classes with a sort of sacred ardour, is nothing other than a gigantic *potlatch*, implicating millions of individuals, and at the end of which many family budgets are faced with lasting disequilibrium' (Lévi-Strauss, 1949, p. 56).

Now I do not doubt that many people overspend at Christmas (as some of us do throughout the rest of the year as well). But the parallel between Christmas and the potlatch seems to me far-fetched in the extreme. In our own society status is largely determined by one's role in the occupational system or by one's birth. There is simply no room for competititve gift-giving to determine status as it may (or may not) have done among the Kwakiutl Indians. A man's prowess in the Christmas present 'competition' will scarcely be known outside his own immediate circle of family and friends. There is nothing of the public character of the potlatch that is essential for status (as customarily defined) to be concerned. At the very most the size of one's present will affect one's standing and reputation within a small circle of intimates.

Perhaps this is all that Lévi-Strauss has in mind, but there is also evidence that competitive giving is actually proscribed in our own society (just as, of course, it may have been among the Kwakiutl). Thus in one study which I carried out the great majority of my respondents agreed that one definitely should not give bigger presents than one received and many of them reported that, when they found they had given bigger presents they would feel 'embarrassed' or 'annoyed – especially if it happens more than once'. Very few gave any indication that their 'success' in giving more than they received had made them feel in any way superior (Heath, 1974a). It is my contention, then, that most people subscribe to the norm that presents between equals should be balanced, over-generosity as much as under-generosity being a matter for censure and embarrassment. Moreover, this embarrassment or censure is much like that experienced when any other social norm is broken and has nothing to do with status. Status, as I understand it, is a relatively *permanent* attribute of an individual (or more strictly of his relationship with others) whereas the infraction of a norm usually leads to no more than a transitory disgrace. One is no doubt vulnerable to this kind of disgrace whenever one ventures to engage in social transactions, but we should not suppose that our status is at stake in the way in which it might have been for the Kwakiutl Indian.

Favours are in many respects radically different from presents. Thus they are almost invariably services rather than material objects, and they are usually services which meet a practical need rather than representing a symbolic value. Nor are there set institutionalized occasions when favours must be given; the timing is more a matter for the participants' discretion. Nor are the participants usually groups; if I do you a favour, I do so on my own behalf and not on behalf of some wider group.

If the present, then, resembles Mauss's total prestation, we might expect the favour to correspond to Blau's concept of social exchange, and I think it is true that his paradigm cases of social exchange – the exchanges of advice in a work group – fall clearly within the category of favours. As we saw earlier, then, the primary norms which we must look for are the norm of reciprocity and the proscription on bargaining. Unfortunately, as so often, we lack the systematic evidence needed to provide a compelling test of these claims. Still, we find that there is almost complete consensus concerning requests for reciprocation. Muir and Weinstein asked their subjects, 'Do you eventually *ask* for a return favour from someone like this (who never repays, although he can)?' and over 90 per cent of their subjects replied that they would not (Muir and Weinstein, 1962). Now if people are unwilling even to ask for a return I am inclined to think that, *a fortiori*, they will hardly be willing to bargain about what that return will be. Here, then, I think we should uphold Blau (although as I remarked earlier I would not be willing to generalize from the favours exchanged by neighbours to those of politicians or businessmen).

With the norm of reciprocity, however, the situation is pleasantly clear and relies little on inference or guesswork. Whatever its application to presents, there can be little doubt that the norm of reciprocity applies to favours. A majority of Muir and Weinstein's subjects were 'more willing to do favours "in return", that is when you owe someone'. Similarly, a majority of my own subjects felt that one should 'preferably' return a favour (although few were prepared to state that one 'definitely' should). There is also the interesting, and widely found, result that the norm of reciprocity applies more forcefully if one actually asked for the original favour in the first place. Thus Bell found that one of his middle-class subjects who was in need of money preferred not to ask his father-in-law outright for the cash. Instead he simply explained his needs to his father-in-law and hoped that he would then do the decent thing. As Bell explains: 'This illustration also shows that the recipient felt less obligation for accepting aid since he did not ask for it; also it illustrates a recurrent mechanism. The money was not asked for, the case was stated and the action was left to the parent. In this way there seems to be at least a partial resolve of the conflict between the stress on independence and actual dependence' (Bell, 1968, p. 92). It thus seems to be the case that the man who volunteers a favour does not have the same right to a return as the man who was asked. The former does so 'of his own free choice' whereas the latter is in a sense coerced (coerced in the sense which we used in chapter 3); he was obliged to perform the favour and is accordingly entitled to a return.

I very much doubt, however, if rights are all that are involved. As I mentioned in the last chapter, Blau seems to see social exchange as governed by the morality of desert, and accordingly the person who volunteers a favour may be felt to deserve some recompense. After all, 'one good turn deserves another' and, if more cogent evidence than our proverb is required, Muir and Weinstein's subjects were also agreed that they felt more obligated than usual if someone 'goes out of his way to do you a favour'; apparently the greater a man's costs, the greater the return which he deserves.

I would, then, wish to distinguish between the rights which the norm of reciprocity may give us and the deserts which our good deeds may entitle us to. Both, I suggest, may be relevant to favours. I would also wish to suggest that considerations of need may be appropriate too. Thus, for example, Latané and Darley found that a request for a dime (accompanied by no explanation) tended to be met with a refusal (although not quite so often as one might have expected). But an explanation of one's need increased one's chances considerably: 'Excuse me, I wonder if you could give me a dime? I need to make a telephone call' raised the chances of getting one from 0.34 to 0.64. And 'Excuse me, I wonder if you could give me a dime? My wallet has been stolen' raised it to 0.72 (Latané and Darley, 1970).

If the institutionalized present, then, is a relatively clear-cut and well-understood institution, the favour partakes of all the dissensus and uncertainty that we might expect of modern morality. Considerations of rights, deserts and needs are all present. This should hardly surprise us, if only because the favour is not institutionalized in the way that the present is. There are no set occasions like Christmas and weddings when specified categories of participants must perform favours for each other; favours can hardly be included in the category of ritual activities with known procedures. Rather they are practical activities performed at the individual's discretion for individual purposes. With favours, therefore, there is much more scope for choice and hence for personal preferences, and much less scope for social norms, in our explanations.

If this is true, then it gives us yet another reason (in addition to the ones above which apply just as forcibly to favours as to presents) for supposing that status will not be closely associated with imbalanced exchanges of favours. If there is less agreement as to the criteria which govern the return, there must also be less scope for any generally recognized consequences for one's status to follow. Does a man lose status, or validate anothers' claim to superiority, simply because he has failed to make a return? But suppose his benefactor did not *need* a return. Can failure be held against him under these conditions? Should he perhaps have found something which his benefactor *did* need? Or suppose a man's return is in line with the other's deserts but not his needs. Does that count as a balanced return, leaving their status equal? Or has he in some sense failed to make a proper return?

As I suggested earlier, there is likely to be no clear agreement on the answers and hence little basis for social ranking. This of course is not to say that people will refrain from finding fault or distributing blame or praise. It simply means that if we wish to find fault, there are always likely to be some grounds on which it can be done. And if we wish to justify our actions, this is not likely to prove too difficult either. Everyone can thus make claims to superiority, or at least equality; but few are likely to accede to others' claims.

The donation: a free gift?

The third main category of gift which I wish to look at is the donation. This, I think, is the least well understood of all. Even the definition is somewhat unclear. Titmuss seems to define it as a gift to an anonymous stranger, but many favours surely come into this category too, so this will hardly do. Nor is the OED very helpful: it defines the donation simply as 'that which is presented: a gift', which is scarcely illuminating. However, one of my own subjects defined it as 'a gift of money to an "organized" cause' and this probably comes closest to the everyday usage of the term. If the archetypal present is the gift of a material object to a friend or relative, if the archetypal favour is a service performed for a friend, neighbour, or even a stranger, then the archetypal donation is a gift of money to an organized charity. True, we may give our blood or our cast-off clothes, and we may give them to a known individual (although we might have to use here the more old-fashioned terms 'alms' or 'charity'), but there can be little doubt that a covenant to Oxfam, say, will count as a donation.

Now, if Titmuss is right, the donation is a 'free gift without any explicit right or expectation to a return'. *Legally,* this is certainly correct. A charity is under legal restrictions as to the purposes for which it can use its resourses and it cannot make any formal return which lies outside these purposes. If, for example, Oxfam began to pay for the clothes and other gifts which it receives, it might be held to be engaging in trade and hence would lose its charitable status. Still, there must be many charities or organized causes whose purposes are in fact the furtherance of potential donors' own ends. Donations by companies to the Conservative Party are not, one suspects, the results of sheer altruism in the way that blood donations may be. Even if the Conservative Party is most scrupulous when in office and shows no partiality in its allocation of building contracts and so on, its avowed policies will still be to help the corporate sector in general, and hence presumably the individual corporation as well. There will thus in practice be a pattern of reciprocity. As with presents, however, we must ask whether this reciprocity has anything to do with the *norm* of reciprocity and I am very doubtful that the answer would be affirmative. Admittedly, we cannot reach any firm conclusion without investigating the specific mores of the Tories and big business and, even if we did, I doubt if they would admit the existence of such a norm to the inquisitive sociologist. But even so I do not think that we need the norm to account for the pattern of reciprocity. It is quite intelligible on other grounds, namely those of naked self-interest.

In other cases, however, such as Titmuss' blood donors, the situation is much clearer. Thus the National Blood Transfusion Service has nothing that it can reciprocate apart from sweet tea. The decision whether to give blood or not to a particular patient is not made by the Service but by quite independent medical staff in the hospitals who have no knowledge of the patient's record of blood donations. Nor does there seem to be much in the way of an expectation of reciprocity. True, Titmuss does report that a 'substantial group of donors gave blood because they thought that in the future they or a member of their family might need it', but the answers which he gives to illustrate this claim do not seem to have much to do with the norm of reciprocity as it is conventionally understood. Thus: 'Someone in my family may one day need blood. I would like to think that someone will be there then, so I give mine knowing that some unknown person will be eternally grateful.' And 'I have a motor bike and someday I may need blood to help me, so why shouldn't I give mine to help someone who may have had an accident?' (Titmuss, 1970, p. 229).

These are not the comments of people giving blood in return for blood that they themselves have received, or even giving blood in order to get some themselves in future. Instead, they are following the morality of 'do as you would be done by', which is not the same thing at all.

So far this broadly supports Titmuss. As he suggested, the individual donor seems to have no explicit right to or expectation of a return.

But Titmuss was wrong to suppose that this makes the donation a 'free gift'. There are other obligations than those of reciprocity. While the recipient may not have to make a return, he is nevertheless not free to do with the donation whatever he pleases. It does not belong to him in quite the same way that goods purchased in a cash transaction are the buyer's. Instead, he must respect the donor's intentions and take care to use it for the purpose for which it was intended. Indeed, my research showed that this obligation to respect the donor's wishes was one of the strongest in the whole morality of gift-giving, applying most forcibly to donations and, to a lesser extent, to presents.

This obligation may be an important one with considerable explanatory significance. It might, at least in part, account for the differing efficiency of the British and American blood donor systems. As Titmuss points out, the British system, which relies on voluntary donations, wastes much less blood than the American ones, which rely on paid donors. A part of the explanation, I suggest, is this. A commercial enterprise, once it has bought the blood, is entitled to do with it what it likes. If it wastes the blood, and thus makes less profit, so much worse for the enterprise, but it is none of anybody else's business. But if an organization wastes what is donated to it and not paid for, then it *is* other people's business, witness the local outcry in the press when Oxfam dumped a quantity of shoes which it had been given (*Times*, 16 July 1969). Those responsible at first tried to justify the dumping on commercial grounds but their superiors quickly overruled them and admitted that the shoes should not have been thrown away whatever the strict conclusions of an economic cost-benefit analysis may have been. Similarly, I would guess, the discovery of unnecessary wastage within the British blood donor system would become a public scandal in the way that it never would in America. It would also have a much more serious effect on the future supply of blood donations than it would in the commercial American systems, and I would not be at all surprised if the British administrators were aware of this. The incentive on them to minimize wastage (and to maintain secrecy) is thus increased.

Let us now return to status and stigma. Here at last we may expect to find some support for the view that the unreciprocated gift leads to loss of status: that 'charity wounds' is not only one of the strongest dogmas of exchange theory but also of popular wisdom. Moreover, the individual who is 'on the dole' is in the kind of socially significant and recognized position that is necessary for status to become an issue. Still, even here, we must expect to find complications. Like most sayings and proverbs the claim that 'charity wounds' is grossly oversimplified. I am not aware, for example, that anyone has seriously suggested that the recipient of a blood transfusion, whether or not he reciprocates by becoming a donor, loses status on that account. Merely to be the recipient of a donation does not seem to be enough. Conversely, most writers seem convinced that the recipient of Supplementary Benefit feels demeaned and derogated whether or not he has in the past paid the taxes from which the Department of Health and Social Security derives its funds. Whether the exchange is balanced or not cannot therefore be the only consideration.

The puzzle may not, however, be a difficult one to solve. The difference between blood donations and supplementary benefits derives, I suggest, from our earlier distinctions between desert and need. That both patient and 'pauper' need support is not disputed, but it is only the 'undeserving poor' whose plight is believed to be their own fault who incur censure and derogation. Similarly we find that patients whose illness is their own fault, notably in the case of suicide attempts and vagrants, are more likely to be derogated by doctors and hospital staff. People who are believed to be responsible for their own misfortunes are the ones who are stigmatized in our society. It is this as much as (or indeed more than) their failure to reciprocate which is crucial. If 'charity wounds', it is because we live in a society that emphasizes the criterion of desert, not need. On this view stigma is not a cultural universal to be found wherever there is unequal exchange but a phenomenon that flourishes above all in the capitalist societies of the west.

15. *Social norms-final and efficient causes*

In this final chapter of criticism I want to look at various aspects of the theories of emergent processes that we met in chapter 7. It will be remembered that we met there a number of rather different theories which tried to do different things and tried to use different methods. There were the theories which looked at the origins of social norms and the way in which they came into being; there were the theories which looked at the consequences of social norms and their functions for individuals or for society as a whole; there were the theories which adopted a rational choice approach to these problems; and there were the theories which adopted various kinds of sociological approach. Rather than subject each of these theories in turn to detailed scrutiny (partly, I must confess, because I do not always have a great deal that is worth saying about them), I prefer to look at some of the main issues that arise with sociological and rational choice theories that tackle problems of this kind. I shall begin with problems in the rational choice approach.

Is it rational to conform?

The question of conformity to social norms is a relatively straightforward one with which to begin. As I have repeatedly emphasized, the fact that there is a social norm does not, according to the rational choice approach, automatically entail that it will be obeyed. Everyone has his price: the benefits of conformity must be compared with the benefits to be obtained elsewhere, and there is bound to be some level of alternative benefits that will successfully tempt the individual into deviance. How high this level has to be will of course depend on the size of the sanctions that are imposed on non-conformists (and on the level of guilt that transgression brings). Take the case of the prisoner's dilemma, for example. Suppose that there is a norm of honour among thieves and that sanctions will therefore be imposed on those who turn Queen's evidence. Will this turn the game into a cooperative one, or will the participants still end up by confessing? Clearly, the answer will depend on the size of the sanctions (ignoring, for the sake of simplicity, the level of guilt). If the prisoner is simply going to be ostracized and ignored by his former friends, he may not think this is a very high price to pay for the chance of getting off scot-free. More strictly, we can see that the sanctions will need to be at least equivalent (in terms of their disutility to the participants) to two years' imprisonment before it will become rational for the prisoners to stay silent. As can be seen from figure 25 sanctions equivalent to two years' imprisonment will leave the prisoner indifferent between confession and silence; the pay-offs from the two alternative courses of action are now identical. Anything less than two years will leave the situation effectively as it was before; the cooperative move will remain irrational, and rational self-interest will dictate confession just as it did before. And anything more than two years will finally tip the balance and make silence the rational course.

We can now reasonably infer, given our commonsense knowledge of people's values, that the sanctions for non-conformity are going to have to be rather extreme ones in the case of the prisoners' dilemma. A bit of censure or ostracism, even a beating-up, is not necessarily going to have much impact. The prisoners are not lightly to be turned away from their self-defeating course of action, and we cannot lightly agree with Blau that 'sanctions convert conduct that otherwise would

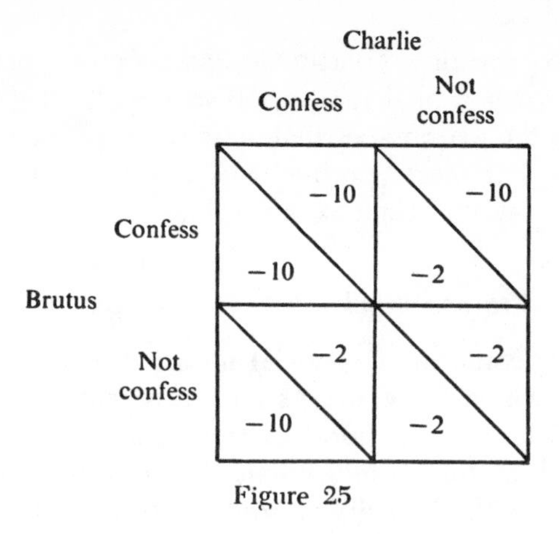

Figure 25

be irrational into a rational pursuit of self-interest' (1964, p. 258). It is not quite so easy to reorganize social life.

Is it rational to enforce norms?

Once the sanctions need to be at all large we run into the more serious problem of why anyone should bother to impose them. I happily assumed above that there was a norm of honour among thieves and that sanctions would be imposed on transgressors, but what is in it for the moral entrepreneur? The people who appear to benefit are the prisoners themselves, not the moral entrepreneur who imposes the sanctions. And even the benefit to the prisoners is somewhat illusory. By the time the sanctions come to be imposed the damage is done. The prisoners have already confessed and punishing them now cannot do anything to alter it. Bygones are bygones for the economic approach, and a confession is indubitably a bygone.

One possible line of defence to these problems is to say that the sanctions are imposed 'pour encourager les autres'. Our moral entrepreneur, like a good rational man, is looking ahead and is concerned to stop others infringing the norm in future. He imposes sanctions now in order to deter others from future transgressions. But in the first place we have to note that the costs of imposing the sanctions are immediate whereas the benefits occur in the possibly distant future. Now as a general rule economists assume that an immediate benefit is more valuable than an identical, but distant, one and that we must therefore discount the future benefits in order to get a fair comparison of their worth relative to the present costs. Accordingly the distant benefits gained from deterrence may dwindle into insignificance in comparison with the present costs. Secondly we should note that 'encouraging the others' only makes sense (from a self-interested point of view) if the moral entrepreneur hopes to deter others from transgressing *against himself* in future, that is if he expects to be caught at some time in the prisoners' dilemma himself. But if he himself is held in prison, the fact that he has sanctioned other people in the past does not on its own provide a cogent reason for his fellow prisoner to stay silent now or for any third party to come to his aid and threaten sanctions. So the distant benefits of moral entrepreneurship tend to evaporate as we get closer to them. Even if the potential moral entrepreneur expects to be caught at some time himself, he has nothing to gain by imposing sanctions on other people now.

This is by no means a full analysis of the problem but I think the general conclusion is warranted that moral entrepreneurship, if it occurs, must be altruistic or moralistic, not self-interested. The moral entrepreneur must be acting out of a desire to enforce norms for their own sake or out of a desire to help other people to achieve benefits. Such a motivation is by no means absurd (and can of course be fitted into a rational choice approach), but I would very much doubt whether motives of this kind would generally be sufficient to lead people into risky or dangerous courses of action. It is no accident that most large-scale societies have a body of *paid* moral entrepreneurs – the police – and do not rely on the voluntary altruism of the public for law enforcement.

So far we have been analysing the rather bizarre and unusual situation of the prisoners' dilemma, where the principal protagonists are held incommunicado by the authorities and are in no position to enforce norms for themselves. Clearly, we must ask whether the logic of the situation changes when this restrictive assumption is removed, and apparently it does. Two crucial conditions are needed to get our prisoners out of their impasse. First, neither must be allowed to make secret deals with the police; neither must be able to act without the other's knowledge. Second, decisions must not be simultaneous; either must be allowed to change his mind and alter his decision at any point. Under these conditions the two prisoners may find it rational to stay silent. For example, if Brutus decides to confess (being tempted by the prospect of getting off scot-free), Charlie will immediately counter by confessing likewise; in this way he reduces his spell of imprisonment from the ten years he gets when he is the only one to stay silent to the eight years that they both get when both confess. Confession, as before, is the rational thing to do. What is different in the present case, however, is that Brutus can work this out and can see that any move on his part will be matched by a move from Charlie. Moreover, he will always have (by definition) the chance to retaliate should Charlie make a move, so there is no need to make a pre-emptive strike. Each can stay silent with impunity until the very last moment. Quite what will happen then is less obvious; perhaps the logic of the prisoners' dilemma will reassert itself and both will simultaneously confess. Or perhaps the final moment will pass before either has a chance to act.

Even with these revised conditions, however, the prisoners' dilemma is not a typical case. Thus, for example it involves only two main protagonists, whereas many situations where norm enforcement arises will involve a larger group of participants. And as the number rises, so we will run into 'public goods' problems. Take, for example, Homans' work group with its norm of output restriction. Enforcement of the norm is assuredly a public good: I get the benefits whether or not I actually do the enforcing and will hence prefer to leave the embarrassing task of disciplining the rate-busters to others. So will everybody else. And so the rate-busters will continue unchecked. True, we may be rescued from this impasse by the small size of the work group. In the classic public goods cases such as that of voting in a general election the large numbers involved meant that my own individual vote could have no appreciable effect on the outcome. But if there are only a few rate-busters who need to be brought into line my personal moral entrepreneurship may bring sufficient benefits to outweigh the costs. Thus the fewer the deviants, the more likely they are to be disciplined. As deviants the world over know, there is safety in numbers.

As well as the number of deviants, the cost of imposing sanctions will also be relevant, and here we may get another example of the so-called exploitation of the strong by the weak. Let us first of all put it in money terms. If I am relatively rich, I will have been able to satisfy most of my more pressing needs and I will be able to turn to less urgent items. Rich men, for example, make greater donations to charitable institutions, are more likely to endow an Oxford college, or to provide a park for the local citizens' well-being than are their poorer brethren. But this is not because they are more philanthropic. The poor man may get just as much satisfaction from the well-being of his fellows as does the rich man, but he simply has other more pressing and as yet unsatisfied wants to deal with. Similarly, in other areas of social life, we may find that the leisured upper classes who have few other things with which to fill their time will be the ones to devote a largest proportion of their leisure to moral entrepreneurship. Again, in a small group, the high-status individuals who are most secure in their social standing and who receive most esteem from their fellows will be the ones most likely to take deviants to task. Since they are relatively long on esteem the resentment which the deviant will turn towards them will affect them less than it would a more marginal member of the group. They can more easily afford to be disliked by the deviant since they get so much liking from elsewhere in the group.

Is it rational to institute norms?

Whereas conformity to norms and their enforcement involve tricky problems, what of their institution in the first place? After all, to promulgate a norm can be a fairly easy matter. Words are cheap. The man who says, 'Let us be sure never to rat on our comrades if we are caught' is not, one would imagine, incurring very great costs by so doing. The costs come when he tries to enforce the norm and make others comply with it. Paradoxically, however, I suspect that the institution of norms will prove to be the area where a rational choice approach in fact has least to offer. My reasoning is as follows. In most of the (rather elementary) applications of rational choice theory at which we have been looking, the participants have a set of *known* alternatives between which to choose. They may not know what the consequences of each alternative are, but at least they know that the choice lies between, say, confessing and staying silent, or between staying with one's husband and going home to mother. In the case of a new norm, however, we are essentially expecting the participants to think up a *new* way of doing things. We are expecting them to engage in some creative thinking (or in the modern jargon some divergent or lateral thinking), whereas our earlier applications required, at most, some deductive or convergent thinking. True, some norms may not require very great powers of creativity, but others surely require considerable feats of originality. I wonder, for example, how many people would have realized that matrilateral cross-cousin marriage is the appropriate norm to institute if one wishes to increase social solidarity.

Now it seems to me that rational choice theory is likely to have most explantory power when modest amounts of deductive reasoning are called for; its predictive value decreases when creative thought is needed by the participants. Thus some norm or institution may be the technically most efficient method of dealing with a problem, but I would only wish to predict that it will be employed if it is already part of the established repertoire of those involved. Norms and institutions are social inventions and involve exactly the same formidable problems that other inventions pose for the sociologist of ideas. The rational choice approach has little to offer here. It can explain what people will do given their beliefs and knowledge of alternatives. It cannot in my view explain how people come to think up new beliefs or appreciate that new alternatives exist. If one could be sure to arrive at the best institutions for our purposes, the history of mankind would have been very different (and probably very much worse).

So much, then, for the rational choice theories of norm formation and enforcement. They are not, I trust, wholly without use although they are clearly no panacea for the sociologist of morality. It would be easy to dismiss them on the grounds that they either make perverse assumptions (as, for example, that men are rational egoists) or that they make trivial assumptions (as, for example, that men can find utility in anything including justice and altruism). Such an easy dismissal would, however, be premature. If we make the assumption of rational egoism, we can at least lay bare the structure of the situation. We can also show what egoistic reasons there are for conformity and so on and *we can then show how much work remains to be done by moral or altruistic considerations.* Just as Weber hoped that his ideal types of rational action could provide a yardstick against which to measure the degree of irrationality in actual courses of action, so we can use rational egoism as a yardstick against which to measure the degree of morality.

Cross-cousin marriage: final and efficient causes

I propose to move on now to Lévi-Strauss's theory of cross-cousin marriage. I shall omit any discussion of the other sociological theories such as Blau's theory of legitimation and opposition largely, as I mentioned above, because there is little that I have to add about them. Let me say that I find Blau's ideas interesting, and, intuitively, his emphasis on shared grievances seems to be correct. However, it is an empirical matter whether the theory is actually sound or not, and unfortunately empirical matters (which are after all the most important) are not ones which can be easily solved by a few pages of *a priori* argument. True, Blau does advance some evidence in support of his theory, but it is rather sketchy and does not get to the crucial factual issues. Since I have already dealt with this elsewhere (Heath, 1971), I shall not weary the reader with further discussion of it. Suffice to say that this theory, like much else in sociology, remains an interesting speculation.

Let us deal, then, with Lévi-Strauss's theory instead. This is particularly interesting since it has been the centre of a controversy in which one of the main protagonists has been none other than Geogre Homans (in partnership with the anthropologist D. M. Schneider). We thus seem to have battle joined between our two main approaches to exchange theory (although, inevitably, matters will not prove to be quite as straightforward as this). Lévi-Strauss, it will be remembered, was primarily concerned with two different forms of unilateral cross-cousin marriage, namely the matrilateral and the patrilateral forms. The matrilateral form, he argued, produced a system of *generalized* exchange in which men of lineage A marry B women, the B men marry C women, and so on. The patrilateral form, on the other hand, produced a system of *discontinuous* exchange; the men of lineage A marry B women and in the following generation B men will in turn marry A women. Next Lévi-Strauss argued that generalized exchange 'allows the realization of a more supple and effective solidarity' and claimed that 'if . . . marriage with the father's sister's daughter is less frequent than that with the mother's brother's daughter, it is *because* the latter not only permits but favours a better integration of the group' (Lévi-Strauss, 1949, p. 448; my emphasis).

As a preliminary skirmish before the main attack Homans and Schneider begin by criticizing the notion that marriage with the mother's brother's daughter favours greater solidarity. Father's sister's daughter marriage, they say, requires at least three lineages just like the mother's brother's form; the men of lineage A may marry B women and may reciprocate in the following generation, but their own women, in the *present* generation, must marry C men. Thus 'any one lineage is linked by marriage to two others in the ring, and the ring can be lengthened indefinitely. On all these counts it meets Lévi-Strauss's requirements for generalized exchange' (Homans and Schneider, 1955, p. 211). Furthermore, they continue, 'We might even go on to argue that father's sister's daughter marriage makes for greater organic solidarity, as the specialization in marriage is determined by generation as well as by lineage, and so creates a more intricate intermeshing of groups' (p. 211).

Homans and Schneider do not press home this attack, however, but proceed to what they regard as their major campaign. They argue that Lévi-Strauss's theory is a *final cause* theory since it is one which accounts for mother's brother's daughter marriage in terms of its beneficial consequences for the society as a whole. They then make the now commonplace criticism (although they were of course making it in the early 1950s) that final cause theories will not do. 'To account for the adoption by a society of a particular institution', they say, 'it is, in principle, never sufficient to show that the institution is in some sense good for the society, however that good may be defined. The weakness in all such theories was pointed out long ago by Aristotle. In his parable, "the house is there that men may live in it; but it is also there because the builders have laid one stone upon another". Or no final cause without an efficient cause' (Homans and Schneider, 1955, pp. 214–15).

Homans and Schneider then proceed to supply an *efficient cause* and thus (in their words) to play Darwin to Lévi-Strauss's Lamarck. That is to say, they are giving an explanation which shows how the marriage rule comes into being, not just why it is 'good' for society. They first suggest that the type of marriage rule may have something to do with linearity. They note that societies in which one finds mother's brother's daughter marriage tend to be ones which are organized in patrilineages. In such societies, they suggest, jural authority over Ego is vested in his father and thus the relationship between Ego and his father is likely to be one marked by respect and constraint. A different relationship, however, grows up between Ego and his mother, who 'is a much more warm and nurturant figure' (Homans and Schneider, 1955, p. 218) and, by extension, a similar relationship grows up between Ego and his mother's brother. He becomes, in Radcliffe-Brown's words, 'a kind of male mother' (Radcliffe-Brown, 1924).

Next, Homans and Schneider suggest that mother's brother's daughter marriage is particularly common in patrilineal societies because of the special nature of this relationship between Ego and his mother's brother in these societies. They write: 'We find in the structure of interpersonal relations the individual motivations, or efficient causes, for the adoption of a particular form of unilateral cross-cousin marriage. . . . As he visits mother's brother often, Ego will see a great deal of the daughter: contact will be established. As he is fond of mother's brother, and as mother's brother and his daughter in the patrilineal complex, the Oedipus complex if you will, are themselves particularly close to one another, he will tend to get fond of the daughter. Their marriage will be sentimentally appropriate; it will cement the relationship. Or, if women are indeed scarce and valued goods, and Ego is in doubt where he can get one, he will certainly be wise to ask his mother's brother, on whom he already has so strong a sentimental claim' (Homans and Schneider, 1955, pp. 219–20).

So far this argument, if true, merely explains why Ego should be likely to marry his mother's brother's daughter. It does not explain why there should be a norm or rule to this effect. But Homans and Schneider are not to be stopped by a minor difficulty like this. They make use of our old friend the proposition that 'the customary becomes obligatory' and argue that 'many egos will develop similar sentiments and behavior toward their respective mother's brothers. In time such sentiments and behavior will become recognized as the right and proper ones: they will be enshrined in norms' (p. 221). As with Blau's norm of reciprocity, then, the norm seems to represent merely a codification of existing practice.

Finally, after dealing with the converse side of father's sister's daughter marriage, Homans and Schneider proceed to test their theory against comparative data. It fares rather well. They find thirty-three societies which practise one or other form of unilateral cross-cousin marriage and show that the predicted association with linearity is statistically significant. The results are as follows:

Preferred marriage	Kin groups	
	Patrilineal	Matrilineal
Mother's brother's daughter	22	4
Father's sister's daughter	2	5

($p = 0.009$ by Fisher's Exact Test)

These results are very impressive, but there are of course some exceptions which do not conform to the general rule. Mother's brother's daughter marriage does sometimes occur in matrilineal societies, and vice versa. After examining these exceptions Homans and Schneider came up with a slightly revised theory. They suggest that it is not *linearity* as such which is important but rather *potestality* (that is, the locus of jural authority). Since, for example, patripotestal societies are not always patrilineal ones, an even better fit can be obtained if we deal with potestality itself instead of linearity. Given this empirical success Homans and Schneider now feel able to conclude that they have rendered Lévi-Strauss's final cause theory wholly redundant. To explain the occurrence of the rule, they therefore imply, one does not need to look at its *consequences* for society but only at the *motivations* of the participants. Once we have the efficient cause theory we can dispense with the final cause.

Not surprisingly, Lévi-Strauss takes exception to all this. In particular he objects to the psychological character of Homans and Schneider's theory. He seems to agree with Durkheim's dictum that 'Every time that a social phenomenon is directly explained by a a psychological phenomenon, we may be sure that the explanation is false' (Durkheim, 1895, p. 104), and he accuses Homans and Schneider of reverting to 'old errors' which he hoped that anthropology had outgrown (Lévi-Strauss, 1963, p. 322).

This raises a popular, if misguided, criticism of Homans in particular and of exchange theory in general. Homans' approach, it is often argued, is 'psychologistic' or 'reductionist'. It tries to explain the social in terms of the psychological and is therefore defective. But this is, frankly, a rather perverse criticism. In assessing an explanation we should first look to see if the conclusion can be derived logically from the premises. If it can (and Homans' usually can), our next step is to check whether the premises are factually sound. If our explanation passes both these tests, then it is very hard to see how it can be rejected. To introduce some third criterion dealing with the character of the premises tells the audience about the nature of one's prejudices but little else. If we object to the theory we must show that either its logic or its facts are shaky. We cannot just dismiss it *a priori* because it is 'psychological'.

Consider, then, the logic of the explanation. It is worth noting first that, as an elementary matter of logic, conclusions about sociological variables cannot be drawn from premises which deal *solely* with psychological ones. (This may be what Durkheim had in mind). We cannot draw conclusions about x and y from premises which deal only with p and q: x and y have to appear somewhere in the premises as well (although of course they may do so in the guise of *sigma p* and *sigma q*). Turning to Homans and Schneider we find that their logic is impeccable. One of their main premises is that potestality (surely a sociological variable) shapes the character of inter-personal relations, and another is that customary behaviour will become enshrined in norms (surely another sociological variable). Indeed, looking at the explanation in this light we could say that Homans and Schneider are explaining the rules of cross-cousin marriage in terms of potestality and that it is therefore a sociological not a psychological explanation!

If the logic is satisfactory, then, let us look at the facts. Perhaps Lévi-Strauss has a hunch that the facts will not support an explanation of the kind that Homans and Schneider present and perhaps this is the main source of his objection. Now the overall correlation between potestality and marriage rules seems well enough established and Lévi-Strauss has few grounds for criticism here. (He does in fact raise some rather silly statistical objections, but these are unfounded. See Homans, 1962, p. 252). But what about the intervening mechanisms? Here there is much more room for doubt and in particular Lévi-Strauss appears to be unhappy with the mechanism whereby the customary becomes the obligatory: '[Homans and Schneider] explain the preference of patrilineal societies for matrilateral marriage in terms of psychological factors, such as the transference of an adolescent's emotional feelings to his maternal uncle's group', he writes. '*If such were the case, matrilateral marriage would be more frequent; but it would not have to be prescribed*' (Lévi-Strauss, 963, p. 322; my emphasis). This I take to be akin to the point I made earlier. If people do something anyway, there is no need to have a norm prescribing it. *In rational choice terms* there is nothing which the participants gain by it. The norm is redundant. It is a waste of time prescribing things that people are going to do even if they are not prescribed.

Of course, there is no need for Homans to restrict himself to a rational choice explanation. Indeed, his theory of cross-cousin marriage makes virtually no use of rational choice theory at all. His psychology here is more that of Freud (as in his reference to the Oedipus complex), and it is perfectly possible that there really are non-rational psychological processes whereby the customary becomes enshrined in norms. Whether Homans and Schneider are right or not is a straightforward matter of fact. My hunch is that they will be proved wrong, but I have as little evidence to refute their proposition as they have to support it.

Lévi-Strauss's rebuttal of his opponents is then, at best, inconclusive. But there is another much more vigorous, sustained and famous attack on Homans and Schneider from Rodney Needham. Needham's work has produced one of the more extraordinary episodes in academic debate, and while it has little real significance for exchange theory, it is perhaps worth relating as an object lesson to textual critics. Needham takes Homans and Schneider to task from time to time on their somewhat casual and slipshod reading and translation of Lévi-Strauss. For example, their 'translations from the French do not always show the minute care for literal exactitude that one could wish' and while their errors seem small, it is nonetheless 'a trifle disturbing when so much hangs on a precise comprehension of the text' (Needham, 1962, p. 16). In particular, says Needham, Homans and Schneider failed to realize that Lévi-Strauss's theory dealt only with *prescriptive* marriage whereas they themselves were concerned in the first place with *preferences,* not prescriptions. To be sure, says Needham, Lévi-Strauss gives his critics some basis for their errors since he 'persists in the unfortunate use of the word "preferred"' but 'the tenor of his explicit definitions' and the cases which he actually studies make it clear that he is concerned to analyse prescriptive rules of marriage, not preferential ones.

This might seem to be a serious criticism of Homans and Schneider but, remarkably, the ground was cut from under Needham's feet when Lévi-Strauss came to write an introduction to Needham's own translation of *The Elementary Structures of Kinship.* This is what he said: 'Following Needham, several writers today assert that my book is only concerned with prescriptive systems, or, to be more exact (since one needs only glance through it to be assured of the contrary), that such had been my intention had I not confused the two forms. But if the champions of this distinction had been correct in believing that prescriptive systems are few and far between, a most curious consequence would have resulted: I would have written a very fat book which since 1952 has aroused all sorts of commentaries and discussions despite its being concerned with such rare facts and so limited a field that it is difficult to understand of what interest it could be with regard to a general theory of kinship' (Lévi-Strauss, 1969, p. xxxi).

So far, then, Homans and Schneider seem safe and Needham's care for literal exactitude seems misplaced, but another of Needham's points is far more damaging, and I have little doubt that Homans and Schneider do seriously misinterpret Lévi-Strauss. Their preliminary attack, it will be recalled, concerned the solidary consequences of the different marriage rules, and they suggest that father's sister's daughter marriage may actually make for greater solidarity than mother's brother's since it entails greater specialization in marriage. Now if Homans and Schneider suppose that Lévi-Strauss's argument is concerned with specialization (as they seem to), they must be wrong. They have attributed to Lévi-Strauss ideas which properly belong to Durkheim. For Lévi-Strauss the crucial point is that the patrilateral form does not constitute 'an overall system' in the way in which the matrilateral form does. The patrilateral form produces a closed structure in which 'a woman is ceded in the ascending generation, a woman is acquired in the descending generation, and the system returns to a point of inertia' whereas the matrilateral form produces an open structure in which each marriage constitutes a link in a single chain (Lévi-Strauss, 1949, p. 444). This may be vague but it is nothing to do with specialization.

Still, there is a crucial issue here which none of our writers deals with adequately. It is all very well for Lévi-Strauss to assert that generalized exchange allows a greater solidarity, and it is all very well for Homans and Schneider to doubt it, but what we actually need is some evidence, and this is signally lacking. If Lévi-Strauss's assertion is true, there are some interesting implications: generalized exchange does not occur only in the case of matrilateral cross-cousin marriage but also, in a rudimentary form, in the case of blood donations, wedding presents and perhaps with social welfare benefits. Do these institutions generate a greater solidarity than do market exchanges or other (social) forms of direct exchange? It would be nice to think so, but we have no basis for giving an answer at the moment. It is indeed a sad reflection on exchange theorists (myself included) that a hypothesis which has been with us for quarter of a century has not yet received a single decent test.

To turn to more amenable issues, Needham also takes Homans and Schneider to task for their overall characterization of Lévi-Strauss's theory. This theory, they say, asserts that mother's brother's daughter marriage is more common '*because it is better* for society' (their italics). Needham objects to these 'morally evaluative terms' in which they represent the theory. It is highly curious, he says, that 'in their little book Homans and Schneider . . . use the word "better" twenty-four times, the word "good" eleven times, and the word "goodness" three times' whereas 'there are only two places in his 639 pages where Lévi-Strauss uses the word "better" in connection with matrilateral cross-cousin marriage' (Needham, 1962, p. 18). Still, Lévi-Strauss should say what he means. It is no good to say, as Needham does, that Lévi-Strauss puts the words 'better structure' in quotation marks or that he emphasizes 'that this superiority is purely formal, and that his analysis in this respect is devoid of explanatory value' (p. 18), for what Lévi-Strauss in fact says is: 'Admittedly, this analysis is based on external characteristics and is hence devoid of explanatory value. But this is not the case with the difference in the functioning of the two systems, which is itself a result of these apparently insignificant peculiarities of the structures' (1949, p. 444).

In any event, it is hard to see what the fuss is about. We can easily get rid of the morally evaluative term 'better' and formulate the theory in more neutral terms which should be acceptable to both Needham and to Homans and Schneider. Needham himself provides the neutral terms. He writes: 'What Lévi-Strauss is saying, as I interpret his argument, is that some institutions work more efficiently than others, and that those which are less effective are less likely to persist' (Needham, 1962, p. 27). I am a little unhappy that Needham does not specify for whom or for what the institutions are effective, but apart from this it seems an entirely acceptable formulation of a functionalist argument. It may not be self-evidently a teleological or final cause theory, but whatever we choose to call it, it is certainly a quite different kind of theory from the one which Homans and Schneider present. Essentially it looks at the consequences of different institutions and suggests that some have greater survival value than others. It does not tell us how any particular institution came into being in the first place; it simply tells us what its likely fate will be once it actually has come into existence.

The battle between our rival theories is still very much with us, then. Homans and Schneider have given us an account of the way in which the different marriage rules may have come into existence, an account which pays particular attention to the motivations of the participants. And Lévi-Strauss and Needham have given us an account which ignores the rules' origin and deals only with their consequences. But is it in fact a battle that needs to be fought at all? Might not both motivations and consequences be needed? Might we not institute a practice for one set of reasons, discover that it has various unintended consequences, and modify our practice accordingly? Thus a strict rationalist might argue as follows: the participants institute a practice in the light of their existing goals and expectation; however, the practice has various unintended consequences which feed back and impose additional costs (or benefits) on the participants; they therefore modify (or maintain) their behaviour accordingly.

Note that this scenario requires the existence of feedback from the unintended consequences. Without this feedback there is absolutely no reason why the participants should modify their behaviour in the slightest even if it has the most dire effects for 'the society'. But this surely cannot be a very onerous requirement. Dire effects for society must surely have dire implications for society's members too, and if they do not I would be hard put to see why we should worry about them. Our rationalist scenario does, however, have a second requirement as well, and this is a much more onerous one. It is the requirement that the participants actually connect the feedback with the original behaviour. Marrying your father's sister's daughter may have all kinds of unpleasant consequences for you, but if people who are contemplating marriage never connect the two there will be no grounds for expecting them to behave any differently from their predecessors.

It is not difficult, however, to write alternative scenarios which avoid this problem. Thus, for example, the original practice might have unintended consequences which alter the situation facing some second group of actors; this second group might modify their behaviour, thus altering the situation facing a third group, and so on, eventually returning to the people who initiated the original practice. Of course there is no reason for this feedback sequence to have equilibrating effects of the kind required by functionalists; a disequilibrating cycle is equally plausible (the classic case being the Marxist one where the capitalists unintentionally set in train a series of events which eventually result in their own overthrow). But the crucial point which I want to make is that the unintended consequences of men's actions can be of crucial importance for sociological explanation and are ignored at one's peril. I would also wish to make the point that they can, in principle at least, be incorporated into rational choice theories, introducing a welcome dynamic aspect to the theories. Much exchange theory, like much elementary economics, takes the form of comparative statics in which we simply compare the choices which people make under different situations. But there is no need to restrict ourselves to this. We can easily construct theories (as in slightly more advanced economics) where choices at time one have consequences for the choices made at time two, and so on. We should not underestimate the practical difficulties involved in establishing what these consequences are, but we should at least take care not to shun them altogether.

But where, it may be asked, does all this leave Homans and Schneider, Lévi-Strauss and Needham? It is one thing to show that the efficient cause and the final cause theories can in principle be reconciled, it may be objected, but it is another to effect the reconciliation in this particular case. And I fear that I would have to agree. Still, I would suggest that taking account of the unintended consequences of marriage arrangements begins (but no more) to explain why those arrangements should be prescribed and enshrined in social norms. Very simply, people in a patrilineal society who fail to marry their mothers' brothers' daughters are imposing costs on others in the form of reduced solidarity and thus provide a reason why norms should be established. So long as one's marriage has no consequences for other people, there is no 'need' for norms to be instituted; once it does, the norms become a little more intelligible. They do not, alas, become completely intelligible. Solidarity, after all, is a collective good and there is little incentive for any one individual to do anything about achieving it. (Nor, I should add, does this kind of argument explain why father's sister's daughter marriage should be prescribed in matrilineal societies.)

We come then to an impasse. Functionalist (and quasi-functionalist) theories of the kind that Lévi-Strauss (and Blau) propose can show why norms are needed but do not show the mechanisms whereby they come into existence. Efficient cause theories like conventional exchange theory can explain why people should behave in certain ways but are not particularly good at showing why norms should actually be instituted and enforced. It is easy to see, then, why Homans should be attracted by the notion that the customary simply becomes obligatory; it disposes of our rationalist difficulties at a single stroke. And perhaps indeed it is correct. I must confess that I have nothing better to offer and must concede to Homans a victory at least on points.

16. Conclusions

I do not propose to weary the reader with a point-by-point recapitulation of all the conclusions reached so far. What I propose to do instead is, first, to compare the different exchange theories with one another and, second, to contrast them with the other main approaches which predominate in sociology at the present. I cannot promise that this chapter will be a 'primitive orgy after harvest' of the kind that Homans gives us but, like Homans, I must ask the reader for license since my characterizations of the various approaches will be necessarily brief and possibly tendentious.

The different exchange theories: rational choice versions

One point which should be well established by now is that exchange theory comes in many shapes and sizes. The main contrast on which I have concentrated is of course that between the 'economic' or 'rational choice' theories on the one hand and the 'sociological' ones on the other. But even this is too simple. While there may be a family resemblance between the 'economic' offspring of Homans, Blau and Olson, for example, they are equally clearly cousins, not siblings. No economist could have written *Social Behaviour: Its Elementary Forms* and no sociologist could have written *The Logic of Collective Action.* The 'rational choice' theories are alike in their concern with men's behaviour and in their attempts to explain behaviour in terms of the goals that men have and the alternatives open to them. But they differ in the models of man that they use. The man that Downs and Olson write about is a very different creature from that described by Homans or by Thibaut and Kelley.

Consider, first, the model of man used in the 'pure' economic theories of Downs and Olson. He is a man with fixed, given preferences whose utility depends solely on the quantity of goods or services that he himself possesses. He is uninfluenced by feelings of envy or (less happily) by feelings of justice. Instead, he pursues his own private self-interest in a straightforward single-minded fashion. In the case of economic man assistance received in the past or obligations owed to others are immaterial; bygones are bygones. All that he is concerned to do is to maximize the future stream of benefits that he will receive, and to this end he selects the course of action that will maximize his expected utility. Changes in his behaviour are thus to be explained by changes in the situation and alternatives that face him: the man faced with a private good thus behaves differently from the one faced with a public good; the man on his own behaves differently from the man in a crowd. But these different experiences leave the economic man untouched. His behaviour may change as his environment changes, but he himself remains the same throughout.

Next we have the 'social' model of man who perhaps appears most clearly in the work of Thibaut and Kelley. He is still a maximizer but he tries to maximize a rather wider range of satisfactions. He seeks status and social approval as well as material gains, and he is also concerned to avoid such intangibles as anxiety and guilt. Indeed, anything 'whereby a drive is reduced or a need fulfilled constitutes a reward' (Thibaut and Kelley, 1959, p. 12). Social man also suffers from feelings of envy or of relative deprivation; he compares himself both with his contemporaries and with his own past. The level of satisfaction which he derives from a given outcome is thus not invariant over time and place, and his behaviour has to be explained not only in terms of his present situation and expectations but also in terms of his past history of satisfactions.

There is also a third model of man which appears in the pages of Homans' *Social Behaviour*. This is 'Skinnerian' man (named after the American behavioural psychologist B. F. Skinner). Skinnerian man is based on the common pigeon. He is not a forward-looking maximizer endowed with sophisticated reasoning powers but a practical creature who learns from experience, avoiding what has proved painful in the past and seeking out what has proved rewarding. He differs therefore from economic or social man (*pace* Homans, who thinks they are the same) in his criteria for selecting behaviour. Whereas economic man will, for example, logically deduce that his best strategy in the prisoners' dilemma is to confess, Skinnerian man will simply rely on his past experience in similar situations: if something worked last time, he will try it again; but if confession landed him with eight years in gaol last time, he will try to stay silent next time. Thus, says Homans, 'if in the past the occurrence of a particular stimulus-situation has been the occasion on which a man's activity has been rewarded, then the more similar the present stimulus-situation is to the past one, the more likely he is to emit the activity, or some similar activity, now' (Homans, 1961, p. 53). Skinnerian man is also liable to emotional outbursts, quite unlike economic or social man, who remain impassive throughout. If Skinnerian man does not get what his past history taught him to expect, those who have baulked him must look out. If he had always got off with two years in the past, the man who turns Queen's evidence and puts him behind bars for ten can expect trouble (trouble which, as we saw in the previous chapter, he would have had no reason to expect had he been dealing with a rational economic man).

Now it would be easy to dismiss all three of these models as unrealistic caricatures of what man is really like and hence as over-simplified models which can have no value for sociology. But this would be a mistake. We cannot decide *in vacuo* what is or is not an acceptable model of man. They are essentially tools for the performance of an explanatory job and the crucial test is whether they work or not in practice. We can never have a completely accurate and realistic model of man and there will always have to be some compromise with realism if we are to have a workable tool.

The same applies if we are trying to compare the different models. We cannot decide *in vacuo* whether the Skinnerian model is better or worse than the economic model. It depends on the job we want it for. True, the jobs that economists and behavioural psychologists try to do are often very different from those of the sociologist and so we might guess that the tools needed will be rather different too. And a survey of the topics which we have covered in this book would tend to confirm this judgement. We have from time to time found it useful to assume that men's utility depends on their relative, not their absolute, wealth, that they derive utility from remaining true to their principles, and so on. The social model of man looks to be our most useful tool. But a different range of topics might have given us a different answer. In some contexts the assumptions of the economic model may be a very good approximation to reality (or at least to those aspects of reality which are relevant for the purpose at hand); in others they may be wildly erroneous. But there is nothing to be gained by deciding the matter beforehand. My *guess* is, as I have said, that the social model will most often prove useful, but I do not wish to pretend that this is anything more than a guess.

All this may sound as though I am adopting the Friedmanite position which asserts that the *only* relevant criterion in judging a theory is its predictive power – a position that is anathema to most sociologists. But this is not the stance that I wish to take (nor is it indeed the position that I have been adopting). My position, rather, is that the explanatory significance of assumptions may vary. Every theory makes explicit certain assumptions which it holds to be relevant to the matter in hand, and it consigns other, hopefully irrelevant, assumptions to the category of 'other things being equal'. Thus the economist does not actually deny that people have feelings of envy or justice, but he holds that these are distributed randomly with respect to the behaviour which he is concerned to explain. The crucial question for the model-builder, therefore, is whether he has included the relevant attributes in his model and excluded the irrelevant, and of course a very good test of this is his model's actual predictive power. But this does not mean that the model-builder is entitled to include *anything* in his model which yields a good prediction. Models can yield the 'right' results for the 'wrong' reasons and that is why it is crucial to check the accuracy of the assumptions that are included. Predictive power is a necessary, not sufficient, condition for a satisfactory explanation.

The different exchange theories: sociological versions

In view of what I said earlier, we should expect the sociological versions of exchange theory to be attempting rather different jobs from the rational choice ones, and indeed this is often what we find. Whereas the rational choice theories set out to explain men's *behaviour,* the sociological ones are more concerned with *rules, values* and *institutions.* Thus one of Mauss's main aims seems to be to describe the morality of the gift in pre-industrial societies; one of Blau's is to show the conditions under which new values such as legitimation and opposition ideals emerge; and one of Lévi-Strauss's is to account for the prevalence of different rules of cross-cousin marriage. These are all matters left quite untouched by the rational choice theories and they are matters on which they would have had little to offer in any event.

The sociological theories are radically different in their general form, too. Whereas the rational choice versions take the form of deductive theories in which conclusions are more or less rigorously derived from specified assumptions, the sociological ones are discursive and descriptive. Thus they describe the morality of social exchange, and assert that as an empirical matter of fact rather than as a matter of logical inference certain consequences will follow. They are not systematic theories in the way that the rational choice ones are.

Still, the sociological theories are like the rational choice ones in at least one respect – no two of them are identical. The differences between Mauss, Blau and Lévi-Strauss are as great as, or greater than, those between Downs, Homans, and Thibaut and Kelley. Blau could no more have written *The Elementary Structures of Kinship* than could Downs have written *Social Behaviour: Its Elementary Forms.* The differences between our sociological writers cannot, however, be so easily ascribed to the differences in their models of man. It is much harder to pin down the precise models which Mauss or Blau is using, and I must at the outset admit that anything I have to say about them is speculative in the extreme.

Mauss, to begin with, is primarily concerned with 'words and meaning' (1925, p. 2). As I understand him he is seeking to describe the institutions of gift exchange and of total prestation and he tries to do so by establishing the rules and meanings involved. This is clear enough in the case of the obligations to give, to receive, and to return, but it is also present, I think, when he turns to the solidary consequences of social exchange. Here, as I understand him, he is saying that the *meaning* of a gift is a declaration of friendship or alliance. He is not concerned so much with the psychological or emotional reactions to gift exchange as with the socially given meanings which such acts have for the participants. If I had to infer a model of man from Mauss's writings it would thus, I think, have to be the cognitive model of the symbolic interactionists (a model which we shall be looking at later).

With Blau it is very different. While he is of course, like Mauss, concerned to describe the rules and norms governing social exchange, meanings as such receive little emphasis. Rather, he seems concerned with psychological reactions. *Feelings* rather than meanings are what Blau talks about. Thus he says that 'only social exchange tends to engender feelings of personal obligation, gratitude and trust' (Blau, 1964, p. 94). Or again: 'As the members of an oppressed collectivity communicate their feelings of outrage, hostility, and revenge to each other, the social consensus that emerges among them legitimates these feelings and reinforces them' (p. 251). We thus have a kind of reactive model of man, a man who *responds* to the world rather than interpreting it.

Inevitably, Lévi-Strauss is quite different again. True, his starting points too are rules and norms – in this case the rules governing the exchange of women, rules such as the incest taboo or the prescription that one should marry one's mother's brother's daughter. But Lévi-Strauss does not appear to be so concerned with the meanings of these rules for the participants or with the feelings they engender but rather with the 'structural possibilities' that they allow. Thus the greater solidarity of mother's brother's daughter marriage lies not in the different feelings that it engenders but in the fact that it constitutes an overall system, whereas father's sister's daughter marriage 'is incapable of attaining a form other than that of a multitude of small closed systems' (Lévi-Strauss, 1949, p. 445).

It is difficult to see precisely what kind of model of man would be implied by an argument of this sort, but Lévi-Strauss does give us some clues. He asserts that there are certain fundamental structures of the human mind (such as the puzzling 'exigency of the rule as a rule' (1949, p. 84). These structures operate in an unconscious fashion and (in Needham's words) 'their social products are shaped by the inherent viability or otherwise of their possible permutations' (Needham, 1962, p. 28). I find this all rather opaque, but we can be sure of one thing: it is a model of man quite unlike any that Blau, Homans or Thibaut and Kelley would use.

It would be tempting to say now that the sociological versions are trying to do different things from the rational choice ones and from each other and hence that there is no real competition between them. Each, on this view, would have something to contribute within its own field. But this pleasantly egalitarian solution is, I fear, too simple. It is certainly true, as I said earlier, that they are often attempting to do different things; but it is one thing to attempt – another to succeed. The sociological theories, even more so than the rational choice ones, involve pretensions rather than achievements. It is doubtless an interesting idea that matrilateral cross-cousin marriage allows greater solidarity than does the patrilateral form, but at the moment it is no more than an interesting idea. It is certainly a commonplace that shared experience of oppression generates opposition ideals, but we must not mistake a commonplace for a well-substantiated fact.

This may sound rather hard on the sociological versions of exchange theory in comparison with the rational choice ones, which got off rather lightly. But there is in fact a crucial difference between the two. The sociological versions are not really tools which can be used to tackle a variety of jobs; rather they are half-finished jobs in their own right. Thus Blau's theory of opposition is really no more than the proposition that groups which experience unjust treatment are likely to develop opposition ideals. If this turns out to be false, that is the end of the theory. Indeed, the proposition is the theory. There are no new inferences which can be drawn from it; nor is the proposition itself one which can be drawn from, or incorporated into, any more general body of theory. It stands or falls on its own. In contrast the rational choice versions do constitute more systematic theories from which a variety of inferences can be drawn. And if one particular inference fails (for example, the inference that working wives have more power within the family than those who stay at home), this does not destroy the entire theory. Admittedly part of the theory would have to be changed – some of the premises would need to be modified; but the rest remains unscathed and can be combined with new premises to give new (and hopefully more accurate) predictions.

This must not be taken to imply that the rational choice theories, since they are more systematic, are therefore superior to the sociological ones. As Homans himself has said: 'Give me a man's actual findings, and I care not what theory he may have built them into' (1961, p. 9). One well-substantiated proposition may be worth a great deal more than a clumsy and badly designed multi-purpose theory. What follows from this distinction between tools and half-finished jobs, however, is that the criteria for assessing them are (up to a point) different. If the job, when completed, turns out to be unsatisfactory, we might sensibly decide to start again and do it in a different way. But if a tool turns out to be ineffective for a particular purpose, we do not throw it away; we would be sensible to keep it by us in case it comes in useful for something else.

Even this may seem somewhat unfair to the sociological versions of exchange theory. Surely, it may be objected, a Maussian or a

Lévi-Straussian approach can be inferred from their writings, and these approaches would surely constitute tools in just the same way that the rational choice theories do. They may be less explicit, but they are still there. This is doubtless true, but I would be surprised if these approaches, once discovered, turned out to be anything other than the conventional approaches of sociology and anthropology. We do not have, I would claim, any special sociological approaches to social exchange; what we have are simply the standard approaches such as functionalism and symbolic interactionism which can be applied, among many other things, to the explanation of social exchange. Indeed, we could go even further and suggest that the same is true of the rational choice theories. As their very name implies, their general domain is that of choice; exchange is merely one part of that domain. The very term 'exchange theory' thus becomes a misnomer. What we in fact have is a variety of general theories and approaches some of which, notably the rational choice ones, have been introduced to sociology through the writings of Homans and Blau on exchange, others of which are established residents. All of them can be applied, to a greater or lesser extent, to the study of social exchange, but that is all that really holds them together. What I propose to move on to, therefore, is a comparison between the rational choice approach, broadly defined, and the main sociological approaches which are current today. I shall begin with the microsociological approaches.

Rational choice and microsociology

One common approach in sociology, more popular in the 1950s than it is now, is what might be called the normative approach. According to this approach, behaviour is to be explained in terms of the norms and roles governing the actor in question. Thus we explain reciprocation in terms of the norm of reciprocity; we explain voting in terms of the duty of citizenship to vote; we explain family power structure in terms of the sub-cultural expectations of the group in question. This is of course the approach which Duesenberry had in mind when he said that 'Economics is all about how people make choices. Sociology is all about why they don't have any choices to make.' It is also the approach that Wrong pilloried as the 'oversocialized conception of man' (1961, pp. 183–93), and it is of course an approach that has been a target from time to time throughout this book. It has been my argument that people usually *do* have choices to make, not least the choice whether or not to conform to the appropriate norms and role expectations. There is always some possible alternative course of action, and the costs of non-conformity are merely one set of costs to be weighed in the balance along with all the others.

Still, the normative approach is not quite as dead as one might have guessed from all this. Sometimes the alternatives are relatively insubstantial and we have, for all practical purposes, explained a given action by showing the norms involved. The most famous example of this is the act of voting. Given the 'public goods' problem we can hardly account for voting in terms of the expected effect it will have on the selection of a government. One's own individual vote can hardly be expected to swing the balance between one party and another and so on an instrumental view voting can hardly be rational (unless electors have bizarre views about the probability of a tie between the two parties). The explanation simply has to be in terms of the intrinsic benefits of voting, notably those of affirming one's allegiance to a political party and to the democratic process.

True, we can always incorporate this explanation into a rational choice framework. We can always say that people derive utility from affirming their political allegiance and it may at times be useful to include this as part of the individual's utility function. However, all we have done is to *re-describe* the explanation in a different language. To say that someone derives utility from the act of voting in itself conveys much less information than the information that the voter is affirming his allegiance to a political party or that voting is a normative expectation of citizens in a democracy. To refer to normative expectations, for example, is to indicate that there are shared and recognized expectations deviations from which run the risk of censure. All of this is missing from the rational choice account.

The game of re-describing other people's explanations in one's own language can easily be played in reverse, too. Some recent writers, for example, have suggested that rationality is simply 'a kind of social norm' and that is is merely one of many possible decision rules that can be employed in social exchange, others being altruism, competition, reciprocity and so on (Meeker, 1971). (Presumably we now need meta-decision rules to enable us to choose between decision rules, and so on *ad infinitum.*) It is easy to see how on this view all behaviour can be reduced to rule-following behaviour just as on the previous one all behaviour could be reduced to utility maximization. But this would be just as much a mistake as it would have been in the previous case. In the first place, I would wish to maintain a distinction between a decision rule and a social norm, the crucial point being that infractions of norms (but not necessarily of decision rules) bring a risk of social sanctions, the risk of sanctions being one of the things that a person takes into account when reaching a rational decision. The man who fails to reciprocate when he should have done so *by definition* runs the risk of censure. But if a man chooses to minimax rather than maximize expected utility, that is his own business. True, in a society such as our own which places such a high premium on science and logic, the man who fails to choose rationally may be derided: 'Whatever did you want to do that for?' people may ask even if it *is* none of their business. But in principle there is still an important distinction between those rules which are socially sanctioned and those which are not; decision rules, I suggest, usually come into the second category.

But there is also a second, more important, objection to this reduction of rational choice theory to a rule-following theory. To concentrate on the rules which people follow is to ignore the central explanatory variable of rational choice theory, namely the *alternatives* that are open to the actor. To say that someone is behaving rationally or that he is following a rational decision rule is only to give the first step in the explanation. We also need to know what were the alternatives that made this the rational course of action to follow. We do not obviate the need for a full-blown rational choice theory by expanding the scope of the normative paradigm; more probably we obscure the need by doing so.

A second approach with which we can contrast the rational choice one is the now fashionable one which places the emphasis on the *cognitive* rather than the normative side. Symbolic interactionism with its emphasis on cognitive meanings is perhaps the most notable version of this. The crucial assumption of this approach is, as Rose puts it, that 'all social objects of study . . . are "interpreted" by the individual and have social meaning. That is, they are never seen as physical "stimuli" but as "definitions of the situation"' (Rose (ed.), 1962, p. x). Accordingly, the individual's definition of the situation becomes a crucial explanatory variable.

A closely related approach is Jarvie's 'logic of the situation'. The crucial assumption here is that individuals 'have intelligible ends . . . and have acted rationally faced with their situation, where "their situation" includes their knowledge and beliefs' (Jarvie, 1964, p. 36). This, with its emphasis on rationality, sounds as though it is a variant of the rational choice approach, and so it is in parts. But the weight of Jarvie's explanation of cargo cults (his chosen field) is in fact borne by a cognitive explanation. The strange practices of the Melanesians in building jetties and airstrips in expectation of the cargo are to be explained, Jarvie says, in terms of their beliefs and doctrines, doctrines which are attempts on the part of the Melanesians to account for the white man's material success and their own endless poverty. They are attempts to account for the problem posed by the white man and the (very limited) facts known about him, and they are necessarily attempts to do so within the existing magico-religious framework of the culture. The doctrines happen (unfortunately for the Melanesians) to be false, but, *given the existing native framework*, they are entirely rational attempts to explain the intellectual problems which they face.

Jarvie's work brings out the importance of the distinction between the rationality of a man's beliefs and the rationality of his actions. Accordingly it brings out the distinction between the conventional rational choice approach that we have been dealing with up to now and the logic of the situation that Jarvie employs. The former tries to explain what someone will do given his knowledge and beliefs about the situation and the alternatives open to him. Knowledge and beliefs are taken to be a datum, not a problem, and explanatory interest focusses on the alternatives open to the actor. The latter seeks first to explain why a man's beliefs about the situation take the form they do and only then to account for his behaviour in terms of them. Knowledge and beliefs now become the centre of explanatory interest.

Both approaches are undeniably important, although as usual their explanatory significance will vary from one topic to another. People, of course, must always have some beliefs about the situation, but in some cases these beliefs will not pose any problems for all practical purposes; in others they will. Thus the beliefs of the Melanesians about the coming of the cargo pose a problem; those of Blau's law enforcement agents do not, or at least not to the same extent. Whether we choose to concentrate, then, on the beliefs which an actor has or on the alternatives which are open to him should depend not on some metaphysical preference for one type of theory over another but on the puzzle which we are trying to solve and on the explanatory pay-off which it has for that puzzle. Thus if we are puzzled by the social construction of reality, we would necessarily turn to the logic of the situation or to some other cognitive explanation such as ethnomethodology. The rational choice approach does not pretend to offer us any guidance here, and we would be silly to ask it for any. But if we are concerned to explain men's actions, the rational choice approach is one possible source of an answer, and the issue becomes (in the language of statistics) which variable – alternatives or beliefs – can explain more of the variance. If beliefs are shared, they cannot, *ex hypothesi*, explain any of the variance; if they vary, they can (at least in principle) begin to contribute towards an explanation. But how large a contribution they can make will be a matter for empirical investigation, not dogmatic assertion.

It may be objected at this point that the choice of an approach is not the simple either/or matter that I have implied it to be. While the emphasis of Jarvie and the symbolic interactionists may be on the cognitive side, it is not exclusively so; and while the emphasis of the rational choice approach is on the alternatives open, it could choose to treat beliefs as a variable in the same way that it can incorporate values. Indeed, if we stretch our approaches in this way, we end up with an amalgam closely resembling the action approach of Max Weber and his followers. This, as Cohen describes it, makes the following assumptions:

'(i) The actor has goals (or aims, or ends); his actions are carried out in pursuit of these.

'(ii) Action often involves the selection of means to the attainment of goals . . .

'(iii) An actor always has many goals; his actions in pursuit of any one affect and are affected by his actions in pursuit of others.

'(iv) The pursuit of goals and the selection of means always occurs within situations which influence the course of action.

'(v) The actor makes certain assumptions concerning the nature of his goals and the possibility of their attainment.

'(vi) Action is influenced not only by the situation but by the actor's knowledge of it.

'(vii) The actor has certain ideas or modes of cognition which affect his selective perception of situations.

'(viii) The actor has certain sentiments or affective dispositions which affect both his perception of situations and his choice of goals.

'(ix) The actor has certain norms and values which govern his selection of goals and his ordering of them in some scheme of priorities' (1968, p. 69).

This looks like (and is) a giant amalgam of the normative, cognitive and rational choice approaches. Goals, means, situations, modes of cognition, norms and values are all included. The only (surprising) omission is that of rationality itself. Accordingly, it looks to be a more general approach than any of the others at which we have looked; it appears to encompass the earlier ones and hence, presumably, is to be preferred. Has not the history of science taught us that more general theories have superseded the less general? But such a preference for the action approach would be the result of an unduly hasty and cursory reading of the history of science. The action approach is not playing Newton to the rational choice's Galileo. For the action approach is just that – an approach, not a theory. It does not, as it stands, explain anything that has resisted the attempts of the earlier approaches. Indeed, as it stands, it does not explain anything. Rather, it is, as Cohen describes it, merely 'a set of near-tautological assumptions which structure the mode of cognition of social inquiry' (Cohen, 1968, p. 94). In contrast the rational choice approach, despite its name, *does* contain a number of systematic theories; it has its share of near-tautological assumptions, but it also has concrete theories of power and price, collective action and coalition formation. We would be foolish to abandon concrete theories, however limited their scope, in favour of a set of near-tautological assumptions. When action theorists have produced the theories to go with their assumptions, we may have some sensible grounds for preference; in the meantime there is no real ground for a competition.

However, I do not want to leave the action approach as the only one without a prize in this Caucus-race where everyone else has won one. If we treat the action approach simply as a compendious tool-kit of assumptions and variables to be drawn upon as the occasion demands, then I cannot find fault with it (beyond its strange omission of rationality). True, my guess is that the action theorists will rarely want to use all his nine assumptions on a single explanatory job; his actual explanations, when they appear, will look very like normative, cognitive or rational choice ones as the case may be. To explain social behaviour we really have very little alternative to looking at men's values, beliefs, and situations, and if the action approach reminds us of that it is doing a good job.

Rational choice and macrosociology

At the macro level we find two dominant approaches in conventional sociology. On the one hand there are the various versions of functionalism and systems theory; on the other the various schools of Marxism or of so-called conflict theory. The former are concerned primarily with systems, their needs and their functioning; the latter with the structure of interests and the conflicts that arise from them. The former is typically associated, particularly of course in the case of Parsons, with the normative approach at a micro level, while the latter, as Cohen has suggested, is typically associated with a model of instrumental rationalism (1968, p. 79). Let us begin with our old friend functionalism.

As we have already seen, functionalism is very different from the general run of rational choice theory. Rational choice theory typically tries to explain differences in rates of behaviour and it tries to do so in terms of the actors' goals and the alternatives open to them. Functionalism, in contrast, is typically concerned with institutions and institutionalized behaviour and attempts to describe the contributions which they make to the functioning of the system as a whole. Put like this the two approaches are simply not in competition. They are doing different jobs and it would therefore be foolish to wish to choose between them.

However, as we saw in the previous chapter, it is not always as simple as this. Thus one might try to use rational choice theory to give the 'efficient cause' of an institution; one might, following Homans, try to show how it was rational for the actors to institute a particular social arrangement. And one might also, following Blau, try to use rational choice theory in a quasi-functionalist manner; one might try to show what contributions a particular social arrangement makes not to the functioning of the system but to the payoffs of the individuals concerned.

Still, we have not got a real competition under way yet. We may try to use rational choice theory in a quasi-functionalist way, but it is still only *quasi*-functionalist. The contributions which a social norm makes to individuals' pay-offs is not identical to the contributions which it makes to the working of the system as a whole. They are somewhat different foci of interest and I do not see that we can prohibit one or enforce the other. I happen to think that it will be a great deal easier, as a purely practical matter, to discover what the individual pay-offs are, and this, if correct, would not be unimportant. But it would still not clinch the matter.

No, a competition gets under way not when functionalism tries to *describe* the contribution which an institution makes to the working of the whole but when it tries to *explain* the institution itself in terms of the contribution which it makes. It is only at this stage that functionalism comes to provide a 'final cause' theory of the kind that Homans castigated and it is only here that we begin to get a competition with a rational choice or with some other efficient cause theory. But it is, one might be pardoned for thinking, a competition between the halt and the blind in which it would be difficult to detect a victor. To show the origins of an institution may not be as easy as Homans imagined; if any degree of creativity were required or shown by actors the sociologist is likely to be in trouble. But even to explain its origins will not necessarily account for its persistence, and to account for its persistence we shall have to do more than show the benefits which it brings whether to the system or to the individual actors; 'public goods' problems should be familiar enough to us by now to understand that rational individuals will not always support institutions that benefit them. Ideally, as I suggested in the previous chapter, we might begin by showing an institution's origin and then demonstrate the feedbacks (or lack of them) which reinforce (or otherwise) the original behaviour. But it is one thing to map out ideal strategies; another to follow them; and while I would assert that a rational choice approach is as good a strategy as any for explaining the origins and persistence of social institutions I would not for a moment claim that it will actually be a very effective one.

When we turn from functionalism to the various conflict theories, however, we are even harder put to discover any real competition. The theories are either trying to do quite different things from rational choice theory or else they are trying to do the same thing but using virtually the same method with which to do so. Thus conflict theory, says Rex, in its simplest form 'starts by assuming two parties with conflicting aspirations or aims . . . in the process of conflict the actors might be expected to look for allies who will add to the strength of the sanctions they can bring to bear against the other side. Allies will be found who have a similar situation and out of the alliances there will emerge groups structured for participation in conflict' (Rex, 1961, p. 122). The only effective difference between this and the theories of coalition formation which we met in chapter 4 is the lack of rigour possessed by conflict theory. Coalition theory, by making strict assumptions about rationality, can yield some precise predictions about the coalitions which will or will not form; it thus actually becomes a *theory*, not just an approach. Conflict theory, in contrast, is much vaguer in its assumptions and correspondingly reaches the much vaguer conclusions that groups (of unspecified character and composition) will emerge. Coalition theory, then, is a more rigorous form of conflict theory; it is not really a competitor at all.

The situation is almost as simple when we turn to Marxism. This of course covers a much wider spectrum of issues than does rational choice theory and indeed it seems prepared to turn its hand to anything of sociological interest. Thus it looks not only at men's behaviour but also at their ideas and their institutions; it looks not only at conflict but at the situation which gives rise to it and at the determinants of that situation. Its ambitions are perhaps only matched by those of evolutionary functionalism and are nowhere near approached by rational choice theory. Still, there are some common concerns to both approaches, and here again, I would claim, we will discover that they use common methods. Marx may have had a determinist and materialist conception of history, but when he gets down to the business of actually explaining men's behaviour we find that he has a model of man which sees man as choosing rationally between alternatives in the light of the situation facing them. Thus in accounting for the proletariat's relative passivity in June 1849 in France, Marx wrote: 'To begin the revolution at this moment against the will of the Mountain meant for the proletariat, decimated, moreover, by cholera and driven out of Paris in considerable numbers by unemployment, to repeat the June days of 1848 uselessly, without the situation that had forced this desperate struggle. The proletarian delegates did the only rational thing' (Marx, 1850, p. 98). Again, this lacks the rigour of the classical rational choice theories; the assumptions are not spelt out in detail and the conclusion is not logically deduced from them. It has, rather, the characteristics of the vaguer action approach, where the main lines of the argument are sketched and the details are left to the reader's imagination. And indeed this is probably the most that can be expected in historical explanation. But it should still be clear that this is only a variant of the rational choice approach (or perhaps the other way round); these are not two radically different alternatives to explanation, merely more or less rigorous and detailed versions of a common general theme.

I would conclude, therefore, that some variant of the rational choice approach has long been with us and is long likely to remain so. We may argue about the precise variant which we are to use, but I do not think that there can be much argument that some variant or other must remain a standard tool of the mainstream sociologist. I do not deny that men may follow rules and interpret their environment; they may also be driven by unconscious desires, innate drives or conditioned reflexes (to move more into the territory of psychology) but to claim an imperialist monopoly for any of these approaches would be as foolish as it would be in the case of the rational choice approach.

Bibliography

Abrahamson, B. (1970), 'Homans on exchange: hedonism revisited', *American Journal of Sociology*, 76:273–85

Adams, J.S. and Jacobsen, P.R. (1964), 'Effects of wage inequities on work quality', *Journal of Abnormal and Social Psychology*, 69:19–25

Andenaes, J. (1952), 'General prevention – illusion or reality?', *Journal of Criminal Law, Criminology and Police Science*, 43:176–98

Anderson, M. (1971), *Family Structure in Nineteenth Century Lancashire*. Cambridge: C.U.P.

Arensberg, C.M. and Kimball, S.T. (1940), *Family and Community in Ireland*. Cambridge, Mass.: Harvard University Press

Arrow, K.J. and Hurwicz, L. (1972), 'An optimality criterion for decision-making under ignorance', in C.F. Carter and J.L. Ford (eds.), *Uncertainty and Expectations in Economics: Essays in Honour of G.L.S. Shackle*. Oxford: Basil Blackwell, pp. 1–11

Bailey, F.G. (1969), *Stratagems and Spoils: A Social Anthropology of Politics*. Oxford: Blackwell

Banks, J. A. (1954), *Prosperity and Parenthood*. London: Routledge & Kegan Paul

Barry, B. (1965), *Political Argument*. London: Routledge & Kegan Paul

(1970), *Sociologists, Economists and Democracy*. London: Collier-Macmillan

Barth, F. (1966), 'The analytical importance of transaction', in *Models of Social Organization*, Royal Anthropological Institute Occasional Paper No. 23. Glasgow: Royal Anthropological Institute, pp. 1–11

Bass, F.M., Pessemier, E.A. and Lehmann, D.R. (1972), 'An experimental study of relationships between attitudes, brand preference, and choice', *Behavioral Science*, XVII:532–41

Baumol, W.J. (1961), *Economic Theory and Operations Analysis*. Englewood Cliffs, N.J.: Prentice-Hall

Becker, G.S. (1960), 'An economic analysis of fertility', in Universities–National Bureau Committee for Economic Research, *Demographic and Economic Change in Developed Countries*. Princeton, N.J.: Princeton University Press, pp. 209–31

(1968), 'Crime and punishment: an economic approach', *Journal of Political Economy*, 76:169–217
Bell, C. (1968), *Middle-class Families*. London: Routledge & Kegan Paul
Blau, P.M. (1955), *The Dynamics of Bureaucracy: A Study of Interpersonal Relations in Two Government Agencies*. Chicago: University of Chicago Press
(1964), *Exchange and Power in Social Life*. New York: Wiley
Blood, R.O. (1963), 'The measurement and bases of family power: a rejoinder', *Marriage and Family Living*, 25:475–7
Blood, R.O. and Wolfe, D.M. (1960), *Husbands and Wives: The Dynamics of Married Living*. New York: Free Press
Boas, F. (1897), *The Social Organization and the Secret Societies of the Kwakiutl Indians*. United States National Museum, Report for 1895. Washington, D.C., pp. 311–38
Bott, E. (1957), *Family and Social Network*. London: Tavistock
Boulding, K.E. and Davis, J.A. (1962), 'Two critiques of Homans' 'Social Behavior: Its Elementary Forms', *American Journal of Sociology*, 67:458, 459
Burgess, E.W. and Cottrell, L. (1939), *Predicting Success or Failure in Marriage*. Englewood Cliffs, N.J.: Prentice-Hall
Buric, O. and Zecevic, A. (1967), 'Family authority, marital satisfaction and the social network in Yugoslavia', *Journal of Marriage and the Family*, 29:325–36
Caplow, T. (1968), *Two Against One: Coalitions in Triads*. Englewood Cliffs, N.J.: Prentice-Hall
Codere, H.S. (1950), *Fighting with Property: A Study of Kwakiutl Potlatching and Warfare, 1792–1930*. Monographs of the American Ethnological Society, XVIII. New York
Cohen, P.S. (1968), *Modern Social Theory*. London: Heinemann
Coleman, J.S. (1966), 'Foundations for a theory of collective decisions', *American Journal of Sociology*, 71:615–27
(1973), *The Mathematics of Collective Action*. London: Heinemann
Curtis, E. (1915), 'The Kwakiutl', in *The North American Indian*, Vol. 10. Norwood, Mass.: Plimpton Press
Davenport, W. (1960), 'Jamaican fishing: a game theory analysis', *Yale University Publications in Anthropology*, 59:3–11
Davidson, D., Suppes, P. and Siegel, S. (1957), *Decision-making: An Experimental Approach*. Stanford, Calif.: Stanford University Press
Davis, J. (1972), 'Gifts and the U.K. economy', *Man* (N.S.), 7:408–29
Deutsch, M. (1964), 'Homans in the Skinner box', *Sociological Inquiry*, 34:156–65

Downs, A. (1957), *An Economic Theory of Democracy.* New York: Harper & Row

Duesenberry, J.S. (1960), 'Comment', in Universities–National Bureau Committee for Economic Research, *Demographic and Economic Change in Developed Countries.* Princeton, N.J.: Princeton University Press, pp. 231–4

Durkheim, E. (1895), *Les Règles de la méthode sociologique.* Paris: Alcan. (Page references in the text are to the edition by G.E.G. Catlin, trans. S.A. Solovay and J.H. Mueller as *The Rules of Sociological Method* (New York: Free Press, 1964))

(1897), *Le Suicide: étude de sociologie.* Paris: Alean. (The page reference in the text is to the edition by G. Simpson, trans. J.A. Spaulding and G. Simpson as *Suicide: A Study in Sociology* (London: Routledge, 1952))

Edwards, W. (1954), 'The theory of decision-making', *Psychological Bulletin,* 51:380–417

Ekeh, P. (1974), *Social Exchange Theory: The Two Traditions.* London: Heinemann

Festinger, L. (1957), *A Theory of Cognitive Dissonance.* Evanston, Ill.: Row, Peterson

Firth, R. (ed.) (1967), *Themes in Economic Anthropology.* London: Tavistock

Gamson, W.A. (1961), 'A theory of coalition formation', *American Sociological Review,* XXVI:373–82

Goldschmidt, W. (1969), 'Game theory, cultural values, and the brideprice in Africa', in I.R. Buchler and H.G. Nutini (eds.), *Game Theory in the Behavioral Sciences.* Pittsburgh, Penna.: University of Pittsburgh Press

Gouldner, A.W. (1960), 'The norm of reciprocity: a preliminary statement', *American Sociological Review,* 25:161–78

Gross, N., Mason, W.S. and McEachern, A.W. (1958), *Explorations in Role Analysis.* New York: Wiley

Heath, A. (1968), 'Economic theory and sociology: a critique of P.M. Blau's *Exchange and Power in Social Life*'. *Sociology,* 2:273–92

(1971), 'Review article: exchange theory', *British Journal of Political Science,* 1:91–119

(1974a), 'The norm of reciprocity revisited'. Unpublished paper

(1974b), 'The rational model of man', *European Journal of Sociology,* XV:184–205

Heer, D.M. (1963), 'The measurement and bases of family power: an overview', *Marriage and Family Living,* 25:133–9

Hirschman, A.O. (1970), *Exit, Voice, and Loyalty: Responses to Decline in Firms, Organizations, and States.* Cambridge, Mass.: Harvard University Press

Homans, G.C. (1961), *Social Behaviour: Its Elementary Forms*. London: Routledge & Kegan Paul

(1962), *Sentiments and Activities: Essays in Social Science*. London: Routledge & Kegan Paul

(1967), *The Nature of Social Science*. New York: Harcourt, Brace & World

Homans, G.C. and Schneider, D.M. (1955), *Marriage, Authority and Final Causes: A Study of Unilateral Cross-cousin Marriage*. New York: Free Press. (Page references in the text are to the reprint in Homans (1962))

Hotelling, H. (1929), 'Stability in competition', *Economic Journal*, 39:41–57

Jarvie, I.C. (1964), *The Revolution in Anthropology*. London: Routledge & Kegan Paul

Jensen, G.F. (1969), '"Crime doesn't pay": correlates of a shared misunderstanding', *Social Problems*, 17:189–201

Kapferer, B. (1972), *Strategy and Transaction in an African Factory*. Manchester: University Press

Latané, B. and Darley, J.M. (1970), 'Social determinants of bystander intervention in emergencies', in J. Macaulay and L. Berkowitz (eds.), *Altruism and Helping Behavior*. New York: Academic Press, pp. 13–27

LeClair, E.E. and Schneider, H.K. (1968), *Economic Anthropology: Readings in Theory and Analysis*. New York: Holt, Rinehart & Winston

Lévi-Strauss, C. (1949), *Les Structures élémentaires de la parenté*. Paris: Presses Universitaires de France. (Page references in the text are to the revised edition, Lévi-Strauss (1969))

(1963), *Structural Anthropology*. New York: Basic Books

(1969), *The Elementary Structures of Kinship*. Revised edition. Translated by J.H. Bell and J.R. von Sturmer; R. Needham (ed.). London: Eyre & Spottiswoode

Lewin, K., Dembo, T., Festinger, L. and Sears, P.S. (1944), 'Level of aspiration', in J.M. Hunt (ed.), *Personality and the Behavior Disorders*. New York: Ronald

Lieberman, B. (1960), 'Human behavior in a strictly determined 3 × 3 matrix', *Behavioral Science*, V:317–22

Lipsey, R.G. (1975), *An Introduction to Positive Economics*, 4th edn. London: Weidenfeld & Nicolson

MacCrimmon, K.R. and Toda, M. (1969), 'The experimental determination of indifference curves', *Review of Economic Studies*, XXXVI:433–52

Malinowski, B. (1920), 'Kula: the circulating exchange of valuables in the archipelagoes of Eastern New Guinea', *Man*, 51:97–105

(1922), *Argonauts of the Western Pacific.* London: Routledge & Kegan Paul

(1926), *Crime and Custom in Savage Society.* London, Routledge & Kegan Paul

Marx, K. (1850), *The Class Struggles in France 1848–50.* First published as a series of articles in *Neue Rheinische Zeitung, Politisch-ökonomische Revue,* 1850. (Page references in the text are to the edition by P.M. Dutt. London: Martin Lawrence, 1934)

Mauss, M. (1925), 'Essai sur le don: forme et raison de l'échange dans les sociétés archaïques', *Année Sociologique,* n.s. 1:30–186. (Page references in the text are to the edition translated by I. Cunnison as *The Gift: Forms and Functions of Exchange in Archaic Societies* (London: Cohen & West, 1966))

Meeker, B.F. (1971), 'Decisions and exchange', *American Sociological Review,* 36:485–95

Merton, R.K. (1957), *Social Theory and Social Structure.* Revised edition. New York: Free Press

Miller, D.L. (1974), 'Social justice'. Unpublished D.Phil. thesis, Oxford University

Muir, D.E. and Weinstein, E.A. (1962), 'The social debt: an investigation of lower-class and middle-class norms of social obligation', *American Sociological Review,* 27:532–9

Mulkay, M.J. (1971), *Functionalism, Exchange and Theoretical Strategy.* London: Routledge & Kegan Paul

Needham, R. (1962), *Structure and Sentiment: A Test Case in Social Anthropology.* Chicago: University of Chicago Press

Olson, M. *jnr* (1965), *The Logic of Collective Action: Public Goods and the Theory of Groups.* Cambridge, Mass.: Harvard University Press

Olson, M. *jnr* and Zeckhauser, R. (1966), 'An economic theory of alliances, *Review of Economics and Statistics,* 48:266–79

Piddocke, S. (1965), 'The potlatch system of the southern Kwakiutl: a new perspective', *Southwestern Journal of Anthropology,* 21: 244–64

Piliavin, I.M., Rodin, J. and Piliavin, J.A. (1969), 'Good Samaritanism: an underground phenomenon', *Journal of Personality and Social Psychology,* 13:289–99

Radcliffe-Brown, A.R. (1924), 'The mother's brother in South Africa', *South African Journal of Science,* 21:542–55. Reprinted in *Structure and Function in Primitive Society* (London: Cohen & West, 1952)

Radford, R.A. (1945), 'The economic organisation of a P.O.W. camp', *Economica,* 12:189–201

Rawls, J. (1972), *A Theory of Justice.* Oxford: Clarendon Press

Razak, W.N. (1966), 'Razak on Homans', *American Sociological Review*, 31:542–3

Read, D.W. and Read, C.E. (1970), 'A critique of Davenport's game theory analysis', *American Anthropologist*, 72:351–5

Rex, J. (1961), *Key Problems of Sociological Theory*. London: Routledge & Kegan Paul

Riker, W. (1962), *The Theory of Political Coalitions*. New Haven: Yale University Press

Robbins, L. (1932), *An Essay on the Nature and Significance of Economic Science*. London: Macmillan

Roberts, J.M., Strand, R.F. and Burmeister, E. (1971), 'Preferential pattern analysis', in P. Kay (ed.), *Explorations in Mathematical Anthropology*. Cambridge, Mass.: M.I.T. Press

Rose, A.M. (ed.) (1962), *Human Behavior and Social Processes: An Interactionist Approach*. London: Routledge & Kegan Paul

Ross, E.A. (1921), *Principles of Sociology*. New York: Appleton-Century-Crofts

Safilios-Rothschild, C. (1967), 'A comparison of power structure and marital satisfaction in urban Greek and French families', *Journal of Marriage and the Family*, 29:345–52

(1970), 'The study of family power structure: a review 1960–1969', *Journal of Marriage and the Family*, 32:539–52

Sahlins, M.D. (1965), 'On the sociology of primitive exchange', in M. Banton (ed.), *The Relevance of Models for Social Anthropology*. ASA Monographs 1. London: Tavistock, pp. 139–236

Salisbury, R.F. (1962), *From Stone to Steel*. Melbourne: University of Melbourne Press

Sharp, L. (1952), 'Steel axes for stone-age Australians', *Human Organization*, 11:17–22

Shurmer, P. (1971), 'The gift game', *New Society*, 18:482

Simmel, G. (1908), *Soziologie, Untersuchungen über die Formen der Vergesellschaftung*. Leipzig: Duncker & Humblot. (The page reference in the text is to *The Sociology of Georg Simmel*, trans. and ed., K.H. Wolff (New York: Free Press, 1950))

Simon, H.A. (1955), 'A behavioral model of rational choice', *Quarterly Journal of Economics*, 69:99–118

Smithies, A. (1941), 'Optimal location in spatial competition', *Journal of Political Economy*, 49:423–39

Stevens, S.S. (1968), 'Ratio scales of opinion', in D.K. Whitla (ed.), *Handbook of Measurement and Assessment in Behavioral Sciences*. Reading, Mass.: Addison-Wesley, pp. 171–91

Stouffer, S.A. et al. (1949), *The American Soldier*. Princeton, N.J.: Princeton University Press

Taylor, M. and Laver, M. (1973), 'Government coalitions in Western Europe', *European Journal of Political Research,* 1:205-48
Thibaut, J.W. and Kelley, H.H. (1959), *The Social Psychology of Groups.* New York: Wiley
Titmuss, R.M. (1970), *The Gift Relationship: From Human Blood to Social Policy.* London: Allen & Unwin
Tittle, C.R. (1969), 'Crime rates and legal sanctions', *Social Problems,* 16:409–23
Tullock, G. (1967), *Toward a Mathematics of Politics.* Ann Arbor: University of Michigan Press
Von Neumann, J. and Morgenstern, O. (1944), *Theory of Games and Economic Behavior.* Princeton, N.J.: Princeton University Press
Waller, W. and Hill, R. (1951), *The Family: A Dynamic Interpretation,* by W. Waller; revised by R. Hill. New York: Dryden Press
Wilensky, H.L. (1956), *Intellectuals in Labor Unions.* New York: Free Press
Wrong, D.H. (1961), 'The oversocialized conception of man in modern sociology', *American Sociological Review,* 26:183–93

Index